To
_____

From
_____

Date
_____

Visit Christian Art Gifts website at www.christianartgifts.com.

Rest in Me: 365 Devotions to Restore Your Soul

Published by Christian Art Gifts, Inc.

Previously published as *The Daily Dose: 365 Days to a Healthy Soul*. First printing by Paladin Publishers in 2018.

Rest in Me: 365 Devotions to Restore Your Soul © 2022 by Lina AbuJamra

Designed by Allison Sowers

Cover and interior images used under license from Shutterstock.com.

Scripture quotations have been taken from *The Holy Bible, English Standard Version*. (ESV)® Text Edition: 2016. Copyright © 2001 by Crossway Bibles, a publishing ministry of Good News Publishers.

Scripture quotations from the *New King James Version of the Bible*, Copyright © 1982 by Thomas Nelson. Used by permission. All rights reserved.

Scripture quotations from the *New American Standard Bible*. Copyright © 1960, 1962, 1963, 1968, 1971, 1972, 1973, 1975, 1977, 1995 by The Lockman Foundation.

Scripture quotations from the *Holy Bible, New International Version*®. Copyright © 1973, 1978, 1984, 2011 by Biblica, Inc.® Used by permission. All rights reserved worldwide.

Scripture quotations from the *Holy Bible, New Living Translation*. Copyright © 1996, 2004, 2007, 2013, 2015 by Tyndale House Foundation. Used by permission of Tyndale House Publishers, Carol Stream, Illinois 60188. All rights reserved.

Scripture quotation from *The Holy Bible, Modern English Version*. Copyright © 2014 by Military Bible Association. Published and distributed by Charisma House.

Scripture quotation from the *Amplified Bible*. Copyright © 2015 by The Lockman Foundation, La Habra, California 90631. All rights reserved.

Scripture quotation from the *Amplified Bible, Classic Edition*. Copyright © 1954, 1958, 1962, 1964, 1965, 1987 by The Lockman Foundation.

All rights reserved under International Copyright Law. No part of this publication may be reproduced, stored, in a retrieval system, or transmitted in any form or by any means—electronic, mechanical, photocopy, recording, or any other—except for brief quotations in printed reviews, without prior permission of the publisher.

ISBN 978-1-63952-100-5

Printed in China

27 26 25 24 23 22
10 9 8 7 6 5 4 3 2 1

Rest in Me

365 DEVOTIONS
to Restore Your Soul

Lina AbuJamra

Christian art gifts®

Fresh Starts

*Call to Me and I will answer you, and will tell you
great and hidden things that you have not known.*
Jeremiah 33:3

Today is the first day of the rest of your life. It's the beginning of a new year. If you know me at all, you know that I'm all about fresh starts. New pages. Second chances. Grace poured out over and over again. I can't think of anything more exciting than the first day of the new year to shout out fresh start! No matter how great or how challenging your last year was, today is a new day, an opportunity to start again.

I wonder what the new year will bring for you? Will it be your year of breakthrough? Will it be your year of finally finding the victory you've been hoping for? Will you use every day you're given for God's glory? Will you do what it takes to change, even if it hurts a little at first?

The good news is that you're not in this alone. God is on your side. His grace will sustain you. His spirit will empower you. His Word will be your guide. All God wants is for you to take that first step toward Him. Ask Him to show you what He wants for you this year. Ask Him to whisper a word of hope to set the tone for the next twelve months.

Tell Him your hopes and your dreams. Make new commitments, and ask Him to help you keep them.

Questions: *Ask God to give you a word or a verse (or both) to set the tone for the new year. Listen as you read His Word, and hear Him speak personally and specifically to you.*

DAY 1

Love the Word

Do your best to present yourself to God as one approved, a worker who has no need to be ashamed, rightly handling the word of truth.
2 Timothy 2:15

How's your Bible reading plan for the new year going? If you haven't thought about it yet, today is a good day to stop and consider it. I know we're only two days into the new year. I know you're still adjusting to the post holiday blues. But if you're looking to deepen your walk with the Lord this year, and if you're looking for growth this year, and if you're looking to get stronger this year, there is only one sure way to do it. Get into God's Word.

Immerse yourself in His Word. Meditate on it, and chew on it daily. God's Word is sure; it makes wise the simple. His Word is right; it rejoices the heart. God's Word is food for your soul, light for your path, wisdom when you need it, and hope no matter what you're facing.

Let me ask you again: How's your Bible reading plan going? If you don't have one yet, today is your chance to start one!

Questions: *Consider going through the entire Bible this year! Or simply take some time and find a year-long Bible reading plan and a journal. Write down your resolve to be in the Word daily.*

In the Wilderness

He has known your wanderings through this great wilderness.
These forty years the Lord your God has been with you; you have not lacked a thing.
Deuteronomy 2:7

If I know my way around one place, it's the wilderness. I've been there more times than I care to count, and it seems like I land there more often than I ask for. One of the advantages of time in the wilderness is that I've gotten really good at figuring out the best way out of it: You can either complain your way out of the wilderness, or you can praise your way out of it.

The first response is rooted in fear. Fear leads to complaining and despair. Fear that God won't show up in the wilderness is crippling. Then there's the way of faith. Faith sings its way through the wilderness. Faith rejoices in the dry season. Faith looks up instead of around and knows that eventually the wilderness is just a season. It will surely pass.

If you're in the wilderness right now, decide how you're going to get through it, and remember that complaining your way through the wilderness will only drag it out. Now you choose, but I'd recommend praise!

Questions: *How are you responding to the season of wilderness in your life right now? What are simple steps you can take to learn to praise your way through the wilderness?*

God of Miracles

*Now restore us again, O God of our salvation.
Put aside Your anger against us once more.*
Psalm 85:4

I love miracles—all sorts of miracles. But do you want to know what my favorite miracle in the Gospels is? Out of all the miracles that Jesus did, by far and above my favorite is this one: the second one. If you don't know, I can explain it.

Remember the feeding of the 5,000? It was a great miracle. But the better miracle was the second time Jesus did it—when He fed the 4,000. And have you heard the miracle where Jesus asked Peter to put his net into the deep after fishing all night and catching nothing (Luke 5)? It was a great miracle indeed. But the even better one was the second time Jesus did the same miracle again in John 21.

Of all the miracles recorded, it's always the second miracle that I love the most because it's a reminder that God is always willing to do it again—if He showed up once, He will surely do it again. If He answered your cry for help, He's willing to do it again. He's the God of second chances.

So what miracle are you hoping God will do in your life but feel you don't deserve? You might be surprised. God might just do it again.

Question: *List some of the ways God has shown up in your life in a miraculous and awesome way. Take a minute and ask Him to do it again!*

Be Pure

Blessed are the pure in heart, for they shall see God.
Matthew 5:8

Is purity realistic? To listen to popular culture today, the conclusion is clear: Purity is not realistic at all today. To hear the world according to Hollywood tell it, purity is undesirable and unhealthy. But as a board certified medical school graduate and a real doctor, let me assure you that purity is in fact good for your health.

Purity has never caused anyone to die or land in the hospital, even for a short visit. Purity, it turns out, is not bad for your body or your soul. In fact, according to God's Word, purity is the way to happiness. In 1 Thessalonians 5, Paul reminds us that purity is God's will for us. God does have a plan for us whether we're single or married, and it is to pursue purity.

So forget about Hollywood and forget about popular culture. The key to peace and joy and freedom is simpler than we've made it. Flee sexual immorality. Choose holiness. Love God and honor Him. And remember that God never asks us to do anything He won't give us the ability to carry out. He's our good, good Father.

Questions: *Are you making choices in your life that are leading you to more consistent purity? Are there some things in your life that you must resolve to cut off in order to pursue purity?*

He is in Control

*And the men marveled, saying, "What sort of
man is this, that even winds and sea obey Him?"*
Matthew 8:27

Do you ever wonder how anyone who calls themselves a follower of Jesus spends one second worrying about anything?

I was in Jordan with a friend a while back and felt claustrophobic and scared. The environment was foreign. The challenges around me sounded massive. The night around me felt really dark. I wanted to go home. Because I'm a verbal processor, I expressed my frustrations out loud. My friend listened in agreement, but didn't say a thing. I figured she'd fallen asleep in the darkened room when suddenly she whispered: "Even the winds and waves obey Him."

It was all I needed to hear. I knew what she was talking about. The disciples had been stuck in a boat on a dark and stormy night. They were afraid. They felt alone. They wanted to be on safe land. Instead, Jesus showed up and quieted the storm. The disciples were amazed. They stood in awe and wondered at the Son of God. They were a step closer to understanding who He is.

Are you a step closer to knowing Jesus today? Maybe the storm you're in will help you see Him even more clearly.

Questions: *Do you ever wonder why God allows storms in our life? How does knowing our God can quiet a storm help encourage you in facing what's to come?*

DAY 6

Deny Yourself

If anyone would come after Me, let him deny himself and take up his cross daily and follow Me.
Luke 9:23

Have you thought about what it means to call Jesus your Lord lately? We're living in a time when many call Jesus their Lord. But did you know that you can't call Jesus your Lord and treat His ways as a mere suggestion?

Today many call Jesus Lord, but few are doing what He commands. Few love their enemies, few give without expectation, few are willing to deny self and serve others. It's easy to say Jesus is Lord, but true Christianity moves past the words to doing what Jesus asks.

Are you treating His ways as mere suggestions, or are you the real deal? Are you living as a Christian with this one goal in mind? To glorify God no matter what you're going through, or are you focused on getting what you want at any cost? In every area of your life, you must choose to live the way of Jesus or your self-centered way. And how you live day after day will always tell the real story—do you just call Jesus Lord, or is He indeed Lord of your life?

Questions: *What are some of the ways in your life that you are not living as a true follower of Jesus Christ? Are you willing to make some changes in those areas?*

Setting Right Goals

*One thing I ask from the Lord, this only do I seek;
that I may dwell in the house of the Lord all the days of my life,
to gaze on the beauty of the Lord and to seek Him in His temple.*
Psalm 27:4

Someone recently asked me what my goals were in this season of my life. I immediately thought about some of the things I'm trying to accomplish. I thought about numbers and impact and growth. Then I paused to consider.

In Psalm 27:4 David said, "One thing I ask from the Lord, this only do I seek; that I may dwell in the house of the Lord all the days of my life, to gaze on the beauty of the Lord and to seek Him in His temple." Most of us have been there before, but truth be told, we're easily distracted. We're distracted by the noise in our lives. We're distracted by the stuff that we have. We're distracted by our dreams. Eventually we will learn that lesser things will never satisfy us. They will always leave us empty.

What's your goal in this season of your life? Is it financial security or marriage? Is it professional advancement or a desire for more travel? Haven't you figured it out by now? You'll never find the peace your soul longs for until God becomes your #1 goal. Everything else pales in comparison.

Questions: *What is your #1 focus and goal in this season of your life? What are some specific ways you can seek the Lord more intentionally?*

DAY 8

God at Work

And I am sure of this, that He who began a good work in you will bring it to completion at the day of Jesus Christ.
Philippians 1:6

Have you ever had a season in your life where you couldn't see God at work clearly enough? Did it make you wonder whether He was really doing anything at all?

One of the most fascinating books in the Bible is the book of Esther. In the entire book, God's name is not mentioned once! Not once is there reference to God, yet the entire book so clearly points to His presence. On every page of the book of Esther, God is at work in the details, even when we can't see it clearly. Even when His name isn't mentioned. God was working behind the scenes setting the stage to save His people. God was at work defeating the enemy of His people. God was at work protecting the queen.

If you're going through a season where God's presence isn't clear, don't doubt it for a moment, He's at work even when you can't see it clearly. He's faithful to the end. He sees you even when you can't see clearly.

Question: *Meditate on the faithfulness of God. How does the truth that God is faithful to you impact the way you view your present trial?*

Happiness

You make known to me the path of life;
in Your presence there is fullness of joy.
Psalm 16:11

Is it possible to be truly happy? It's a question I've been asked a million times. Is it possible to be happy, or do happy people just fake it really well?

We're all living in a mirage that we'd be happy if we finally got the one thing we long for. If you're single, that could be marriage. If you're married, it might mean the perfect kids. If you're a professional, a promotion might be your dream. But I ask you again, is it possible to be truly happy?

In Psalm 16:11 David wrote this: "You make known to me the path of life; in Your presence there is fullness of joy." David understood that the secret to happiness is not in our circumstances but in God's presence. The secret to happiness is to dwell in the shelter of the Most High and not in the cave of negativity or the trap of discontentment or the pit of self-pity and despair.

So yes, it is possible to be truly happy, but it only happens when you make God's presence your home.

Questions: What's the one thing you think you still need to be happy? What practical steps can you take to experience more of God's presence in your life?

Return and Rest

*For thus said the Lord God, the Holy One of Israel,
"In returning and rest you shall be saved; in quietness and
in trust shall be your strength." But you were unwilling.*
Isaiah 30:15

Anytime I have the opportunity to sign books, I catch myself jotting down the reference to one of my favorite verses in the Bible. Isaiah 30:15 has become the theme for my life. I can easily become overrun by all the noise in my life and overwhelmed by all I have to do. It's easy for me to forget about God. But Isaiah's words are a reminder to us that we can't forget who God is.

Rest and quietness are precious commodities in today's world, but without them we cannot connect with the Lord. Elijah learned that lesson in a cave after watching an earthquake and a storm. He soon understood that God often shows up when it's quiet enough for a whisper.

How much time are you carving out in your day for rest? How still are you during the course of the day? Isaiah's words remind us that not everyone was willing to take God up on His offer. Not everyone found strength for the road, but only those who heeded the words of the Lord.

Questions: *What does it look like practically speaking to "return and rest" in today's culture? How can you carve out more time with the Lord each day?*

Settle Your Priorities

*But seek first the kingdom of God and His righteousness,
and all these things will be added to you.*
Matthew 6:33

Do you take God's Word seriously, or do you just say that you do? Most of us are very familiar with Matthew 6:33. Seek first the kingdom of God, and all these things will be added to us. We say it and perhaps to a certain extent we might even believe it—technically speaking. But practically speaking is a whole different matter.

Practically speaking our families come first. Or maybe it's our kids' soccer games. Or our work meetings. Or our free time. When it comes to "me" time, most of us become very dogmatic about it. We figure God wants us to rest, and that means time set aside for us to binge on our favorite Netflix show, or catch up on ESPN.

While all of these things I mention are not bad per se, God's Word is clear. Make Him your priority, make His kingdom central to your life, and your family and kids and work and self will line right up the way they're supposed to.

Is your life out of sync? Perhaps it's because your priorities are too.

Questions: *What are you prioritizing in your life right now? Where do you spend the majority of your time each day?*

DAY 12

More than You Think

*Why, even the hairs of your head are all numbered.
Fear not; you are of more value than many sparrows.*
Luke 12:7

My mom is a bird lover. She has a few feeders in her yard, and when we go to Starbucks in Florida, I catch her throwing little pieces of bread to the sparrows. It makes me laugh because if their fate was left to my mom, those sparrows might die. She's not there enough to feed them what they need.

The good news is that God cares for the sparrows. He feeds them and provides for them and knows their needs. While my mom's kindness is noted, the sparrows' reliance is on their God. Back in Jesus' day sparrows were not worth much. They were the cheapest bird to buy. And out of all the birds He could have used as an example, Jesus picked the sparrow to let His disciples know exactly how much He loved them.

If Jesus cares for the sparrow, does He not care so much more about you? And if my mom has enough mercy to feed a little bird at Starbucks, how much more the God who created you sees your need and stoops low to meet it?

Question: *In what ways has God provided for your need this week?*

DAY 13

Don't Be Afraid

*I praise God for what He has promised. I trust in God,
so why should I be afraid? What can mere mortals to do me?*
Psalm 56:4

Some days it feels like everyone is against me—whether I'm driving my car or at the store, it's like one big conspiracy trying to take me down. It's me against the mortals. You ever felt this way?

In Psalm 56:4 David says, "I praise God for what He has promised. I trust in God, so why should I be afraid? What can mere mortals to do me?" When we're up against the mortals, it's important to refocus. Mortals can't touch us. They can't take us down. They can't even make us stumble. God is in control of our lives. He's the One who's shaping us into His likeness, even through the trials that come from mere mortals.

The moment you get your perspective off the mortals in your life and fix it on the One who is in charge of your life, you will find freedom—even freedom enough to love those mere mortals.

No one can touch you. God's got your future and your days in His hand. Now praise Him for His promises and get on with your day.

Question: *Who are you most afraid of and why? Pray through your fears, reminding yourself that God is your safety no matter who you're up against.*

Battling Temptation

In your struggle against sin you have not yet resisted to the point of shedding your blood.
Hebrews 12:4

Battling temptation is serious business. Most of us forget that fighting temptation is hard work. We assume that because it doesn't magically happen in our lives, then something must be wrong with us. Maybe we don't have the same amount of Holy Spirit power that others do. How wrong we are.

Proverbs 5 is the story of a man who becomes lured by sin and falls for it—leading to disaster. The chapter starts with an admonition, a warning of sorts: "My son, be attentive to my wisdom; incline your ear to my understanding." You can almost hear the writer beg the listener to pay attention. Be on guard. Fight the battle for holiness.

Later in the New Testament, the writer of Hebrews said that in our struggle against sin, we have not yet resisted to the point of shedding our blood. If you're finding the struggle against sin to be hard work, that's normal. That's expected. But it's possible to overcome it.

As we submit to God and resist evil, we can live victoriously no matter what.

Question: *What's your plan to fight the most common temptations that are thrown your way each day? If you don't have a plan, go ahead and develop one right now.*

Answers to Prayers

*Ask, and it will be given to you; seek,
and you will find; knock, and it will be opened to you.*
Matthew 7:7

When it comes to prayer, sometimes we get exactly what we ask for. I recently asked God for more patience. Do you want to know what happened? Trials, detours, and delays came my way. I asked Him for more intimacy. A deep aching loneliness came over me, like a longing for more. I asked for more faith, and suddenly a situation of such deep need, and no way to provide for myself.

Then it hit me. As I prayed and asked God for more, He gave me exactly what I'd asked for. God knows exactly where to apply pressure to produce what we need.

The trials in your life are not meant to harm you. They're answers to prayer, meant to grow you in the areas that you've asked for. The point is not to stop asking God for what we need, but to trust that He's a God who answers our prayers in wisdom and in love.

Then start seeing in your life God's finger exactly where you need it.

Questions: *What are some of the things you're praying for? Can you consider how God might be answering your prayers, even though you might not have seen it clearly before?*

DAY 16

Clean Up

*Do not be conformed to this world,
but be transformed by the renewal of your mind....*
Romans 12:2

I am a neat freak, a total minimalist. I like to keep things simple and clean. Whether you're a minimalist or not, most people understand that the only way to fill our closets with new stuff is to get rid of the old, which means that before we even think about buying new stuff, we need to do some major housecleaning.

Jesus said, "No one puts new wine into old wine-skins. If he does, the wine will burst the skins...new wine is for fresh wineskins" (Mark 2:22). So when it comes to our thought life, the only way to fill up with fresh thoughts is to eradicate the old. The only way to renew our mind is to get rid of what's rotting in it.

For some of us, that means getting serious about cleaning up. Some habits we will have to change. And the things we love and think we can't live without? It might be time to dump those habits in the trash bin, and make room for what's new and pleasing to the Lord.

Questions: *What occupies your thought life? Are there some things you need to clean up and replace with what's new?*

Live to the Hilt

This is the day that the Lord has made; let us rejoice and be glad in it.
Psalm 118:24

Jim Elliott is one of my spiritual heroes. He was a missionary who lived all out for Jesus, and his testimony continues to shout how great God is. Jim Elliott once said, "Wherever you are, be all there. Live to the hilt every situation you believe to be the will of God."

When it comes to our lives, there is no wiser counsel. On any given day, God is able to change our circumstances, but He is far more interested in changing our hearts through our trials. We know that God is good and if God is able to and if God is good, then no matter where we find ourselves today, God has allowed us to be there for a reason.

Now think about Jim's words. If you're a follower of Jesus and seeking to obey the Lord, then wherever you find yourself today, choose to be all there. Don't wish you were somewhere else. Live to the hilt. Believe that you're in God's will, because by God's grace, you are.

Questions: *What's your general attitude about your life right now? Do you find joy in the details of each day? How can you make sure you are living each day to the hilt?*

DAY 18

Loving God's Word

Oh how I love Your law! It is my meditation all the day.
Psalm 119:97

How deeply do you value God's Word? Do you tend to down-play it in your day-to-day life? Some people minimize the importance of the written Word of God. They claim Jesus is the living Word and the only One worth pursuing. While I agree that the point of reading God's Word is to connect with the living Word of God, Jesus, I wonder what Jeremiah would have thought of this sort of thinking? In Jeremiah 15:16 he said, "Your words were found, and I ate them, and Your words became to me a joy and the delight of my heart."

I love God's Word. I meditate on it and need it deeply in my life. It is a lifeline when I'm hurting and an anchor when my world is shifting. And while God's Word is not an end in and of itself, it is still by far the best way to get to know the Father and the best way to grow stronger. It is indeed food to be eaten daily.

So how much time are you spending eating God's Word each day?

Questions: *What's your relationship with the Word of God? Do you spend time reading it? How does it point you to Jesus, the living Word of God?*

The Potter's Hand

So I went down to the potter's house, and there he was working at his wheel. And the vessel he was making of clay was spoiled in the potter's hand, and he reworked it into another vessel, as it seemed good to the potter to do.
Jeremiah 18:3-4

Have you ever tried to step into the way of an artist? If you know any artists, then you know that when it comes to the work they're doing, you better stay out of their way until they're done. And if you're watching from afar, you never know what they're working on until they're done. What looks like rubbish to you right now is often a masterpiece in the hands of the artist who won't stop until the masterpiece is done.

In Jeremiah 18, God compares Himself to a potter working on a piece of clay. He's molding it to perfection. When He notices that it's spoiled, He reworks it until He's fully satisfied with it.

The analogy is obvious. You and I are the clay, and God is the potter. He's got a perfect vision of the person He's shaping us to be and won't stop until He's completely satisfied with who we're becoming.

This potter is trustworthy. He knows what He's doing. So get out of the way and let Him do what He does best.

Questions: *Do you believe that God is working out His best work in you? Can you thank Him for the process even when it's painful?*

DAY 20

Sudden Stops

*For My thoughts are not your thoughts,
neither are your ways My ways, declares the Lord.*
Isaiah 55:8

Few things are more annoying than sudden stops. One minute you're cruising along hardly paying any attention when the car in front of you suddenly stops, forcing you to stop too. It's jarring and sudden, but it's these stops that often keep us from crashing. It's these stops that keep us safe. While sudden stops might mean a delay in our plans, they're meant to get us where we're going and to make it there in one piece.

Perhaps you've been forced to stop suddenly. You were cruising along when all of a sudden an unexpected and unwanted stop has forced you to slow down.

Quit sulking about your fate. Stop worrying about the delay. God is not stressed by your sudden stop. He knows all about it and is with you in it. Your sudden stop is meant to slow you down and protect you.

Thank God for the sudden stops in your life and use the time to give Him praise.

Questions: *Why do you think God allows us to stop suddenly on the road to where we're headed? Can you stop and give Him praise for your unexpected delay?*

Pray in Faith

Elijah was a man with a nature like ours, and he prayed fervently that it might not rain, and for three years and six months it did not rain on the earth.
James 5:17

Prayer is the language of the believing, yet most believers struggle to pray. Again and again in my life, I'm brought to the place where I have to confess: I'm not that great at praying. I typically do it when I'm desperate. While we claim to believe God, our actions reveal that the reason we don't pray is that we don't really believe. See, prayer is the language of the believing.

In James 5 we're reminded of Elijah, a man like us, who prayed and saw God move in massive ways. The difference between Elijah and us is that he believed. He believed that God answers prayers. He believed that God hears us when we pray. He believed that God moves when we ask Him to. Yet Elijah had a nature just like ours. He got tired and sometimes depressed. He got scared and sometimes frustrated, but over and over again, Elijah prayed.

Won't you start practicing the language of the believing? Won't you start praying like Elijah did? Who knows? God might just answer you today.

Questions: *How's your prayer life? If you really believe that God answers prayers, how would that change your prayer life?*

Be Still and Wait

*Be still before the L̲ord and wait patiently for Him;
do not fret when [people] succeed in their ways.*
Psalm 37:7

You don't need a long list of do's and don'ts to make it in your Christian life. The Christian life is much more simple and direct than that. In Psalm 37:7 David summed it up like this: "Be still before the L̲ord and wait patiently for Him; do not fret when [people] succeed in their ways."

It's easy to get riled up when others look like they're doing better than you are. It's easy to get disappointed when your life seems to be on hold, always waiting for God's promises to come to pass in your life. If anyone knew anything about waiting, it was David. He gave us two pieces of advice to help us make it through the waiting: Be still before the Lord, and wait patiently for Him. Be still and wait. Stop and listen. Pause and breathe.

You might be tempted to fix your situation and position yourself just right. But you don't need to do that. Simply stop and be still; then wait for God to unfold His will in your life. When it comes to advice that will help you make it, it doesn't get any better than this.

Question: *What aspects of God's character make it easier for us to be still and wait instead of panicking and comparing ourselves to others?*

DAY 23

Free Indeed

For freedom Christ has set us free; stand firm therefore,
and do not submit again to a yoke of slavery.
Galatians 5:1

What's holding you hostage today? While many of us look free, we're too often held hostage by negative emotions like worry and anxiety and fear and despair. Or we're held hostage by self-pity and complaining. Before we know it, instead of overflowing with joy, we become discouraged, prisoners of our own negative emotions.

Are you familiar with these places? There is a better way. Jesus paid the price on the cross so that we could be free. We are free in Him. We can change. We can escape our prisons of despair. And it starts when we choose to praise.

Paul was in a prison cell when he wrote these words in Galatians 5:1: "For freedom Christ has set us free." No matter what difficult circumstances you're facing today, stop and give God praise. Thank Him for the privilege of experiencing His freedom. Recognize that you are free indeed. Pretty soon you'll see, there's no prison that can keep you hostage. You're more free than you feel.

Questions: *What negative emotions are holding you hostage today? Does knowing that Christ paid the price for your freedom motivate you to live in the freedom that is yours in Him?*

DAY 24

Trust God's Heart

*And I will wait for the Lord who is hiding His face
from the house of Jacob; I will even look eagerly for Him.*
Isaiah 8:17

Do you ever long for God to give you clear answers for your questions? We all want answers. We've got questions and if we're honest, we can't understand why God doesn't speak more clearly to us. Henry Nouwen once said, "Getting answers to my questions is not the goal of the spiritual life. Living in the presence of God is the greater call."

I get so caught up in needing God to answer me. I get frustrated and hurt by His silences. But I'm starting to see that His silence is a gift. He's growing my faith through seasons of silence. He's teaching me to trust Him. He's calling me to a higher place—the place of His presence.

There is no greater sign of spiritual maturity than the willingness to settle into God's presence even when He seems silent. To trust that in His goodness He's not withholding any good thing from us.

Do you trust the Father enough to settle for His silence? Are you willing to try?

Questions: Have you ever been frustrated by God's silences? What are some promises God gives that you hang on to in seasons of silence?

Choose to Obey

Has the Lord as great delight in burnt offerings and sacrifices, as in obeying the voice of the Lord? Behold, to obey is better than sacrifice.
1 Samuel 15:22

It's easy to get so focused on the outcome that obedience becomes secondary. Too often I get caught up in what I want. I pray about it. I align it with what I think is God's plan for me. I even find a verse to support it. In the process I can forget all about obedience. I start to mumble and complain. When God delays I numb my frustration with what I know better than wasting my time on.

I get so hung up on the outcome that I lose sight of obedience. It's easy to get that way and forget that God loves obedience even better than sacrifice. God sees in our obedience a submission to His will, a trust in His love, a willingness to wait.

Are you so hung up on the outcome that you're cutting some corners in your walk with God? Have you given in to old addictions, or found comfort where you shouldn't, or are you choosing to obey no matter what?

Obedience glorifies God, especially when the outcome isn't clear. Obedience says yes when it feels like saying no, simply because of who God is.

Questions: *What are some areas in your life you've been compromising in? Where do you need to trust God and obey Him more?*

Come Away

My beloved speaks and says to me:
Arise, my love, my beautiful one, and come away.
Song of Solomon 2:10

I used to think that the Song of Solomon was for the married couples and honeymooners. I was wrong. Every word on every page of the Song of Solomon is an invitation. God is wooing us to Him in this song. He's inviting us to walk closer with Him.

In chapter 2, verse 10, we hear the sweetest invitation of them all. It's an invitation to God's heart. "My beloved speaks and says to me: Arise, my love, my beautiful one, and come away." This is God's invitation to His people to come away with Him. It's His invitation for you to come away with Him, to step closer, away from the noise of this world and draw nearer. It's His invitation for you to greater intimacy with Him.

How are you responding to His invitation? Are you shaping your day around it, or are you too busy to notice? There's no greater invitation than this one. Won't you say yes to Him right now?

Questions: When was the last time you stepped away from the cares of this world to run into God's arms? What competes the most with your time with God?

Don't Panic

*His way is in the whirlwind and storm,
and the clouds are the dust of His feet.*
Nahum 1:3

Do you dread the storms in your life? You don't need to. Most of us freak out at the storms in our lives. Like the disciples, we panic in our boats, storm tossed by the wind, while we look at Jesus sleeping and wonder how He could do this to us. It seems unfair to us that Christ would sleep while we suffer.

In Nahum 1:3 we're told that God's way is in the whirlwind and storm and that clouds are the dust of His feet. It's not that God doesn't care. Quite the opposite. It's that God rules over the storms of our lives. He's unrattled by the storms and has perfect peace because when He speaks, the winds and waves obey Him. I love that picture of God walking on the clouds like dust. His way is in the whirlwind and storm.

Don't fret the storms in your life. God's presence might just surprise you, even in the storm. He's closer than you think. He'll never let you go.

Questions: *What storm are you facing right now? How does knowing that clouds are the dust of God's feet encourage you to stand strong in the midst of your storm?*

Rest Up

When my heart is overwhelmed
lead me to the rock that is higher than I.
Psalm 61:2

When I was in medical school, I had a favorite verse. It was Psalm 61:2: "When my heart is overwhelmed lead me to the rock that is higher than I." Seems like in those days I was always overwhelmed by something. Yet somehow the moment I would pray the words of King David, my heart would find its resting place.

These days I still get overwhelmed. I try to control my circumstances. I fight and I strain until I finally slow down enough to open God's Word. The pages still fall to Psalm 61:2. When my heart gets overwhelmed, God still leads me to the rock that is higher than I. I'm reminded that the same God who got me through med school will get me through my present struggles no matter how big they are. He's the rock my heart rests in when nothing else will do.

Won't you run to Him right now if your heart feels overwhelmed?

Question: *What circumstances are overwhelming you right now? Memorize Psalm 61:2 and pray it to the Lord today.*

Cut it Off

And if your right hand causes you to sin, cut it off and throw it away.
Matthew 5:30

I had a tree in my yard that became a big problem. Whenever I checked my patio, I noticed the same thing: There was bird poop all over my patio furniture. Aggravated, I'd clean it all up. Over time I tried everything from owl scarecrows to hanging a string over my patio to waving a plastic bag on a pole. Nothing worked.

I finally figured it out—a solution that would work. I hired a guy to cut off the parts of the tree where the birds sat. And just like that, the problem was gone.

When it comes to the sin in our lives, many of us try to manage the problem like I did but realize we can't. The only thing that will work is to find the root of the problem and cut it off.

Jesus once said that if your right hand offends you, cut it off. Just like my tree, some things have to be cut off for our hearts to feel clean. I hope you're ready to do some surgery. I hope you're ready to feel clean.

Questions: *Is there a pattern of sin in your life that keeps you defeated? Are you willing to do whatever it takes to live a life of holiness?*

Wake Up

Watch therefore, for you know neither the day nor the hour.
Matthew 25:13

The only way to make it for an early morning flight is to know about it ahead of time and set your alarm for it. Then you've got to wake up for it and stay awake.

Multiple times in the New Testament we're told to wake up, to stay awake, to watch out because we're living in the last days and don't know when Christ's return is. These words were not meant to lull us to sleep, but to prepare us.

When the news around the world gets bad, don't panic. Wake up and take note of what's happening instead. When sexual promiscuity seems to be increasing and hatred and violence are on the rise, open your eyes, sleeper, and connect the dots. Don't miss the signs of the times.

Jesus is coming back, and it's closer than most of us really think. Wake up to the urgency of the need around you. Spread hope. Speak truth. Shine brightly. You have been given a mission today. Your purpose is to show your world who Jesus is by the way that you live and the depth of your love. Care about others. Point to Jesus. Might He come back today?

Question: *If Jesus were to come back today, how would you spend your last day on earth?*

DAY 31

Eyes on God

For who is this uncircumcised Philistine, that he should defy the armies of the living God?
1 Samuel 17:26

How did David find the courage to battle Goliath when nobody else did? Remember the story of David and Goliath? Not one man of the army of Israel mustered enough bravery on that day to take on the giant. David was too young for battle. He wasn't even supposed to be at the battlefield. But he showed up and won the victory over the giant that day.

The reason David was able to defeat Goliath was simple: While everyone else's eyes were fixed on Goliath, David's eyes were fixed on his God. It didn't occur to David that any giant stood a chance against Jehovah, because God was so much bigger than the giant.

As you face your own giants today, are your eyes fixed on your obstacles, or are you looking at your God? Only a true vision of who God is will give you the courage that you need to win your battles today. Fix your eyes on Jesus and live!

Question: *Make a list of the giants you're facing right now. Then think about the Lord. Fix your eyes on God and all that He is. Can any of your giants stand a chance against the Lord?*

Extravagant Worship

*Therefore I tell you, her sins, which are many, are forgiven —
for she loved much. But he who is forgiven little, loves little.*
Luke 7:47

What's the most extravagant thing you've ever done? Was it a big ticket item you bought just because? Or a party you dressed up for? How about in your worship?

There was a woman who once went a little bit crazy in worship. She was a woman with a past that should have stopped her but didn't. She walked right up to the front of the room, opened the most expensive bottle of perfume, and poured it on the feet of Jesus. As if that wasn't enough, she got down on her knees and washed His feet with her hair. The people standing around were horrified. "Why the extravagance?" they asked. "Why the humiliation?"

See, she understood what they did not. She was worshipping the Messiah who would later pour out His body in extravagant love for us. Her extravagance was more appropriate. It was glorifying to God.

So let me ask you again. What's the most extravagant thing you've ever done in worship? Maybe it's time to turn things up a notch.

Questions: *How do you express yourself in worship before the Lord? How thankful are you for all He has done for you?*

Prayer Power

She was deeply distressed and prayed to the Lord and wept bitterly.
1 Samuel 1:10

Have you ever had a problem so big no human could fix it? Some problems are so big no one can fix them. In 1 Samuel 1 Hannah had this sort of problem. She couldn't have kids. And even though her husband loved her deeply, he couldn't fix this problem for his wife. No matter how hard he tried, all his actions were wasted.

Hannah finally got to her wit's end, and did the only thing any of us can when we're given a problem that no human can fix: Hannah finally took her problem to God. She prayed. And prayed. She prayed so hard that the priest thought she was drunk. Eventually, God answered her.

Are you facing a problem that you can't fix? Are you dealing with a problem that no human can fix? How about taking it to God instead? How about leaving it at the feet of Jesus and trusting that He will do what no human has the power to do? Who knows? God might answer you when you finally choose to pray.

Questions: *How much time are you really praying about the problems in your life? Are you a fixer, tempted to fix other people's problems? What if instead you simply prayed for them?*

He Still Loves You

I have loved you with an everlasting love; therefore I have continued My faithfulness to you. Again I will build you up, and you shall be built.
Jeremiah 31:3-4

Do you ever wonder if you've crossed the line? If perhaps this time God might not answer if you call on Him? Sometimes I over-repent. I knowingly sin and still find myself hungry for forgiveness. It's in those moments that I'm thankful for Jeremiah 31:3-4. Over and over again God reminds us that He's a God who will do it again. He loves us enough to forgive us again. He's faithful enough to bless us again.

While we might feel hopeless at our own weakness, God knows us so well and still loves us so much. Again, He will build us up. Again, He will give us joy. Again, He will bear His fruit in our lives.

No matter what you bring to the table today, God is able to heal you again. And as surely as God has promised it once, He will surely do it again. There's no God like our God. There's no love like God's love. Won't you run into His waiting arms right now? He longs to remind you that you'll find Him—again!

Questions: Is there a pattern of sin in your life that makes you feel like you don't deserve God's love? If you were sure God loves you no matter what, what would you say to Him right now?

DAY 35

Daily Disciplines

Rather train yourself for godliness.
1 Timothy 4:7

When I was a kid, my parents put me in Girl Scouts. We were living in Beirut at the time, and I vaguely remember putting on the uniform every Saturday and making my way to the great wilderness at my school's playground.

To be honest I barely remember learning anything of value during those years. Yet today my mother might tell you that my drive for adventure was birthed during those years in Girl Scouts. She might tell you that my adrenaline-seeking spirit was massaged during late night campfires. My mom is correct.

While some things we do in this life might feel useless and hard to remember, our very character is shaped by them. For example, showing up to church week after week or reading your Bible day after day might feel like a waste at times. But over the course of your life, you will find that your very character is shaped by the disciplines that you adopt.

What kind of disciplines characterize your life today? You'll be able to tell by the person you're becoming.

Questions: *What are some of the disciplines that you have adopted in your life? What are some you need to work on?*

DAY 36

In Control

*Now in putting everything in subjection to him,
He left nothing outside his control.*
Hebrews 2:8

Have you ever tried to run your world and failed miserably at it? It's usually not until I hit rock bottom that it hits me. I'm not in control, and it's the best feeling in the world. I don't have to fix everything all the time or have all of the answers. I don't have to save the world. But there is Someone who can.

There is a Superhero among us, and He's waiting to save the world. He's in control and no earthly mess intimidates Him. No political argument can take Him down. His name is Jesus, and He is full of grace. He is the light that makes a way through the darkness when it feels like nothing else will. He's completely in control of everything, and it's the most liberating feeling in the world.

You can take a deep breath. God's presence hushes the whispering lies in your head and gives you the grace to go on. There's not a detail of your life that He doesn't know and will work out in season.

Questions: *What weighs you down today? Will you stop for a moment and leave it at the feet of Jesus in prayer?*

List Makers

*Whoever abides in Me and I in him, he it is that
bears much fruit, for apart from Me you can do nothing.*
John 15:5

I am a list maker. I love everything about having the list. I love crossing things off and seeing my list shrink. When it comes to living life by the list, one of the mind-sets I've developed over the years is the idea that Jesus must be at the top of my list.

While the idea of Jesus at the top of a list sounds great at first glance, it's not the way we're meant to live. It's an idea that gives us a false sense of comfort. But too often, it pushes us into a lifestyle of striving harder to please God, holding us by the noose and wearing us down.

In an effort to make a God-honoring "list," we sometimes miss the very heartbeat of what it means to be a Christian, a follower of Jesus. Instead of living by the list with Jesus at the top of the list, we're meant to live with God at the core—Jesus at the center of it all.

No matter what you're doing today, if Jesus is at the center of it all, you're sure to find the abundant life He promised.

Questions: *Is Jesus a part of your day, or is He the center of all that you do? How can you live your life aware of Jesus at the center of it all?*

Weary in Waiting

But David strengthened himself in the L<small>ORD</small> his God.
1 Samuel 30:6

I finished speaking at an event recently when a woman came up to me and said, "I loved your message. I'm still waiting on the Lord, but I'm weary in the waiting."

I knew what she meant. I get weary in the waiting too. When the waiting drags out, every step that I take feels like a ton of bricks. Every prayer feels unanswered. God's presence seems far. But we're not alone in our weariness. A few of the greats felt it too. Abraham was weary in the waiting. Moses became weary during his forty years in the wilderness. Saul got weary, and his impulsiveness lost him the kingdom. The list goes on.

Weariness in the waiting is common but not fatal if you treat it right. In 1 Samuel 30:6, David was weary in the waiting, but he strengthened himself in the Lord. He ran to the Lord and hid in God's presence for safety.

If you're weary in the waiting, you can find your strength in the Lord today too. Won't you hide in His presence until victory is yours?

Questions: *Where do you go when you get weary in the waiting? How do you respond when you feel weak?*

DAY 39

God Hears

And the Lord said to him "I have heard your prayer and your plea, which you have made before Me."
1 Kings 9:3

Do you ever feel like no one is listening to you? No matter how loud I speak, some days it feels like no one is listening to me. It's the most aggravating feeling in the world. Even when I repeat myself three times, I can barely get those who love me to listen.

In 1 Kings 9:3 Solomon has just finished pouring his heart out to God. He's laid out his deepest thoughts to God. In answer, God tells Solomon, "I have heard your prayer and your plea." Solomon had watched his father, King David, speak to God over and over again, and he'd learned what we must never forget: We worship a God who hears. He listens to us when we cry out to Him. He's never deaf to our voices. He never ignores our pleas. Whereas other people might gloss over our words, God listens to every breath of our hearts. He hears us. He knows us.

If you're feeling unheard today, lift your voice up to the Lord. He's a God who listens. He's a God who hears.

Questions: *How good of a listener are you when it comes to hearing from God? Do you ever stop long enough to listen when you pour out your heart to Him?*

DAY 40

Happy

*You make known to me the path of life; in Your presence
there is fullness of joy; at Your right hand are pleasures forevermore.*
Psalm 16:11

I'm one of those people who has to fight for happiness. When someone asks me if I'm happy, I freeze. Happy? What do you mean, happy? I wonder. It's like I hardly ever allow myself the freedom to be happy. It's almost like I'm afraid of happy, afraid to concede to happy lest nothing ever changes in my life ever again, afraid of resigning myself to this present reality, right here, right now.

Yet when Jesus is at the center of our lives, happy is what we should be. In 1 Kings 10:8 the queen of Sheba came to the house of Solomon, and after a thorough investigation concluded: "Happy are your men! Happy are your servants, who continually stand before you and hear your wisdom!"

Whenever God is at the center of our lives, happy should be the state of our hearts. Are you happy today, or are you afraid of happy? Let God have His way in your life and find happiness in the fullness of His presence.

Questions: *Is your happiness dependent on your circumstances, or do you find your happiness in the reality of God's presence? How can you tell?*

DAY 41

Satisfied

*Delight yourself in the Lord,
and He will give you the desires of your heart.*
Psalm 37:4

We all have desires. We want some things, many of them reasonable and godly. We love verses that tell us that God will give us the desires of our heart as we delight in Him. We hang on to the hope God will give us what we want—eventually. But the moment we realize that God hasn't given us what we desperately want, we struggle.

Why does God hold back what seems so good for us? We miss what He's trying to teach us in the delays. Psalm 18:30 gives us the answer: "This God—His way is perfect; the word of the Lord proves true; He is a shield for all those who take refuge in Him." God in His sovereignty always has a reason for every delay we face. He knows what we need and gives us a place to hide while waiting for His plans to unfold.

Are you taking refuge in Him right now, even if you haven't been given the desires of your heart yet? Are you finding your satisfaction in Him alone while you wait? He is all you need and more.

Questions: *What are some practical ways you can delight yourself in the Lord today? How can you tell if you're finding your satisfaction in Him alone?*

Wrestling with God

But Jacob said, "I will not let You go unless you bless me."
Genesis 32:26

Do you ever feel like you're in a wrestling match with God? Do you ever wonder if you stand a chance in a wrestling match with God?

In Genesis 32 Jacob is in a wrestling match with God. Stuck in a dark place, overwhelmed by fear and uncertain of his future, Jacob met God and finally had it out with Him. When facing his deepest fears he didn't turn to his family, and he didn't call his friends. In his darkest hour only God would do. So he wrestled with the Almighty and wouldn't stop until he received God's blessing.

The outcome was awesome: Jacob did get his blessing, but he also got a limp. God took his hip out of socket, and it stayed that way forever. Jacob had been marked by God's presence, and everyone who saw him knew it.

Are you seeking God's face for an answer to your problems? Don't stop seeking Him. Hang on to Him for dear life. God will always answer. And His presence will leave a mark on you forever.

Questions: *What are you wrestling with God over right now? Are you about to let go, or will you keep on asking for His blessing?*

Forgiveness Heals

For if you forgive others their trespasses, your heavenly Father will also forgive you, but if you do not forgive others their trespasses, neither will your Father forgive your trespasses.
Matthew 6:14-15

Some people are hard to forgive. They've hurt you and they've shown no remorse. They don't seem to deserve your forgiveness. Yet Matthew 6:14-15 creates a small problem for the follower of Jesus. There seems to be a connection between our forgiving others and our Father forgiving us.

The truth is that anyone who has tasted and received the forgiveness of God understands his own unworthiness. Anyone who has been forgiven by God understands the value of mercy and grace. It becomes easier to forgive others as we meditate on Christ's forgiveness of us. Most of us are not as great and as perfect as we've led ourselves to believe. We are broken, needy people who have been forgiven. We are broken, needy people just like that one who is hard to forgive.

Receive Christ's mercy, and you'll find it so much easier to extend mercy to others. Hold back and find your heart has hardened just a little.

Questions: *Who is the hardest person in your life to forgive? How does seeing how much Christ has forgiven you make it so much easier for you to forgive the one who has wronged you?*

DAY 44

Exposed

> *Moses did not know that the skin of his face*
> *shone because he had been talking with God.*
> *Exodus 34:29*

Not long ago the lights on my deck stopped working. I had a short in the fuse, and it would require a fortune to fix. So I decided to switch to solars. I didn't realize how much in awe I would be staring at these solars. All day long the lights are exposed to the sun. Then when night comes, they have all they need to light up the darkness.

When it comes to your walk with Jesus, you are a lot more like the solar lights than you think. The more you're exposed to the sun, the brighter your light will shine. Just like Moses, as you sit in the presence of the Son and allow Him to fill you completely, something happens deep in your heart. Then when night comes, you don't even need a switch. You'll shine brightly because of what you've been exposed to.

If your light is dim in the darkness, it might be because you've not been exposed long enough to the Son.

Question: *What are some ways you can expose yourself more consistently with God's Son?*

DAY 45

Restored

*Restore to me the joy of Your salvation,
and uphold me with a willing spirit.*
Psalm 51:12

Do you ever notice what you do after an agonizing failure? If you're like me, you might be tempted to run to the familiar, straight back to your comfort zones. You might drown your sorrows in a bowl of ice cream, or veg in front of your favorite Netflix series. You'll do anything that feels safe and numbs out your sorrow.

In John 21 Peter did the same: When his life didn't turn out like he expected it to, he went back to his fishing boat. He reverted to the life he had before Jesus had radically changed it. But what I love most about John 21 is that Jesus didn't allow Peter to wallow in self-pity at all. No—Jesus showed up instead and restored Peter completely. Peter's worst nightmare became the launching pad for the rest of his life.

Jesus is committed to healing you. He will meet you in your brokenness and turn everything around for His glory. He's the God of second chances.

Questions: *Where do you turn to numb your pain when you're hurting? Are you willing to receive God's grace that is offered to you in your pain?*

DAY 46

Heart Matters

For out of the abundance of the heart the mouth speaks.
Matthew 12:34

Here's a physiological fact—or maybe it's mostly a spiritual reality, but it's the truth. When it comes to our bodies, there is a heart-mouth connection. In other words, what flows out of our mouth is a reflection of what's in our hearts. In other words, if you want to diagnose the state of your heart, just listen to the words that you speak. If you're always whining and complaining, then your heart is surely not trusting God. But if you catch yourself singing praise, odds are your heart is focused on Jesus. It's easier than you think.

Your words diagnose your heart—every single time. If you're not sure how you're doing, just ask those closest to you and they'll tell you—simply by listening to the words of your mouth—exactly how healthy your heart is.

Jesus said it like this: "Out of the abundance of the heart the mouth speaks." How is your mouth doing? Or maybe the better question is: How's your heart really doing?

Question: *Take a look at the pattern of words that routinely come out of your mouth. What do they reflect about your heart?*

Even If

Our God is able to rescue us...
But even if He does not...we are not going to serve your gods.
Daniel 3:17-18

Sooner or later we all face tough stuff. And when the going gets tough, it's easy to question God.

In Daniel 3, three friends named Shadrach, Meshach, and . were facing some pretty challenging circumstances. They had every reason to doubt that God would come through for them. When the king asked them to turn their back on their God, they responded without wavering: "Our God whom we serve is able to rescue us from the furnace of blazing fire, and He will rescue us... But even if *He does* not...we are not going to serve your gods or worship the golden image that you have set up" (vv. 17-18).

These three men were resolved to trust God no matter what would happen to them. Their faith remained unshaken despite great turmoil. And God came through for them.

If you're up against some tough stuff right now, would you resolve to believe God even if it doesn't look like He's with you right now? In due season, you'll see, He's closer than you think, and even the fire can't touch you when God is in your midst.

Question: *What are some ways you can become an "even if" Christian, unshaken by your circumstances no matter what?*

Past the Past

*But one thing I do: forgetting what lies
behind and straining forward to what lies ahead.*
Philippians 3:13

When it comes to moving past your past, one of the greatest obstacles is the "been there, done that, and keep failing" cynical approach. I know this state of mind very well. I've lived there before.

Until we're willing to allow God to break us free of this kind of thinking in our lives, we'll always be living in our past. The only way to overcome this sort of negative thinking is to rest our minds on the truth of who God is. God's mercies are new every morning, His steadfast love is so strong He'll never turn His back on us.

If you're stuck in a cycle of "been there, done that," your story is far from over. Because Jesus has risen from the dead, you have the power to overcome sin. Better yet, in Christ you are now dead to sin. Stop believing lies and embrace your identity in Christ. You are a new creation. The old is passed away. All has become new. Today is the first day of the rest of your life.

Questions: *What are some things in your past that you need to move past? How does your identity in Christ give you the power to do that?*

Think About It

As he [a man] thinks in his heart, so is he....
Proverbs 23:7

Do you ever think about what you're thinking about? In Proverbs 23:7 God tells us that "as [a man] thinks in his heart, so is he." In other words, it's important to think about what we're thinking about.

Have you ever stopped long enough to think about that, or is your mind occupied with your worries today? Are you resting your thoughts on the greatness of our God or on the size of your trials?

Stop and think about it. What you think about defines who you become. If you're tired of feeling worn out, perhaps it's time you rest your mind on Jesus. His love is steadfast, His faithfulness never ends, He is a God of second chances, and He's got your life under control.

Think about what you're thinking about, and if it's not leading to peace, chances are you're not thinking what's right and what's true.

Questions: *What do you spend most of your day thinking about? How can you train your mind to think about God more?*

Transitions

*Remember not the former things nor consider the things of old.
Behold, I am doing a new thing; now it springs forth, do you not perceive it?*
Isaiah 43:18-19

Transition. It's just another word for change. If you're like me, a creature of habit, transitions can be tough. I like stability and knowing where everything is all the time. Yet God uses transitions to move us into our destiny.

In Isaiah 43:18-19 God says, "Remember not the former things nor consider the things of old. Behold, I am doing a new thing; now it springs forth, do you not perceive it?" The best part about these words is that God places them smack dab in the middle of Isaiah 43, a chapter about God's love.

In Isaiah 43 God reminds us that when we go through the rivers, they won't overwhelm us, and through the fire, it won't burn us. If you're feeling the weight of a transition today, take heart. Your circumstances might be changing, but remember that God never will. His presence is with you, and His love is steadfast no matter what. There's no need to be afraid.

Questions: *What sort of changes are you going through right now? How does the reality of God's love encourage you to overcome the fear of change?*

Part of the Family

*See what kind of love the Father has given to us,
that we should be called children of God; and so we are.*
1 John 3:1

There are privileges that come with being the child of someone who is unique and awesome. If you're your parents' child, you don't have to ring the doorbell to come in. You don't have to be invited by phone to come to dinner. You don't have to wonder if you'll be going on the next family vacation with the family. It's expected because you're part of the family.

Whether you grew up in a loving home or a broken one, there is a comfort of home that we all yearn for and want. John captures that spirit of love in 1 John 3:1. He reminds us of what it's like to be home. To be loved. To be part of God's family. No wonder John calls himself the beloved disciple and the disciple whom Jesus loved.

John, like no one else, understood the full privileges of what it means to be a child of God. He leaned on Jesus at the Last Supper because he received Christ's love.

Have you received Christ's love for you? Are you living like you're part of the family of God? In John 1:12 we're promised that the moment we receive Christ, we're given the right to be called God's children. Adopted, loved, invited, included. Beloved, that's who we are!

Questions: *How would you live differently if you truly felt like part of God's family? What are some things you might tell God or ask of Him? Have you been acting like a visitor, or do you know who you are?*

Negotiators

*For You have done wonderful things,
plans formed of old, faithful and true.*
Isaiah 25:1

Do you ever feel like you're negotiating your way through your life? My friend is a single mom. She thought she'd be married forever, but then her husband left her unexpectedly. Now she acts like a negotiator, always trying to do what's best for the kids, balancing the needs of everyone, and trying to make right choices.

Maybe you're not negotiating parenthood, but your issues are with your siblings or your colleagues, or even your church family. While it's tempting to want to negotiate our way through life, it's not necessary. It is only as we rest in the Lord and in His perfect ways that we can let go of a role God never intended for us in the first place.

Your life is safe in the arms of the Father, and not even a messy divorce or demanding boss can ruin it. God is in control of your life and future. You can turn your negotiating to Him. He's got your back both now and forevermore.

Questions: Where in your life are you most tempted to take on the role of negotiator? Would you confess to God that you're not going to try to control that difficult situation anymore?

Not by Might

*Then he said to me, "This is the word of the L*ORD *to Zerubbabel: Not by might, nor by power, but by My Spirit, says the L*ORD *of hosts."*
Zechariah 4:6

Have you ever considered why we love verses like Zechariah 4:6? I don't know about you, but I've lived long enough by now to recognize that I simply don't have enough strength. I don't have enough resources. I don't have enough wisdom.

No matter how hard I work, it never seems enough. No matter how good my intentions, they always seem short of what's expected. No matter how deep my love for missions or others, inevitably I want to escape it all. And God knows that.

Not only does He know it, but He designed us in such a way that we would be completely and utterly reliant on Him. But then He gives us His Spirit. If you're a follower of Christ, the Spirit of God indwells you. He is your comforter and strength. He's your teacher and corrector. He's your guide.

So while you and I might not be able to accomplish much on our own, we become unstoppable by the power of the Spirit. Will you ask the Spirit of God to help you today?

Question: *In what areas of your life do you feel powerless and helpless? Ask God's Spirit to help you in your place of need.*

DAY 54

Believe God Now

No eye has seen a God besides You, who acts for those who wait for Him.
Isaiah 64:4

First, God makes the promise, then comes our receiving the promise; and finally comes the hard part: waiting for the promise to be fulfilled. That's where true faith must show up. That's where true faith grows. I call it life in the gap.

Mary, the mother of Jesus, typified life in the gap. After being told she was chosen to carry the Messiah, she submitted to God even though His plan sounded crazy to her human mind. In Luke 1:45 we're told, "Blessed is she who believed that there would be a fulfillment of what was spoken to her from the Lord." That's life in the gap.

I'm sure you're familiar with that place. If you're living between the promise and the fulfillment of the promise, you're not alone. Like Mary, resolve not just to receive God's promises in submission and trust, but be willing to wait for the fulfillment of the promises. When you do, you too will be called blessed.

Question: *What are some ways you can show God you trust Him while waiting to see His promises fulfilled in your life?*

Overcomer

And this is the victory that has overcome the world—our faith.
1 John 5:4

Do you feel stuck? On the verge of defeat? Overwhelmed? God's way is better. God's plan for you is to overcome. To conquer. To defeat. To soar. To soar above your present circumstances.

In 1 John 5:4 we're told: "And this is the victory that has overcome the world—our faith." We overcome through our faith in the resurrected Jesus! Nothing can stand against our faith in God. You might feel like your faith is small, but remember that it's not the size of your faith but the size of your God that matters. He's the God who rose from the dead and conquered death and the grave.

Faith is your shield against the onslaught of the enemy. Yeah, you're an overcomer even if you don't feel like you are. God says that you are more than a conqueror through Christ, and nothing will ever separate you from His love.

Go ahead and lift your head high. You're a child of the King. It's who you are. It's God's plan for you. It's your destiny. Now live like it, won't you?

Questions: *Do you feel like an overcomer, or do you feel defeated by your circumstances right now? How does knowing who you are in Christ change your whole attitude today?*

No More Fear

The fear of man lays a snare, but whoever trusts in the Lord is safe.
Proverbs 29:25

What you fear determines how you feel. You either live with the fear of man or with the fear of God. The ramifications are deeper than you think. Proverbs 29:25 says that *fearing people is a dangerous trap, but trusting the Lord means safety.*

When it comes to overcoming fear in your life, you need to consider who you're living in fear of. Ask yourself: Am I more worried about what "they" think about me or about what God thinks? Am I saying yes to them when I should be saying no? And am I choosing to be silent when I should be speaking truth?

One of the best ways to tell if you're controlled by the fear of man is to check your moods. If you're constantly weighed down by worry and driven to despair, you're living for man. But if you're able to find freedom no matter what happens around you, and if you're able to stay strong despite your trials, then you're on to something. You're living in the fear of the Lord, and that's where wisdom begins.

Questions: *Who do you fear more than anything else? If you were to live fearing God more than you fear man, how would that change your behavior today?*

DAY 57

More than Enough

*And my God will supply every need of yours
according to His riches in glory in Christ Jesus.*
Philippians 4:19

Some days it feels like I just don't have what it takes to get the job done. Do you ever feel like that? I often feel like I'm not good enough, not smart enough, and not resourced enough. Yet over and over in His Word, God shows us that we don't ever have to be strong enough to need Him.

Consider David and Goliath or the feeding of the five thousand. All God ever asks of us is only what we have—what's in our very hands. And all God ever does is only what we can't do. All God fills is exactly what we offer Him. God has a way of always using what is broken in our lives.

It was only when Gideon smashed the jars and when Jesus broke the bread that the miracle took place. God doesn't need you to be more than enough. He's the One who is more than enough, and He longs to meet you in your point of need.

Give Him all you've got and watch Him do what you could never do on your own. God is able, and that's more than enough for today.

Questions: *In what areas in your life do you feel like you don't have what it takes? Are you striving to do it all on your own, or are you willing to trust God with what you hold most dear?*

Resurrection Power

That I may know Him and the power of His resurrection.
Philippians 3:10

Lord, I need a breakthrough! Have you ever prayed this prayer to God? Maybe you're there right now. You're on the verge of giving up. You're barely holding on to the hope that someday, somehow, God is going to show up. That's a really great place to be. You're closer to breakthrough than you think.

A breakthrough is defined as movement beyond the enemy's front line of defense. And when it comes to spiritual breakthrough, God specializes in crossing enemy lines when it looks impossible and when you feel like there's nothing more you can do.

Do you feel like you've waited forever for the Lord to show up? When Jesus hung on the cross, breakthrough looked hopeless; yet three days later God miraculously raised Jesus from the grave.

Oh, your story might look like it's over right now, but the same power that raised Jesus from the dead is yours in Christ today. Breakthrough will come in God's perfect timing, and nothing can stand in His way.

Questions: *Where do you long for breakthrough in your life right now? Will you pray and tell God that you'll wait for His timing no matter how long it takes for breakthrough to come?*

Pressure Points

For this is the will of God, your sanctification.
1 Thessalonians 4:3

We all have a dark side. Most of us walk around with one likeable public persona, but reserve another dark side for those who know and love us best (for instance, our family). But when the pressure of life squeezes us a little, our dark side comes to the surface when we least expect it—like on the phone with the customer service rep or at the poor lady at the airport. Yet it's God's grace that allows us to be pressed in order to see who we really are.

We are a work in progress, always in need of God's grace, but it's only when our worst self shows up that we'll admit our need for change. In 1 Thessalonians 4:3 Paul reminds us, "This is the will of God, your sanctification." God will make sure that our dark side shows up in order to remind us that we're in need of His grace more than we realize it.

If your dark side shows up today, confess your sin to Him quickly, and ask Him to change you where you need it the most.

Questions: *When was the last time you were pressed? How did you respond? What might God be trying to change in you through the pressure that you're feeling?*

Remember Truth

For the righteous falls seven times and rises again.
Proverbs 24:16

My mom jokes that as she's getting older she's developing amnesia. She started that joke when she was sixty, and truth is, she doesn't forget much.

Too many of us have developed a sort of spiritual amnesia that forgets the most important things. We forget who we're supposed to be. We forget God's Word. We forget our promises to God. We forget who we are and whose we are.

When we find ourselves in places of forgetting, the only thing we can do is to stop and remember; and nothing will flood your memories with truth like God's Word. By God's grace when we remember God's Word, we're reminded that we can indeed start afresh each new morning. We can go back to our places of resolve.

Proverbs 24:16 reminds us that even though a righteous man falls seven times, he will still get up. It doesn't matter how many times we fail God, or veer from our intentions, every day is a chance to receive God's mercies again.

Let's grab on to God's promises, even when we feel we've blown it. Let's get back in the Word and remember the truth about who we are and who God is no matter how deep our amnesia seems to be!

Questions: *What truth of God do you need to be reminded of today?*

Wonderful Places

*He who dwells in the shelter of the Most High
will abide in the shadow of the Almighty.*
Psalm 91:1

What's the most wonderful place you've ever been? There's a group I follow on Instagram called "Wonderful places" that shows some of the most amazing places on this earth. Every time I see a picture, I yearn to go there. It also fills my heart with wonder that God has created these wonderful places for us to enjoy and to reflect His glory.

Think about it. Yet as beautiful as these places are, God has given us an even more wonderful place to dwell, and it's closer than you think.

David understood it. In Psalm 16:11 he wrote that "in Your presence is fullness of joy; at Your right hand are pleasures forevermore." And in Psalm 91:1 he said that "he who dwells in the shelter of the Most High will abide in the shadow of the Almighty."

Oh, there are many wonderful places on this earth, but the most wonderful place of them all is to stay tucked safe in the shelter of God's arms. If you're looking for wonderful, it starts right here!

Questions: *What's the most beautiful place you've been? How awesome is it to know that God's presence is even more beautiful than that? How can you intentionally hide in Him today?*

Unchanging God

I am God, and there is no other; I am God, and there is none like Me...
I have spoken, and I will bring it to pass; I have purposed and I will do it.
Isaiah 46:9,11

One of my biggest fears in life is that I'll screw up God's plans for my life with my own bad decisions. Yet when it comes to God and His ways, we can hold on to the hope that God never changes. He's the same yesterday and today and forever. His plans are sure and secure.

In Isaiah 46:9-11 God reassures us with these words: "I am God, and there is no other; I am God, and there is none like Me, declaring the end from the beginning and from ancient times things not yet done...I have spoken, and I will bring it to pass; I have purposed, and I will do it."

Nothing will change God's plans for your life. He always perfects what concerns you. When you're tempted to look at your circumstances and wonder what went wrong, God sees past your circumstances. He knows what you need and when you need it and will accomplish all that pertains to your life in due season.

His plans for you never change. You don't need to be afraid.

Question: *When your past comes knocking with regret and condemnation, will you stand strong in the truth of who God is and His unchanging promises for you?*

Wonderfully Made

*I praise You, for I am fearfully and
wonderfully made. Wonderful are Your works.*
Psalm 139:14

If you could change one thing about yourself, what would it be? If I'm being honest, I'd probably change not one but two or three things about myself if I could. And when that list was over, I'd think of at least two more things I'd change about myself.

Most of us aren't convinced that we're beautiful. Yet in Psalm 139:14-16 David wrote: "I praise You, for I am fearfully and wonderfully made. Wonderful are Your works; my soul knows it very well. My frame was not hidden from You when I was being made in secret, intricately woven in the depths of the earth. Your eyes saw my unformed substance; in Your book were written every one of them, the days that were formed for me, when as yet there was none of them."

David was pointing to an important truth: God made you just the way He wanted you to be and wouldn't change one thing about you. He created you just as you are—you're perfect in His eyes. He loves you just the way you are.

Questions: *Think about the two or three things you would change about yourself if you could. Now stop and give thanks to the Lord for those very things you hate.*

DAY 64

Not Forgotten

Can a woman forget her nursing child, that she should have no compassion on the son of her womb? Even these may forget, yet I will not forget you.
Isaiah 49:15

I'll never get over the story of God choosing David to be the next king of Israel. God sent Samuel to anoint the next king of Israel. After going through all his other brothers, the family almost forgot about David. David was out in the fields tending sheep. He was doing what he was supposed to be doing, and everyone almost forgot about him. Except for God.

God hadn't forgotten about David. He hadn't lost sight of His chosen one. And just in the nick of time, God led Samuel to David. There was never a chance that the future king of Israel would ever miss his own anointing. God would find him no matter how hidden David's road seemed to be on that fateful day.

Do you ever feel forgotten? You don't have to be afraid. The same God who sought David out in the fields has His eye on you today. He'll never lose sight of you. He'll never forget you. You just keep on tending sheep.

Question: *Memorize today's verse and give thanks to God who has not forgotten you.*

Don't Compare

For I know the plans I have for you, declares the Lord,
plans for welfare and not for evil, to give you a future and a hope.
Jeremiah 29:11

One of the most dangerous things you can do is compare your story to everyone else's. Just because you went to the same high school or roomed together in college doesn't mean that God has the same plan for your life. Yet so much of our time is wasted comparing stories.

Life never seems fair when we give in to the trap of comparison. But consider God's point of view. God is sovereign over all. There's nothing He can't do, and there are no accidents in His economy. He sees the end from the beginning, and He's written your story with every little detail. You are where you are today because God ordained it. He isn't perplexed by your current status. He knows exactly what you need and when you need it.

The easiest way to trust God's heart is to fix your eyes on His promises, and stop comparing your story to everyone else's. Freedom comes when you live in the sphere God has placed you in right now.

Questions: *Who do you tend to compare yourself to? What are some practical action steps you need to take to protect yourself from falling into the trap of comparison?*

Growing Up

But solid food is for the mature, for those who have their powers of discernment trained by constant practice to distinguish good from evil.
Hebrews 5:14

Have you ever been stuck in a pothole? The best way to avoid being stuck in a pothole is to know about it before you hit it. You can then slow down and drive around it.

The same principle is true in your life. In order to avoid being stuck in a pit of self-pity and regret, some potholes are best avoided completely. It might be the pothole of an old addiction or the pothole of an old toxic relationship. Learn to watch out for the potholes in your life and drive around them.

The good news is that if you're stuck in a pothole right now, God's grace will get you out of it every single time. But the key to maturity is growing in discernment as you learn to tell where the potholes are in your life and avoiding them completely. Instead of sinking into a pothole, resolve to climb the mountain of God's love and celebrate His goodness.

Questions: What are the most common potholes that get you stuck in your life? What are some ways to learn to see them before you fall into them?

Strong Enough

But David strengthened himself in the Lord his God.
1 Samuel 30:6

Ever feel like the whole world is against you? Like no matter how hard you've tried, no one really understands you? That's where David found himself once. It was a time when David was still living out in the strongholds. He and his men had gone out to war. Back at the camp, tragedy struck. All the women and kids from his village were taken captive by the enemy with no one to protect them.

When David and his men came home and heard the calamity, David's brothers wanted to kill him. David could have caved under the weight of the burden but he did not. David rose above it. In 1 Samuel 30 we're told that when the people spoke of stoning David, he "strengthened himself in the Lord his God." When everyone turned against him, David turned to God. Not only did he find comfort for his broken heart, but David also found victory over the enemy.

Do you feel the weight of your trial today? Won't you seek refuge in the Lord? You'll find Him strong enough to carry your burden and defeat your enemy.

Question: *What are some ways you too can strengthen yourself in the Lord?*

Open Eyes

Open my eyes, that I may behold wondrous things out of Your law.
Psalm 119:18

Two men looked through the bars. One saw mud, the other the stars. Which one are you? I'm ashamed to admit it, but more often than I care to, when I look through the bars I see mud. I have a gift for picking out what's bad in my life. Winters are too cold. Dating is too hard. My clothes are too dated. My cup tends to be half empty. All I see is mud.

Consider David's prayer in Psalm 119. David longed to see beauty. David prayed to see the Lord through His Word. Maybe David had a tendency to see mud too, but his words show that he was committed to change. David's prayer is a reminder that when we can't see things clearly, the best thing we can do is to ask God to change us.

Are you a mud seeing or a star gazing sort of person? God in His grace can open your eyes to behold His beauty too.

Question: *What are some of the wondrous things God has shown you in His Word lately?*

Whispers of Truth

Why do you say, O Jacob, and speak, O Israel, "My way is hidden from the LORD, and my right is disregarded by my God"?
Isaiah 40:27

Are you quick to accuse God of not showing up in your life? Every so often I feel the twinge of self-pity. Has God forgotten me? Has He overlooked His promises to me?

In the stillness of the morning, I read the words of Isaiah 40:27-28: "Why do you say, O Jacob, and speak, O Israel, 'My way is hidden from the LORD, and my right is disregarded by my God'? Have you not known? Have you not heard? The Lord is the everlasting God, the Creator of the ends of the earth. He does not faint or grow weary; his understanding is unsearchable."

God's whisper has a way of reaching the depth of my heart. His Word testifies that He hasn't forgotten me. His Spirit reminds me that He knows exactly where I am. The accusations of the enemy always stop in the light of God's truth. This all-powerful God could change my circumstances if He chose to, but until He does, all I will do is trust and obey. Won't you do that too?

Question: *Whose voice are you listening to today? Read the words of Isaiah 40:27 out loud; then quiet yourself long enough to believe them.*

DAY 70

Fruit Bearing

*Unless a grain of wheat falls into the earth and dies,
it remains alone; but if it dies, it bears much fruit.*
John 12:24

More than anything in the world, I want to bear fruit for God's glory. But do you know how fruit is born? It's not until the seed falls into the ground and dies that fruit is birthed. It's what Jesus meant when He said, "Unless a grain of wheat falls into the earth and dies, it remains alone; but if it dies, it bears much fruit."

Do you want to bear great fruit for God's glory? The more pertinent question is: Are you willing to die? Are you willing to be broken by God? It's this kind of brokenness that leads to more fruit.

Maybe you've asked God for fruit, and instead, all you feel is the pressure of His squeezing fingers. You're confused and you're wondering what happened. Perhaps you're simply being broken while God readies your life for more fruit. Will you surrender to the pain of His touch even when you don't understand it? God brings life out of all that looks broken.

Question: *In what specific ways is God asking you to die to yourself?*

DAY 71

Forgiven and Clean

If we confess our sins, He is faithful and just to forgive us our sins and to cleanse us from all unrighteousness.
1 John 1:9

No matter how hard I try to live for God, I find myself falling for the same temptations over and over again. After a while, even though I ask the Lord for forgiveness, it's harder for me to feel forgiven. Sometimes it's easier to believe the lies that Satan throws our way than the truth of God's promises. We convince ourselves that our sin is too great for God to forgive. We tell ourselves that this time we've crossed the line. But God's Word is clear: As far as the east is from the west, so far has God removed our sins from us (see Psalm 103:12). The minute we confess our sin, God forgives us.

It's never about how we feel when it comes to God's promises. It's about who God is. It's about what He has promised. It's about Jesus' blood shed for our sin. And when it comes to God's Word, God promises that He always forgives those who ask for forgiveness. His love is steadfast no matter how we feel and even when we don't deserve it.

Question: *Have you ever been wrecked and utterly astounded by God's grace in your life? Take a minute and consider how deep His love is for you.*

DAY 72

Fighting Sin

In your struggle against sin you have not yet resisted to the point of shedding your blood.
Hebrews 12:4

When it comes to fighting sin, it's not always a walk in the park. In Hebrews 12 we're told, "In your struggle against sin you have not yet resisted to the point of shedding your blood." I've never thought about this verse too much until I resolved to get serious about fighting sin in my life.

Overcoming your besetting sin will demand every bit of your focus. No, it's not going to be a walk in the park. As God's Spirit convicts you and you get serious about changing, you will need help and accountability to make it. You will need to get serious about praying. You will need to remember who you are. You are dead to sin. Sin has no power over you, but it will take every bit of your focus to win this battle.

While fighting sin is not easy, it's worth every bit of the struggle. So how hard are you willing to fight to overcome sin? How serious are you about victory?

Questions: What is your besetting sin, and what is your strategy to overcome it?

Power Up

And do not get drunk with wine,
for that is debauchery, but be filled with the Spirit.
Ephesians 5:18

I went out of town recently and took my computer, but noticed that I'd forgotten to bring along the plug. After about four hours and twenty-eight minutes, I ran out of battery power. For the remainder of the trip, I couldn't use my computer no matter how hard I tried. No amount of effort was going to get my computer going. The only hope I had was to find a charger and power up my computer again.

As a follower of Jesus Christ, you might be scratching your head wondering why your life feels so powerless. Unless you're regularly powering up your life with the Holy Spirit, no amount of striving will give you the power that you need. Only God's Spirit will give you the fresh power that you long for.

The best way to connect to the Holy Spirit is through God's Word and in prayer. Ask Him for a fresh filling of His Spirit again. Ask Him to fill you anew.

Question: *What are some practical ways that show that you are being filled with the Spirit? Read Ephesians 2:19-21 for some practical insights.*

Turbulence

And He awoke and rebuked the wind and said to the sea, "Peace! Be still!" And the wind ceased, and there was a great calm.
Mark 4:39

In all my years of flying, here's what I've learned about turbulence: No matter how bad the turbulence has been, not once have I ever considered stepping into the cockpit of a plane to take over the flying. Even when the winds get really rough, deep in my soul is the firm belief that the pilot has it under control.

When it comes to the Christian life, most people don't hold to the same confidence. The moment we hit a patch of turbulence, most of us run into the command center and want to assume control. We demand to take the wheel back even though we have zero experience in flying. How offensive our response must be to God. How insulting to the Almighty.

Are you going through some choppy weather right now? Resist the temptation to jump into the cockpit. Let God be God. He doesn't need your help. All He needs is your cooperation. He's going to land you safely if you'll just trust Him.

Question: *In what ways do you tend to take over the control of your life when you hit a patch of turbulence?*

God in the Mess

He drew me up from the pit of destruction, out of the miry bog, and set my feet upon a rock, making my steps secure.
Psalm 40:2

Some days my life feels like one big mess. Despite all my best intentions and plans, I find that the things that I don't want to do I do, and the things I never thought would happen to me have. No matter how I tease it out, some days I look at the sum total of my life and wonder: How did I get here? When did my life become so messy? And just when I start to get weighed down by it all, I look at God's Word, and I see a theme.

God is at work even in the mess. He's a redeeming God. That's the message of the Bible. He is at work in our tears. He is at work when we fail. He is at work when we're too broken to find our way out. God is waiting for us to cry out to Him for help. He's a God who's able to take the mess that we've made and make something beautiful out of it.

Question: *Have you ever had a time in your life where you felt like a mess, but God stepped in and made something beautiful from it?*

DAY 76

Just Enough Light

*I will lead the blind in a way that they do not know,
in paths that they have not known I will guide them.*
Isaiah 42:16

Do you ever feel like you're not sure which way to go? Yeah, me too. On most evenings, I'm more than a little grateful for the flashlight on my phone. It gives me just enough light to see in front of me and keeps me from stumbling.

No matter how hard I try to see everything clearly all of the time, sometimes it feels like I'm walking through a dark tunnel. I'm not sure which way to go. When I'm in that place, I rest in Isaiah 42:16: "I will lead the blind in a way that they do not know, in paths that they have not known I will guide them. I will turn the darkness before them into light, the rough places into level ground. These are the things I do, and I do not forsake them."

Like the light on my phone, God promises to give us just enough light for the step we're on. Now that's a promise I'm going to hang on to. That's a light I'm going to keep on using.

Questions: *What are some tangible ways that God gives us light in the darkness? What is the next step you can take today given the bit of light God has given you?*

DAY 77

No Regrets

*No one who puts his hand to the plow
and looks back is fit for the kingdom of God.*
Luke 9:62

I recently read about William Borden. Born in 1887, he grew up in Chicago with a rich family, but he soon felt the call to become a missionary. Mocked by many who thought his decision a waste, he wrote two words in the front of his Bible: No Reserve.

After graduating from Yale, he was offered many jobs which he rejected. His heart was set on being a missionary in China. Two more words were added to the front of his Bible: No Retreat.

On his way to China, he made a pit stop in Egypt to learn Arabic, which would help him on the mission field. A month later Wiliam Borden contracted meningitis and died. His death shook the world. Many felt his life a waste. Yet, shortly after his funeral, someone found his Bible and noticed that William had added two more words to the front of his Bible: No Regrets.

Borden was a Christian who understood what it meant to live with undivided focus on the Lord. Won't you let his life inspire you?

Questions: *Have you ever taken a big step for God that no one understood? If God asks you to do something hard for Him, would you be willing to say yes?*

DAY 78

Unconditional Love

*There is therefore now no condemnation
for those who are in Christ Jesus.*
Romans 8:1

It's not always easy being a Christian. The temptations are plentiful and failures are real despite the Holy Spirit living in us. Some days, no matter how hard we try to ignore it, it's easy to believe the lie that our sin is just a bit too much for God to handle. But have you considered God's Word? It's filled with people who crossed the line in what we might consider unforgivable ways.

There's David who first committed adultery, then killed his mistress's husband. There's Samson the fool and Lot the self-centered and Jacob the deceiver. The list is long, but the theme is the same: There is no sin so dark that God's love cannot reach. His grace is unending. His mercies never come to an end. They are new every morning.

No matter what you've done in your life, God's grace is yours again if you'll ask for it. If His love doesn't stir you up to love and obey Him even more, nothing else ever will.

Questions: *Do you feel more loved by God when you're more obedient? Why is that kind of thinking not consistent with who God is?*

Promise Maker

God is not man, that He should lie,
or a son of man, that He should change His mind.
Numbers 23:19

God is a promise maker and a promise keeper. There is no greater proof of it than the Christmas story. For four thousand years God had promised that Jesus would come. Many doubted Him. Others turned from Him. Still others mocked God and His people.

In Numbers 23:19 we're reminded that "God is not man, that He should lie, or a son of man, that He should change His mind. Has He said, and will He not do it? Or has He spoken, and will He not fulfill it?" Just as God had promised, after centuries of waiting, Jesus was born in a manger.

Today we're still waiting on the Lord. We're waiting for Jesus to come back. Our hearts long for Him with yearning. Our eyes strain for His return. Some days we might be tempted to want to give up. We might be tempted to doubt. But a look at Christmas is enough to remind us that our God does not lie. He always does exactly what He promises.

Question: What promises are you still waiting on God for?

DAY 80

Winter Seasons

Though the fig tree should not blossom, nor fruit be on the vines...
yet I will rejoice in the Lord; I will take joy in the God of my salvation.
Habakkuk 3:17-18

Where I live, winter means that the leaves are all gone and it's really cold outside. Everything looks barren where there used to be fruit.

It's easy to feel discouraged during the barren seasons of life. It's easy to wonder where God is when every part of your life looks dormant. But don't be fooled by the absence of the leaves. Just because it's winter doesn't mean it's dead. The trees that look dead in the winter are simply getting ready for fruit season.

See, winter is a season that ushers in the spring. Winter is a time to hang on to Habakkuk 3:17-18 that says, "Though the fig tree should not blossom, nor fruit be on the vines, the produce of the olive fail and the fields yield no food… yet I will rejoice in the Lord; I will take joy in the God of my salvation."

Even in winter, our hearts can rejoice. Even when we can't see it clearly, God is at work. If you're living in a winter season right now, just wait. Spring will be here before you know it.

Question: *What are some things you can rejoice in during the winter seasons of your life?*

Satisfied

*Hope deferred makes the heart sick,
but a desire fulfilled is a tree of life.*
Proverbs 13:12

Have you ever noticed that when it comes to most things in life, half the fun is in the anticipation? I think of most Christmas mornings, half the fun is waiting for that moment when I'll finally find out if all my dreams will come true and everything I wished for will lie hidden under that tree. Will the wait have been worth it?

Some years, joy came after a season of waiting, but sometimes, the weight of disappointment felt crushing. I learned to brace myself for disappointment.

Have you approached your life the same way? We wonder if God will show up and if it will in fact be worth the wait. But just like the real meaning of Christmas, none of us ever wake up disappointed. God came to earth in the form of man. We have a Savior, Emmanuel. No one gets the short end of the stick. Jesus loves us. He came for us. He died for us. And He lives for us today.

The long-awaited Messiah is here. Joy is ours for the taking.

Our desire has been fulfilled in Christ.

Questions: *Do you find yourself always longing for more? How can you find all of your satisfaction in Jesus?*

Thrive

I am the vine, you are the branches. Whoever abides in Me and I in him, he it is that bears much fruit, for apart from Me you can do nothing.
John 15:5

When it comes to thriving as a Christian, there are two habits that every Christian desperately needs. First is the habit of being in the Word daily. Second is the habit of guarding what comes into our hearts diligently.

The assumption that some people are just blessed with a more godly DNA than others is not true. The only way to thrive in Christ is to do what He has asked: Abide in Him. In John 15, we're compared to branches of a tree, dependent on Jesus, our vine.

The strategy God gives us to bear fruit is to stay so connected to Christ through His Word and His Spirit that anything becomes possible. When you and I spend time in God's Word intentionally, we fellowship with the Father and hear what He says. When we yield to the Holy Spirit's control of our minds and our hearts, our lives become fruitful. That's how we thrive.

Questions: *How fruitful is your life for Christ? Are you making time for God's Word in your life? Are you fully yielded to the Holy Spirit?*

Easy Living

For it was fitting that He, for whom and by whom all things exist, in bringing many sons to glory, should make the founder of their salvation perfect through suffering.
Hebrews 2:10

One of the biggest lies I've hung on to is the lie that my life should be easy—that I *deserve* an easier life. A look at God's Word shows us that the opposite is true. The Christian life is full and unlike any other, but it's not always easy.

A study of the Scriptures shows that almost every man or woman who followed the Lord Jesus embraced suffering. In Hebrews 2:10 we're told that Jesus Himself was made perfect through suffering. In Matthew 7 Jesus told us that the road is narrow that leads to life, and in 2 Timothy 3 we're promised that all who desire to live a godly life will suffer persecution.

Following Jesus might not be easy, but it's worth every sacrifice we make. Furthermore, by the power of the Spirit we're given everything we need to overcome and live victoriously. You can hang on to hope today no matter what you're facing.

Questions: *What kind of suffering are you going through right now? Does knowing that Jesus suffered just like us encourage you to go on today?*

Believe God

No unbelief made him waver concerning the promise of God, but he grew strong in his faith as he gave glory to God.
Romans 4:20

One of my favorite Bible passages is in Romans 4. It tells the story of Abraham who waited forever for the son God had promised him. There came a point where it became ridiculous to believe God, but still, Abraham believed God. Romans 4:18-21 says that "in hope he (Abraham) believed against hope...he did not weaken in faith when he considered his own body, which was as good as dead...No unbelief made him waver concerning the promise of God, but he grew strong in his faith as he gave glory to God, fully convinced that God was able to do what He had promised."

Are you on the verge of giving up today? Have you given up on your dreams, your hopes, even your God? Have you hung on to God's promises but have noticed you're starting to doubt God? The same God who came through for Abraham is the God who will answer you today. Your faith in Him, when you can't see the answer, greatly glorifies Him.

In Christ we can rest in the truth that God will always do what He promised. There's nothing He cannot do if we'll just trust Him. Won't you make Romans 4 your resting place today?

Questions: What are you still waiting on God for? Will you believe in hope against hope that God will fulfill His promise for you still?

Aim for Love

*"By this all people will know that you are
My disciples, if you have love for one another."*
John 13:35

As a pediatric ER doctor, I get a lot of opportunities to interact with a lot of people. Too often, I have to give people news and information that they don't want to hear and might not agree with.

For example, if they think they need an antibiotic and I have to tell them that they just have a cold and that it will eventually go away on its own, I can feel the friction of the conversation. They don't like it when I tell them what they don't want to hear. But over the years, I've started to make an obvious observation: It's not what I tell people, but how I tell it to them that matters the most.

See, it's not unusual for people to disagree with their doctors. But the ones who still leave happy are the ones who can tell that their doctor really cares about them and is looking out for their best.

Isn't it true in our lives, too? We don't have to be surrounded with people who agree with us to find joy and harmony. We simply have to aim for love. As we aim for love, even our most ardent critic will start to bend to the truth. Always aim for love. Watch Jesus melt hearts in due season.

Question: *Aim for love. Think about how that might look in your life right now—with your family, with your kids, with your coworkers, and with your church folks.*

Seek the Truth

*The heart is deceitful above all things,
and desperately sick; who can understand it?*
Jeremiah 17:9

People are fond of this saying: "Trust your heart. You won't go wrong if you'll just trust your heart." At first, we nod our heads in agreement. But consider Jeremiah 17:9 where God tells us that "the heart is deceitful above all things, and desperately sick; who can understand it?"

By God's standard, the heart cannot be trusted at all. It will always lead us astray. Our hearts might tell us that if it feels good we should do it, but the truth of God's Word is that when we choose to sin, we choose to suffer. Our hearts might tell us to end a marriage because it's hard, or to date a guy because he's cute, but God's Word speaks truth: Marriage is a covenant, and dating has a godly strategy.

While our hearts might lead us astray, God's Word never will. While our feelings might lie, God's Word is the rock on which to build our life. If you're looking for a thriving future in the Lord, stop listening to your heart and start heeding God's Word!

Questions: *Are you tempted to follow your heart, or do you seek God's Word for every decision in your life? In what areas in your life right now might you seek God's Word for guidance?*

Guard Against Sin

Take no part in the unfruitful works of darkness, but instead expose them.
Ephesians 5:11

As a pediatric ER doctor, I get these questions all the time: Is it contagious? Am I going to catch this rash or that cold? And if it is contagious, people will do whatever they can to avoid it and protect against it.

Yet when it comes to our spiritual health, we are far less worried about things that mar our souls and kill our growth. In Ephesians 5 Paul lays it down when it comes to our soul health. As far as sin goes, he says, don't even take part in it. He goes on to say that it is shameful even to speak of the things that people do in secret.

I know it doesn't sound popular, but over and over again in His Word, God commands us to be set apart. To guard against sin. To flee immorality. Yes, we must love people, sinners included, but when it comes to sin, we must protect against the things that will infect our souls. We must choose the kind of purity that welcomes the Almighty and allows us to see Jesus!

Question: *What measures are you taking to guard against sin in your life?*

DAY 88

Overflow

Out of the abundance of the heart his mouth speaks.
Luke 6:45

There's been a huge increase in road rage in recent times. People are driving with an angry intensity like never before.

I saw a news segment of a man and a woman who got in a road argument, and pretty soon they had gotten out of their respective cars and into a fistfight—right there on national news! It made me reconsider what I do and say on the road, but it also got me thinking that we as a people seem to becoming angrier and angrier with time. Violence is brimming over at the mere tip of the iceberg.

Jesus warned us of this in Luke 6:45 where He taught us that out of the abundance of our hearts our mouths speak. Our words and our actions reflect who we really are.

Have you ever considered what comes out of your mouth when you're pressed? Does joy leak out, or do you explode in anger? The only way to overflow with grace is to fill up daily on God's Word. Make room for His Spirit each morning. He's the only One who can fill your tank with joy and peace.

Question: *What comes out of your heart when you're pressed? Watch your reactions today, and ask the Holy Spirit to transform your heart where needed.*

God's Favor

*The Lord bless you and keep you; the Lord make
His face to shine upon you and be gracious to you;
the Lord lift up His countenance upon you and give you peace.*
Numbers 6:24-26

When push comes to shove, we all want to have a little bit more of God's favor. When things go well for us, we claim it's His favor on our life. When we get a big check or hit relationship gold, we feel like God's favor has been poured out on us. But we might be confused about God's favor.

See, God's favor on Jesus led Him to the cross. God's favor on Paul led him to prison. God's favor on Peter led him to be crucified—upside down. And God's favor on John the beloved disciple sent him into exile alone for years.

God's favor is not defined by our desires and our preferred version of the American dream. God's favor is far more than a big house and a fat retirement account. God's favor is His presence. God's favor is His will. God's favor is life and peace no matter what we're facing.

How desperately do you long for His favor in your life today?

Questions: *Have you been confused about God's favor in your life? In what surprising ways has God been showing you His favor in your life?*

DAY 90

We Should Bear Fruit

He is like a tree planted by streams
of water that yields its fruit in its season.
Psalm 1:3

In Psalm 1 God tells us that there are two kinds of people in the world: the person who delights in the Lord, and the one who does not. The person who meditates on God's Word, and the one who ignores it. The person who endures in hardships and still bears fruit, and the one who perishes at the end of the day.

There is a right way and a wrong way to live your life, and there is no better gauge for the kind of person you are than a look at Psalm 1. Do you avoid sin or run to it? Do you delight in God's Word and meditate on it, or do you hardly notice that it's missing in your life?

You might be in the middle of a very difficult season in your life, but you can rest in the knowledge that God promises fruit in due season. As you follow His leading and choose to obey Him, you will be like a tree planted by streams of water. In due season, you will prosper. At the right time, you will bear His fruit!

Don't you long to be the kind of fruit-bearing Christian that God promises you can be?

Question: *Read Psalm 1 and honestly ask God to show you which kind of Christian your life currently reflects. Are you delighting in God's ways or choosing your own?*

Keep Going

*And Gideon came to the Jordan and crossed over,
he and the 300 men who were with him, exhausted yet pursuing.*
Judges 8:4

I've always been intrigued by the picture of the army of Gideon. Remember Gideon? He's the guy who was out threshing wheat when God called him to save His people. Gideon felt weak and powerless. He pleaded with God for a sign. God gave him the sign. And still Gideon balked.

Eventually, Gideon jumped in and gathered an army of men. Though he had thousands, God brought his army down to three hundred. Only three hundred men to fight a huge army of the enemy, except Gideon had God on his side. So Gideon sets off to war energized by God's presence and guidance. Though Gideon knows that God is on his side, he's still human. Pretty soon even the strongest soldiers and most focused humans get worn out. But Gideon didn't stop. Gideon and his army of three hundred had experienced God's presence so keenly that they were indeed exhausted but pursuing.

Have you set out in faith but find yourself tired? Follow Gideon's example. Your fatigue will soon turn to victory as you pursue the goals and dreams that God has put before you. And on that day, it will be worth it all, the trouble and the pain.

Questions: What makes you tired in your pursuit of your calling? What simple ways can you use to restore some strength back into your walk?

DAY 92

Bold as a Lion

*The wicked flee when no one pursues,
but the righteous are bold as a lion.*
Proverbs 28:1

Here's a great definition for "bold": not hesitating or fearful in the face of actual or possible danger or rebuff; courageous and daring. We all admire bold people. We look up to those who seem to be braver than the average. We tell stories of men and women who stood in the face of lions, and walked into fiery furnaces, and stood strong no matter what.

Few things inspire me more than boldness in the faith. I love to hear stories of missionaries who boldly embraced all that God had to offer them, many even suffering for their faith, but courageously daring to stand tall. They are our examples today.

Though you might not feel very bold in your little corner of the woods, in Proverbs 28:1 God calls the righteous bold. And if you know your Bible at all, then you know that those of us who have received Christ are made righteous in Him. Therefore, whether you see it clearly right now or not, you are bold because you are righteous. You don't have to cower and run. You can stand strong no matter what because of who you are in Christ.

Questions: *Are you living boldly? How does knowing that you are bold affect the way you might live today?*

DAY 93

Think Well

*Set your minds on things that are above,
not on things that are on earth.*
Colossians 3:2

It's easy to think about everything around us. We used to just turn the television on and be bombarded with bad news. Now we simply touch our screens and the world comes to life. Stories of murders and racism explode in our faces. Threats of wars and natural disasters abound. Not a day goes by without some bad news flooding our eyes and our minds.

While we might have unique access to global disasters, God knows exactly how difficult our struggle with our thinking is. Paul spent much of his time in prison, and it was in a prison cell that he penned the words to Colossians 3:2. If anyone had reason to think negative thoughts and succumb to fear and defeat Paul did. But Paul had a secret, and by God's Spirit he tells us what it is. Paul learned that the only way to win any battle is in the mind.

As we set our minds, not on the world and what is in it, but on God and His kingdom, everything changes. Joy becomes ours as we think about God's goodness. Our light shines brightly when we refuse fear and rest in His peace.

Let's be people who turn our eyes upward to heaven. Jesus is coming back, and He's in control of our world today.

Question: *What are some practical ways you can turn your mind onto godly thoughts and God's Word as you go through the day today?*

Constructive Criticism

*Behold, blessed is the one whom God reproves;
therefore despise not the discipline of the Almighty.*
Job 5:17

I'm not great at receiving criticism. No matter how kindly it's given, it always seems to sting. I take it too personally and feel so misunderstood.

In the book of Job we meet a man who got more than his share of criticism and almost always unfairly. Yet it was Job who wrote: "Behold, how happy is the man whom God reproves, so do not despise the discipline of the Almighty" (Job 5:17). David agreed with Job in Psalm 119:71 where he said, "It is good for me that I was afflicted that I might learn Your statutes." Both men understood the value of corrective criticism and found in it a wealth of joy.

I have a friend who prays daily that the Lord would teach her to love criticism deeply. I want to be able to pray that same prayer. Instead of cowering in hurt when critiqued, I want to receive it with grace as a gift from the Lord who is using it to shape me into His likeness. Would you pray that same prayer with me?

Questions: *When was the last time you received criticism? How did you receive it? What might God be trying to change in you through this criticism?*

God Is Good

He who did not spare His own Son but gave Him up for us all, how will He not also with Him graciously give us all things?
Romans 8:32

Do you believe that God is trustworthy? I mean, do you really believe it? I confess that when it comes to God's trustworthiness, my faith is sometimes shaky. I want to rest in Him, but I tend to curb my enthusiasm instead. I want to believe Him completely, but I've chosen to guard my hope in the outcome instead.

But here's the truth: Hoping in God for a good outcome demands an unflinching belief in the trustworthiness of God. To lose hope or to withhold hope or to even stifle hope is to refuse to believe in the goodness of God. The only way to maintain this kind of hope is by faith: faith in the promises of God, faith in the character of God, faith in the goodness of God that has been proven to us in Christ Jesus on the cross of Calvary.

The best way to strengthen your faith in the trustworthiness of God is to go back to the cross of Christ. Because Christ died for me, I can rest in Him no matter what I'm going through. Do you believe that?

Questions: *What keeps you from hoping in God for more in your life? Are you afraid to expect God to do above and beyond what you can ask or think?*

Reach Out and Touch

And He said to her, "Daughter, your faith has made you well; go in peace."
Luke 8:48

She's my favorite person in the New Testament. I don't know why I love her so much. Maybe because she showed up alone. Maybe because she seemed so broken. Or maybe because she seemed so small to the casual observer, but was so big in the eyes of the Savior.

I'm talking about the woman with the issue of blood who touched the hem of Jesus' robe. She was scared. She was sick. She was in desperate need for healing. She had no connections and hardly any friends. Alone and feeling invisible, she took one step of faith—and hardly a step. She simply reached out toward Jesus. The best part was that He saw her—really saw her. And when He saw her, everything changed. He saw her small act of faith and responded with love.

Some days I feel like that woman. And all I have strength to do is to reach out and touch just the hem of His robe. Yet it is in those precise moments that I'm reassured that He sees. He knows me so well and heals me completely.

Questions: *Do you ever feel small and invisible in this world? What would it look like for you to reach out in faith to the Lord?*

DAY 97

Changing the World

*So, whether you eat or drink,
or whatever you do, do all to the glory of God.*
1 Corinthians 10:31

There are days, even after a shift of saving lives in the ER and ministering to thousands all over the world, that I sit in the quiet of my house and secretly wonder: Am I really making a dent in this world? Does anyone really care? Is anything really changing because of me?

The temptation to feel insignificant in a big, big world is huge. Everyone else seems to be making a much bigger impact than my measly contribution. But it's in those moments that God whispers this reminder deep into my heart: It's not about changing the world. It's about glorifying Him.

The purpose of our lives is not as complicated as we're told it is. We don't have to be mountain movers. All God wants us to do is to live for Him each day.

Whether you work in the house or in the marketplace, can you honestly and joyfully say "God, Your will be done. I'll praise You even in these circumstances"? When you do, you'll be living a world-changing perspective.

Question: *How can you glorify God in your circumstances right now?*

Clean Up

*If we confess our sins, He is faithful and just to forgive us
our sins and to cleanse us from all unrighteousness.*
1 John 1:9

I have a hate relationship with the laundry. I hate doing it. I went to empty the dryer the other day and was attacked with the onslaught of lint. The lint literally exploded in my face. The reason was that I hadn't bothered to clean out the lint in a while.

Have you ever done that in your life? I'm not talking about laundry anymore. I'm talking about your heart. When we don't make it a habit to regularly confess our sin to God, we never know what will come flying out of it. But there is good news. God promises that when we do confess our sin, though they be as scarlet, they will be as white as snow; though they be red like crimson, they will be as wool. And you and I both know that there's nothing quite like the smell and feel of a fresh load of laundry—lint-free!

Have you confessed your sin to the Lord lately? Why not take a moment and do it right now?

Questions: *What do you need to confess to the Lord today? Will you take a few minutes and ask Him to forgive you?*

Never Too Old

I have spoken, and I will bring it to pass; I have purposed, and I will do it.
Isaiah 46:11

One of the most destructive lies you and I will ever believe is the lie that we're too old: too old to marry, too old to serve, too old to do anything that matters. Too old to thrive. But here's what I do know: When it comes to God and His plans for us, as long as we have a pulse, we're never too old.

Think about it: Abraham was one hundred when he had his first son. Sarah was ninety. Moses was eighty when he started down the road of God's call on his life. Joshua was ninety when he got ready to enter the promised land. And Anna was well past retirement age when she finally held the long-awaited Messiah.

When it comes to God's plans for your life, if you're not dead, God's not done with you yet! Anything can happen today. You're not too old for God and His ways. Don't give up and don't give in to the temptation to fret. God can do anything anytime even when you can't see it clearly.

Questions: *Is there an area in your life that you have concluded is too late for God to change? How do the examples of Scripture encourage you to keep on keeping on?*

Someday

Yet you do not know what tomorrow will bring. What is your life?
For you are a mist that appears for a little time and then vanishes.
James 4:14

Do you have a bucket list? I do and it's full of stuff I dream of doing...someday. For example, I want to see the penguins in Antarctica...someday. And I want to hike Machu Picchu, and bike across Camino de Santiago and walk over the great wall in China...someday. And I want to go on a safari in South Africa...someday. Yeah, there's a whole lot of stuff I want to do...someday. But we can't keep waiting until someday to do the things we're *meant* to be doing today.

In James 4:13-14 we read, "Come now, you who say, 'Today or tomorrow we will go into such and such a town and spend a year there and trade and make a profit'—yet you do not know what tomorrow will bring. What is your life? For you are a mist that appears for a little time and then vanishes."

No matter how hard we try to prolong them, our days are limited. We have no control over the future. Today is all we've been given. Instead of postponing the things we long to do someday, let's make the most of each moment and live out our dreams, starting today!

Questions: *What are some of the dreams you long to fulfill someday? Are there some things you can do today to make the most of every day?*

Resolved

*No one who puts his hand to the plow
and looks back is fit for the kingdom of God.*
Luke 9:62

Do you ever wonder what the difference is between giving up meat for Lent and being a vegetarian? In both cases, meat is denied, but there is one core difference between the two and it boils down to one word: *resolve*.

Most people who give up meat for Lent don't care that much about giving up meat. They're simply in it for a season while a real vegetarian is resolved to live that way because of a change of values deep in his core.

When it comes to living purely and obediently before the Lord, the difference between the Christian who is living victoriously and one who is constantly failing also boils down to one word: *resolve*. Resolve is the commitment to put your hand to the plow and refuse to look back. Resolve is commitment to go on when you'd rather quit. Resolve is possible when your heart has been transformed by the God of resolve.

Have you ever resolved to obey God no matter what? God is resolved to love you no matter what you do and to stay with you no matter where you go! He's a God who will never leave you.

If you're constantly stuck in a cycle of defeat, perhaps you're lacking in resolve.

Question: *Name two or three resolves you have taken in your pursuit of God in the last year. Can you think of one resolve you can make today to deepen your walk with Jesus?*

DAY 102

The Fear Factor

*For God gave us a spirit not of fear
but of power and love and self-control.*
2 Timothy 1:7

How big is the fear factor in your life? Does it lead you down a path you don't want to be on, or are you able to fight it with courage?

Fear is one of the most debilitating emotions in my life. I fear dating. I fear not dating. I fear having kids. I fear not having kids. I fear taking risks. I fear a life of safety. I fear success. I fear failure. Chances are you too struggle with fear.

Did you know that 366 times in His Word, God tells us not to fear? He knows that we need daily reminders against fear! But what if there was a better way to live? What if God wants us to live without fear? Jesus died so that we could be free of fear. God hasn't given us the spirit of fear, but of power and of love and of self-control!

In the battle against fear, there are three critical steps we must take: First, name your fear as specifically as you can. Second, try to identify the lie surrounding your fear. And third, start replacing the lie you're believing with the truth of God's promises. When you do that, you'll feel the fear fall off your shoulders.

Question: *Take a moment and name the biggest fear you're facing right now. Then identify the lie you're believing about that fear. Now replace the lie with the truth of God's promise!*

Don't Fit In

Put on the Lord Jesus Christ and make no provision for the flesh, to gratify its desires.
Romans 13:14

Do you like Netflix? I do. But I came across Romans 13:14 recently, and it made me stop and think. Romans 13:14 says: "Put on the Lord Jesus Christ and make no provision for the flesh, to gratify its desires."

Have you noticed that when it comes to our entertainment, it's easy for us to maintain a high amount of flexibility in what we allow into our homes? We are, after all, post-modern Christians seeking to be relevant and culturally savvy in a world that needs Christ. We want to fit in, to be relatable. So we strategically suck in the culture in every media form possible in an effort to connect with the rest of the world. Yet Paul challenges this strategy.

Paul reminds us that God's approach is different. God instructs us to make no room for the flesh. His strategy to reach the world is to crucify our flesh, to refuse to make space for sin. God is much less concerned with our relevance as He is concerned about our holiness. He cares less about our fitting in to this world than our being set apart while in it. Maybe it's time we make some changes.

Questions: *Have your entertainment choices been pleasing to God? In what ways can you make some changes to result in more holiness?*

DAY 104

Impossible Is Overrated

*Behold, I am the Lord, the God of all flesh.
Is anything too hard for Me?*
Jeremiah 32:27

Some problems in our lives seem too big for us to fix. It almost feels like we're standing in front of the Red Sea hoping it will part. Or like we're looking at Jericho wishing for the walls to come down. Or like we're feeling the heat of the flame hoping we don't burn. Or like we're looking at the hungry mouth of a lion praying he won't bite. Or like we're staring at a starving crowd of five thousand with nothing but a couple of pieces of toast.

Each of these circumstances sounds ridiculous, right? Yet in each and every one of them God showed up in a mighty way. He parted the Red Sea and dropped Jericho's walls and protected three men from the fire and shut the mouths of the lions and fed the starving crowd.

Are you facing a problem in your life that seems too big to handle? Don't forget that we serve a big God. There's nothing He can't do. Impossible is where He often chooses to show up!

Questions: *What impossible situation are you facing right now? Do you believe that God is able to deliver you even where it looks impossible?*

Hearing Clearly

My sheep hear My voice, and I know them, and they follow Me.
John 10:27

Would you still serve God if He forbade you to marry? Or what if He told you to marry a prostitute? Or how about if He told you not to marry someone who didn't believe the same thing as you do?

You might think it crazy, but God did in fact say these things. He told Jeremiah not to marry, and He told Hosea to marry a prostitute and remarry her after she went back to her old lifestyle; and he told Samson not to marry a Philistine because she did not hold to the same beliefs about God that he did.

See, sometimes God asks us to do things that don't make sense to us humanly speaking, but they make all the difference in the world in His eyes. The key is to tune in to His Word and hear Him speak.

In John 10, Jesus promises us that we, His sheep, hear His voice. If you're a child of God, He's promised to tell you exactly what you need to know when you need to know it.

Are you listening to Him in the details of your life? Even more importantly, are you doing what He tells you to do?

Questions: *When was the last time you heard God speak clearly to you through His Word? Did you obey what He told you to do?*

DAY 106

Worth the Pain

We went through fire and through water;
yet You have brought us out to a place of abundance.
Psalm 66:12

I hated my obstetric rotation as a medical student. It looked painful and long and agonizing, and I wasn't even the one having the baby! But after the pain—oh, the joy! After the hurt, what relief! Ask any mother who's birthed a baby if the pain was worth it. Ask her if she'd do it again. You'll hear the same answer: Every second of the pain is worth the joy in the end.

In Psalm 66:11-12 we read, "You brought us into the net; You laid a crushing burden on our backs; You let men ride over our heads; we went through fire and through water; yet You have brought us out to a place of abundance."

Oh, it was painful, but it was worth every second of the pain to see God move. If you're feeling the pressure of the pain right now, don't give up. God's not done with you yet. It won't be long before the pain ends and your tears will turn into joy. Soon you too will be able to say, "It was worth the pain."

I might not be a mother, but I've seen more than my share of babies being born, and I know: there's joy on the other side of the pain.

Questions: *Think about the most painful thing you're going through. What would it look like to have that difficulty turn into joy? Would you trust God to do it—to turn your pain into joy?*

Confident

Let us then with confidence draw near to the throne of grace, that we may receive mercy and find grace to help in time of need.
Hebrews 4:16

I love the word "confidence." It sounds strong and undoubting and firm and certain. It's a word that describes the kind of person I want to be. But for years I've read this Word and confuse the source of my confidence. I suppose I've always felt like I needed to muster up confidence to approach God and pray because He'll give me grace and help when I need it, and I need it a lot. But the confidence that Hebrews 4:16 talks about is a confidence rooted in God.

Our confidence isn't a belief in our own ability to draw close, but in God's sacrifice on the cross making it possible for us to come. Our confidence never wavers because God never wavers. He is our High Priest who paid the price to make a way for us to enter in His presence. Because it's a finished act, He can't take it back.

The price for our sin has been paid. Even on the days that you might feel and know that you're too sinful for God, the fact that He sent Jesus to die on your behalf is the confidence you need to approach His throne boldly and expect the help that you need.

Questions: *How is your prayer life? Do you tend to have more confidence to pray when you're living right? Is your confidence rooted in yourself or in who God is?*

Shelter in the Storm

*When you pass through the waters, I will be with you;
and through the rivers, they shall not overwhelm you....*
Isaiah 43:2

When it rains it pours. Do you ever feel that way? I don't mind a little drizzle, but sometimes it feels like the storm won't let up. The worst part is that I never seem to have an umbrella handy when I'm being drenched by the storm.

In Isaiah 43:2 we read, "When you pass through the waters, I will be with you; and through the rivers, they shall not overwhelm you; when you walk through fire you shall not be burned, and the flame shall not consume you."

It's easy to feel shaken and pummeled by life's circumstances, but God's Word reminds us that we have a shelter in the storm as we turn to God for help. God's presence is a place of rest when we need Him the most. He promises to be with us no matter how deep the river is.

If you're feeling beat up by the storm in your life, take shelter in the Lord. If you need an umbrella to make it, let His love be the banner over you.

Question: *What are some practical ways you can hide in the shelter of God's safety as you walk through the storm today?*

Genealogies

*The book of the genealogy of Jesus Christ,
the son of David, the son of Abraham.*
Matthew 1:1

Genealogies. Do you like them? I don't always like them. I'm middle-aged and never married, and genealogies remind me that I won't ever have one. Yet the Bible is full of them. I came across yet another genealogy while reading God's Word recently. Like all other genealogies, it was long and names were hard to pronounce. Most names on the list weren't famous or well-known.

But each person mentioned in the genealogy mattered. Each name was part of a bigger story, the story of Jesus the Messiah. Whether you and I ever have kids here on this earth, each of us is part of a bigger story, the story of Jesus. Our genealogies tell a lot about us. Our spiritual legacy is the one worth striving for.

What does your genealogy say about you? Whether you're well-known or feel completely anonymous, and whether you have birthed kids or not, your life is part of a much bigger story. Don't let anyone rob you of the joy of your God-given genealogy.

Questions: *Write down your genealogy as best you can. Think about both physical and spiritual relationships; then give thanks to God for His perfect plan in your life.*

Easter Joy

*That He was buried, that He was raised on
the third day in accordance with the Scriptures.*
1 Corinthians 15:4

There are three things that fill me with joy when I think about Easter. First, I rejoice in knowing that though obedience doesn't spare us pain, it always leads to life. Jesus set the example for us at the cross. Though pain was a necessary part of the process, God gave Jesus the strength to make it to the other side. Second, I take joy in the fact that what doesn't make sense right now will always make sense in due season.

On the night of the crucifixion, the disciples felt confused and disappointed until Jesus rose from the dead. After the resurrection, everything made perfect sense. If you're struggling with some stuff right now, hang in there. Every confusing piece of your life will someday make perfect sense!

Finally, I revel in the fact that grace is never beyond our grasp. When Peter did the unthinkable and denied his Lord, he felt like an utter failure. But it was on the cross that Jesus paid the price for Peter's sin, reminding us that there's nothing we can ever do that is out of reach of God's grace. Jesus paid the price for our sin too. Because He died, we too now live. Because He suffered, we rejoice.

Yes, Easter is indeed a time for rejoicing.

Questions: *What gives you the most joy at Easter? Where do you look for hope when you feel like you've failed miserably in your walk with Jesus?*

Resurrection People

For you have died, and your life is hidden with Christ in God.
Colossians 3:3

The day after Easter Sunday is an interesting day of the year. On Easter almost everyone who claims to be a Christian loudly proclaims that Jesus is alive. On the morning after Easter, we get to live it out.

As you consider your post-Easter week, consider two Questions: If Jesus is alive, why are you still so worried about the problems in your life right now? Jesus conquered death. He defeated evil. He overcame the grave. There isn't a situation in your life that Jesus can't walk you through. He is a God worthy of your trust. Secondly, if Jesus is alive, shouldn't you feel just a little bit happier today? It's barely been a day since we took off our pastel outfits and polished off the last of the ham. But what about today?

Is your joy spilling over? Our King is alive, and He's coming back for us soon! He's defeated everything we hate! Let's allow His joy to continue to spill over into our present circumstances. Let's show the world that Easter is more than just a day. The resurrection defines who we are in Christ!

Questions: *Are you living your life in light of the reality of the resurrection? In what ways might God want you to live in greater freedom and joy?*

Thick Skin, Soft Hearts

He will rejoice over you with gladness; He will quiet you by His love; He will exult over you with loud singing.
Zephaniah 3:17

Do you have thin skin? I sometimes do. Say something to me in passing, and it's seared in my mind forever. For example, way back in 1983, my ballet teacher told me I was too heavy and would never be a ballerina. I was nine, and I never danced again. Pathetic? Yet most of us understand that words have a way of staying with us forever if we'll let them.

An angry comment, unwarranted criticism from an ex, like a dripping faucet we replay them over and over again when it's quiet in our house until we can't take it anymore. But what if we let go of the lies and hang on to the truth instead? I want thick skin and a soft heart. I want to meditate on what God says about me instead of believing the lies of the enemy.

He rejoices over me with gladness and exults over me with singing. His promises have a way of thickening my skin and softening my heart, and it makes me less easily offended. That He loves us so deeply changes everything. It sets our hearts on fire.

Questions: *Has anyone ever hurt you deeply with their words? Write it down on a piece of paper; then rip it up into small pieces. Are you willing to let go of the offense right now?*

DAY 113

Bottom of the Ninth

No unbelief or distrust made him waver (doubtingly question) concerning the promise of God, but he grew strong and was empowered by faith as he gave praise and glory to God.
Romans 4:20

The bottom of the ninth might be a term for baseball, but it's pretty fitting for most of us too. It's that stage in the game where it feels like there isn't much time left to turn things around. We feel the pressure to succeed, and the weight of it is heavy enough to bury us.

There was a time in my life when I used to live in the bottom of the ninth until I finally moved out. So did Abraham. In Romans 4:19-21 we're told that Abraham "did not weaken in faith when he considered the [utter] impotence of his own body, which was as good as dead because he was about a hundred years old…No unbelief or distrust made him waver (doubtingly question) concerning the promise of God, but he grew strong and was empowered by faith as he gave praise and glory to God, fully convinced and assured that God was able and mighty to keep His word and to do what He had promised."

When he found himself in the bottom of the ninth, Abraham turned to God. He hung on to God's promises when he needed them the most and never let go. It's the reason he made it safely home, and so will you when you rest your all on God's Word.

Question: *In what area of your life is your faith being challenged? Ask God to give you a promise to hang on to until you make it all the way home!*

DAY 114

For His Eyes Only

For God is not unjust so as to overlook your work and the love that you have shown for His name in serving the saints, as you still do.
Hebrews 6:10

Do you ever feel like you're busting yourself for nothing in the Christian life? Maybe you've taught a Bible study class for decades and have never seen more than a handful of people show up. Maybe you've faithfully driven your car to the homeless shelter week after week unnoticed and unappreciated by anyone for years.

At first, you might have enjoyed it all, but as life got busier you can't help but wonder why your ministry doesn't grow like other people's ministries do. You can't help but wonder if it's worth it all at all, this business of serving the Lord.

Anytime I catch myself in the throes of frustration and fatigue, I go to Hebrews 6:10. The Word of God is salve to our wounded souls. It's water when you're thirsty. It's light in the darkness. God does see every little thing we do. He even sees the love in our acts of worship. He loves it when we serve His children, especially those who are too needy to pay us back with praise.

So go on and keep serving. Rest in His promise. This world is not the end of the road. Eternity is coming.

Questions: *Where are you serving right now? Who are the people God has called you to serve? How can you tell that you're serving in love and for the glory of your Father?*

DAY 115

Recharge

*But whoever drinks of the water that
I will give him will never be thirsty again.*
John 4:14

The only thing I hate about my phone is that it has to be recharged on a regular basis. The more I use it, the faster I need to recharge it. If you know me, you know that it's not lipstick you'll find in my purse. It's a power cord to recharge my phone instead! And if you need to find me, look for the nearest power source, and odds are I'll be there!

How quickly we forget the need to recharge in our daily life. When we feel weak and running out of gas, we think a nap will do, and sometimes we might need one. But when we're burned out, the only thing that will recharge us is plugging back into the power source of life.

Don't wait until you crash to reboot. Instead, be intentional and strategic in recharging several times in the course of the day. As you fill up on God's power regularly, you'll have all that you need to handle all that you face no matter how challenging it is. And the best way to recharge is through the Word of God and prayer.

Questions: *How much time are you spending recharging your soul these days? What are some practical ways you can find to recharge as you go through the day?*

Our Gifts and Calling

Who saved us and called us to a holy calling, not because of our works but because of His own purpose and grace.
2 Timothy 1:9

Most of us think upside down about our gifts and calling. We figure that because we're gifted in an area, like singing, then God will open doors for us to sing for His glory and to be used for His kingdom. But when it comes to God's plans for our lives, God isn't out there looking for someone with precisely our gifts to fit His purposes.

In 2 Timothy 1:9 Paul explains that it is the power of God that has called us to a holy calling, not because of our works but because of His own purpose and grace which He gave us before the ages began. In other words, God *gave* us our specific gifts *in order* to use us in His kingdom! He doesn't use us because we have gifts. No, He gives us specific gifts in order to use us in specific ways! Our calling has less to do with us and everything to do with what God has already purposed for our life.

Do you see how that puts a whole new spin on things? No more striving and worrying about where we fit in. All we must do is trust God to unfold His plan for us daily.

Question: *What are some of the ways God has gifted you? Give Him thanks not just for your gifts but for the specific ways He intends to use you for His glory!*

You Are Not Invisible

So she called the name of the Lord who spoke to her, "You are a God of seeing," for she said, "Truly here I have seen Him who looks after me."
Genesis 16:13

More often than I care to admit, I feel sort of invisible and not in the cool wonder woman sort of way. Sometimes, no matter how hard I try, I wonder if anyone really notices me, especially in the church. When I find myself in that place, no one speaks to my pain like Hagar does.

Do you remember Hagar? She was the woman who had Abraham's son Ishmael, and later was kicked out of Abraham's home by Sarah—Abraham's wife.

I know. It's complicated. Lonely and dejected, Hagar wandered around in the wilderness for a while. And just when she thought she was completely invisible, God saw Hagar and reminded her that He loves her. God opened her eyes and helped her see water, the very symbol of life for the thirsty.

Perhaps today you might feel invisible. You need to remember that God sees you. He knows where to find you even in your loneliest wilderness. He knows you by name, and He's never going to let you go.

Questions: *Have you ever felt invisible, unseen, forgotten by God? How would you react differently if you knew that God could see you right now?*

Look Up

*Set your minds on things that are above,
not on things that are on earth.*
Colossians 3:2

Once in a while, when I need it the most, sleep escapes me. No matter how hard I try to fall back asleep, I can't. Typically, it's because I'm anxious about something.

Have you ever thought about what keeps you awake at night? Is it your finances or your boss? Is it your husband or your kids? Is it your future or your past? Whatever it is that's on your mind, typically what keeps us awake at night has everything to do with our perspectives.

We can either look at our troubles from our perspective or from God's. We can look at God through our circumstances, or we can look at our circumstances from His point of view. When God is big, our problems become small. And when our problems become too big, they block our view of God.

In Colossians 3:2 we're told to set our minds on things above, not on things that are on the earth. It is possible to change our perspectives, but it will only happen when we start looking up.

Question: *What are two or three simple ways you can set your mind on heavenly things and keep your perspective vertical?*

Hungry for More

As a deer pants for flowing streams, so pants my soul for You, O God.
Psalm 42:1

When was the last time you felt hungry for more? I'm not talking about just hungry for food. I'm talking about hungry for more—more satisfaction, more peace, more joy, and more of God. I'm talking about wanting God more than you want anything else in your life. I'm talking about recognizing that God is the source of all you need, and refusing to move on until He gives you more of Himself.

David understood it in the Psalms when he compared his desire for God to a deer panting for water. Moses understood it when he told the Lord he wouldn't go on if the Lord didn't go with them. Joshua understood when he remained in the temple well after everyone else had left. And Hannah understood it while she poured out her soul to God in prayer refusing to leave until God heard her.

What is it that makes some people so much hungrier for God than others? And what about you? Are you hungry for God? Are you hungry for more? Or are you filling up your soul with temporary fills?

Questions: *What are you feeding your soul with? Are you satisfied with God alone, or are you filling yourself with what doesn't fully satisfy your hunger?*

Yielded and Willing

*And when they had brought their boats to land,
they left everything and followed Him.*
Luke 5:11

One of my favorite Christians of all time is D.L. Moody, the great Chicago pastor of old. Someone once told D.L. Moody: "There is no limit to what God can do with a man who is yielded and willing to do His will!" His response was radical and inspiring. He looked at the man who spoke these words to him and said: "By the grace of God, Edwards, I am determined to be that man!" And so he was!

Today Dwight Moody has a college and radio station and church in Chicago that still bear his name. He was a man totally dedicated to God and His ways. He lived what he believed.

When I hear stories like this one about D.L. Moody, I too am inspired and challenged to step it up a bit in my walk with the Lord. Like Moody, I want to be able to say, "By the grace of God, my friend, I am determined to be that woman!" I want God to do through my life above and beyond what my mind can even imagine. Don't you?

Questions: *To the best of your knowledge, are you totally yielded and willing to do God's will in your life? Is there an area in your life where you might be holding back from God?*

DAY 121

Come Out of Hiding

And there is no creature hidden from His sight, but all things are open and laid bare to the eyes of Him with whom we have to do.
Hebrews 4:13

I once heard the story of a young Jewish shoemaker who hid in his sister's farmhouse back in 1945 because he was so afraid of the Nazis. His fear kept him in hiding for thirty-two years. He never heard the news that Hitler was killed. He never heard the news that the Allies had won the war. He used to watch people in the village mill about from the window of his farmhouse. He was eventually accidentally found thirty-two years later.

"If I had not been discovered," he said, "I would have remained in hiding...so I am happy that this happened."

It seems hard to believe that this could happen anywhere, yet think about this: Today many Christians are living in fear exactly like this man. Instead of embracing the freedom we're given in Christ, we hide in fear, uncertain of our future, concerned about our safety. But we don't need to be afraid.

Because of Christ's resurrection, we are free indeed! No more hiding. No more fear. Let's rejoice in Jesus and live the abundant life He's given us.

Question: *In what ways do you stay in hiding because of your fear? It's time to come out of hiding and let yourself be found! Find a faithful friend and share your fears with that friend.*

DAY 122

Transformed by Grace

For the Lord has chosen Jacob for Himself, Israel for His own possession.
Psalm 135:4

Stop for a moment and think about Jacob. I have such a soft spot for him. Here was this total screwup who was a professional liar as a young man. He was lazy at best, and conniving at worst, yet God still loved him deeply and used him mightily.

Grace has often been described as undeserved favor, and there's no better picture of grace than in the life of Jacob. What's most astounding about Jacob is that God's grace outpoured on his life eventually transformed him into a solid man of God.

I love the God of Jacob, this God of all grace. He's the God of Abraham, the God of Isaac, and the God of you and me! He loves us so much He took on flesh and came to earth to give His life as payment for our sins!

If you think you're too much of a screwup for God, just remember Jacob, who started off as a total mess and eventually was used by God to change the world. Yes, God knows each of us so well, and He still loves us so much. Won't you let His love transform you today?

Questions: *How does the story of Jacob inspire you to go on? Are you receiving God's grace in your life, especially in the areas where you feel like a failure?*

DAY 123

Neither Hot nor Cold

I know your works: you are neither cold nor hot.
Would that you were either cold or hot! So, because you are lukewarm,
and neither hot nor cold, I will spit you out of My mouth.
Revelation 3:15-16

As a pediatric emergency physician I've had to face my fair share of vomit, and it's not fun. Ask any mother of a sick toddler, and she'll agree. Most of us see it coming and run! So when God tells us exactly what makes Him want to throw up, we should listen carefully.

In Revelation 3:15-16 God rebukes His followers for developing a lukewarm heart. Writing to the church in Laodicea Jesus says, "I know your works: you are neither cold nor hot. Would that you were either cold or hot! So, because you are lukewarm…I will spit you out of My mouth." The church of Laodicea was rich and self-satisfied and had become just "meh" about God—not too hot nor too cold.

So many modern-day Christians sadly fall into the same category: not too hot, not too cold. Just lukewarm followers of Jesus, unencumbered with surrender, living for personal comfort and success.

God forbid that we stay lukewarm. God goes on to tell us that if we're lukewarm, the only solution is to repent and go back to our first love. Repentance turns up the heat as God fuels the fire in our hearts to live for Jesus.

Questions: *How would you describe your relationship with God today? Hot, cold, or lukewarm? What are some of the things you used to do but don't now that fueled your love for Jesus?*

DAY 124

Trust God's Heart

*Trust in the Lord with all your heart,
and do not lean on your own understanding.*
Proverbs 3:5

Things don't always turn out well for Christians—at least not here on this earth. Think about John the Baptist who, according to Jesus, was the greatest man who ever lived. His head was chopped off while Jesus went about healing people and performing miracles. The whole story doesn't make sense in our favor-oriented, comfort-seeking culture.

We want the story to work out well for us every time. We want God's favor packaged in the American dream on demand for us the moment we ask for it. Yet if God allowed the greatest man who ever lived to have his head chopped off for the sake of the gospel, might it be possible that He would choose for us to undergo hardships at times?

God is always at work. He always does what's best for us even when we can't see it clearly. In the end, you'll never be disappointed. In the end, He'll never let you down! You can go ahead and trust His plans for you even if they don't make a lot of sense right now.

Questions: *What areas in your life don't make lots of sense humanly speaking? How does John the Baptist's story encourage you to keep on trusting the Lord?*

Don't Waste Your Life

Yet you do not know what tomorrow will bring. What is your life? For you are a mist that appears for a little time and then vanishes.
James 4:14

What does God want you to do with the rest of your life? Have you ever stopped long enough to ask God the question, "God, what do You want me to do with the rest of my days? Do You want me to go to the mission field? Are You asking me to give more? Do You want me to help start a church or help disciple more folks?"

It's easy to get caught up with our jobs and our retirement plans and our house payments and our vacations. There is nothing wrong with that per se. But when was the last time you stopped long enough and asked God what specific plans He has for you for the rest of your life?

Don't waste your life here on this earth. Life is too precious to simply coast your way through it. We've been created for a purpose. God will unfold it in time, but let's stop long enough to ask Him the Question: "God, what will You have me do with the rest of my life?" You might be surprised what He'll say if you stop long enough to listen to His answer.

Questions: *When was the last time you asked God what He wanted you to do with the rest of your life? What might God be saying to you in answer to the question?*

DAY 126

On Mission

Go into all the world and proclaim the gospel to the whole creation.
Mark 16:15

Do you ever wonder why? Do you ever wonder why God has left us here on this earth? Do you assume it's simply to grow up and get a job? Or do you believe it's so that you can meet the love of your life?

I remember as a kid wondering why God didn't just take us to heaven after we received Him into our hearts. Today as a middle-aged woman, I still ask God why—why has God left us here on this earth? The answer is simple. We aren't left here on this earth simply to become better versions of ourselves, although by God's grace I do hope we're becoming more Christlike each day. And our mission isn't just to find a husband or a wife or get a great promotion, although all these goals are great goals.

No. The reason we've been left here on this earth is to glorify God by being of service to Him. We've been left on this earth on mission if we choose to embrace it. We are to shine the light of Jesus into a world gone dark, and point others to Jesus every chance that we can. Our mission is to speak the truth clearly, and to love people well.

Do you know your mission? Are you fulfilling it today?

Questions: *Are you living your life on mission? What mission has God given you to accomplish? Be as specific as possible.*

The Good Shepherd

The Lord is my shepherd; I shall not want.
Psalm 23:1

The Lord is my Shepherd. I shall not want. Who doesn't love Psalm 23? Yet in our modern-day world, it's easy to lose the power of the imagery that God intended for us to own.

I can't even remember the last time I saw a shepherd, can you? But think about it. What if we did have our very own shepherd to help us along the way? What would it be like to live with an actual shepherd, someone guiding us along the way, watching for our every need, someone willing to come after us when we get off the beaten path, someone to feed us and hold us and speak to us and love us. Oh, what would it look like to live each day guided by a good shepherd who already knows the way?

Some mornings I wake up and feel I really need a shepherd. I have a feeling you do too. Well, we're in good company. God is our Shepherd. He's leading the way. He sees you and knows your every need and is opening up the way before you. He's not a shepherd who confuses us but a Shepherd who loves and redeems us.

You don't need to see the road; you just need to keep your eyes on the Shepherd. He knows the way.

Questions: *In what areas of your life do you long for leading? How can you fix your eyes on Jesus intentionally today and find the guidance to move forward?*

Don't Give In

*But I discipline my body and keep it under control,
lest after preaching to others I myself should be disqualified.*
1 Corinthians 9:27

The other day I had the urge to eat an ice cream bar. As soon as I finished the first one, I had the urge to eat a second. No sooner did I finish the second, I had this crazy urge to eat a third. Don't worry. I didn't. I didn't because it finally dawned on me what I should have understood immediately: Our urges can't be trusted.

Most of our urges are rooted in our own sinful nature and will typically lead us where we don't want to go.

Paul understood the power of sinful urges. In 1 Corinthians 9:27 he wrote: "But I discipline my body and keep it under control, lest after preaching to others I myself should be disqualified."

As followers of Jesus Christ, we are not victims of our urges. We are subject to God's Spirit who gives us the power to overcome our urges and live in obedience to the Father instead. So don't grab another ice cream bar! Instead, how about reaching out for God's Word to find the strength you need to make it through the day! The more you do that, the more you'll find the urge to turn to God when you need Him the most!

Questions: *What is the biggest urge you give in to on a day-by-day basis? How can you grow your urge to read God's Word daily?*

Unafraid

O Lord, in distress they sought You; they poured out a whispered prayer when Your discipline was upon them.
Isaiah 26:16

Do you know what the most frequent command in the Bible is? You might think it's the command to be holy. Or to stop sinning. Or to tell others about Jesus. Or to love everyone always. While all these commands are great and honorable, they don't make up the most frequent command in the Bible.

If you're looking for the most frequently spoken command that God gives us, it's this: Do not fear. It's that simple. Do not fear. Fear not. Don't give in to fear. Aren't you glad that God knows us so well that He made sure we would never miss this? He knows how easily moved by our circumstances we can become and how quickly we forget that He is in control of everything—always.

There's nothing to fear when God is at the helm of our lives. So no matter what you're facing today, make sure you remember that you don't have to be afraid. God is with you always. He's only a whisper away.

Questions: *What are the prayers you whisper to God when no one is listening? What are the fears behind them? Will you rest in the truth that God hears your whispered prayers to Him?*

DAY 130

What's that Smell?

But thanks be to God, who in Christ always leads us in triumphal procession, and through us spreads the fragrance of the knowledge of Him everywhere.
2 Corinthians 2:14

I have a particularly strong sense of smell—which isn't always convenient in my line of work in the ER. Yet few things are as helpful as our sense of smell.

I can tell from the smell whether an infection is present and how sick a patient is. I can tell from the smell what someone is cooking, and when it's time for supper. I can even tell from the smell if there's going to be a second date or not! It's a pretty amazing gift when you think about it.

Now consider 2 Corinthians 2:14 where Paul says that "through us [God] spreads the fragrance of the knowledge of [Christ] everywhere." As followers of Jesus Christ, our smell should be so distinct and always leave a clear impression of who we truly are. Our words and actions and behaviors and countenances ought to smell so obviously of Jesus that it's unquestionable whose we are.

What do people smell when you walk into a room? Do they long for you to stay, or do they open the windows and hope you leave soon?

Questions: *What smell do you carry when you walk into a room? How can you tell? What needs to change?*

DAY 131

No More Self

If anyone would come after Me, let him deny himself and take up his cross and follow Me.
Matthew 16:24

Do you want to know one of my greatest fears as a Christian? My greatest fear as a Christian is the risk of living my life primarily focused on my "self."

Most of us have become accustomed to making our own decisions regarding our finances, our time, and our hobbies. We are concerned about our needs, our desires, and our futures. We become so focused on our "self" that others become a bit of a bother.

When it comes to God and His ways, there is very little room for self. We all know the golden rule: Love God and love others. Self doesn't even make the list.

If you're like me, it's going to take focus and intentionality to stop making me, myself, and I the center of our world. It's going to take opening our homes to strangers and stepping out of our comfort zones. It's going to take the local church with all its idiosyncrasies to help us find our calling and live it out one God-honoring day at a time. It won't always be easy, but with God's help we can do it.

Questions: *Are you living for self or for others? What are some practical ways you can make your day today less about you and more about them?*

DAY 132

What Matters Most

*Seek first the kingdom of God and His righteousness,
and all these things will be added to you.*
Matthew 6:33

Let me go ahead and say it loud and clear: I can no longer keep up with all that's happening in the world these days. Can you? The amount of information that hits me in the face day after day has become too overwhelming for me to process. I have a sketch of the most important things, but for the most part, everything else has faded into some sort of white background noise I can barely decipher. It's frustrating at best.

Whenever I begin to feel overwhelmed by information overload, I remind myself of Matthew 6:33: "Seek first the kingdom of God and His righteousness, and all these things will be added to you."

We don't have to have everything figured out. We must simply keep first things first in our lives. When it comes to our life, what matters most is God and His ways. Are you making Him a priority in your life today? Are you seeking His face first and foremost? Everything else will fall into place once you go back to what matters the most.

Question: *Make a list of your priorities in life. Now think about how you spend each day. Is your life truly consistent with the things you say are priorities?*

He Does Not Lie

God is not man, that He should lie, or a son of man, that He should change His mind. Has He said, and will He not do it? Or has He spoken, and will He not fulfill it?
Numbers 23:19

There are seasons in my life when I need to know. I mean really need to know. I've hung on for years believing God for a promise. And even though I figure God is good for His Word, there are moments of weakness where I wonder. Will God do what He's promised? Is He completely trustworthy?

I then convince myself of the dumbest thing possible. I use some sort of reverse psychology and tell God that even if He doesn't keep that promise, I'd still believe Him. The arrogance of my thoughts amazes me.

In Numbers 23:19 we meet our God, the God of Israel. He's been a covenant maker and a covenant keeper forever. It's who He is. He never lies. All that He has spoken will come to pass. To ever think we need to cut Him some slack in case what He has promised doesn't come to pass is pure disbelief.

Faith waits on God even when His promises seem far reaching. Faith rests in His character, refusing to make excuses for God's ways. It simply rests in His promises no matter what.

Questions: *What promise has God made you that has caused you to doubt Him? How can you get stronger in faith as you wait for God's promises to be fulfilled?*

DAY 134

Tears in a Bottle

*You have kept count of my tossings;
put my tears in Your bottle. Are they not in Your book?*
Psalm 56:8

I'm not usually much of a cryer, are you? People generally fall into one of two categories: those who cry quickly and those who wait until the tears are like a volcano ready to erupt. I'm the volcano. It's when I least expect it that I feel the weight of my tears building up. The reasons are too many to count—both external and internal.

But regardless of the reasons for the weight of our tears, one of the most intimate aspects of knowing Jesus Christ is the knowledge and the promise that He is a God who is near to the brokenhearted.

Over and over again in the Psalms, God reminds us that He collects our tears in a bottle. He hears our whispered prayers and our loud cries that feel like they're bouncing against the walls. He's a God who is near. He is Emmanuel.

If you're hurting today, or feel brokenhearted, take heart. Jesus is balm for your soul. He's the Prince of Peace, your wonderful counselor, Almighty God. His love surrounds you and will never abandon you. He's a God who is always for you.

Questions: *What makes you cry? How does knowing Jesus understands your pain help you make it through your tears?*

Believing and Doing

*You believe that there is one God. Good!
Even the demons believe that—and shudder.*
James 2:19

When I was in medical school, I learned a whole lot of facts, and I knew a whole lot of stuff. Then I had to actually see patients and treat them. I had to touch them. Suddenly I realized that all the information in the world would never save a life or heal the sick. It's what I do with what I know that is the key to life and healing.

When it comes to our life and faith, it's exactly the same thing. Many of us know a whole lot about God and the Bible. But in James 2:19 God informs us that knowing isn't the issue. He says, "You believe that there is one God. Good! Even the demons believe that—and shudder." Even the demons believe!

What matters even more than what we say we believe is how it translates into our daily living! The extent to which we act it reflects the extent to which we believe it. God wants us to be not just hearers of the Word but doers of it too!

Questions: *Are you generally living with what you say you believe? Are there some areas in your life where you believe one thing but are living out a completely different life?*

Lost and Found

*May the God of hope fill you with all joy and peace in believing,
so that by the power of the Holy Spirit you may abound in hope.*
Romans 15:13

Have you ever lost something you can't find? I lost my phone once. I looked everywhere for it and finally did the inevitable: I asked my sister to call me. I found the phone exactly where I had last left it, inside my closet!

As difficult as it is to misplace a phone, the most dangerous thing I have a habit of losing is my hope in the Lord. One minute it's there, and the next I can't seem to find it. Hope has a way of disappearing when I need it the most. When that happens, the best thing I can do is to call out to the Lord, and then I call a trusted friend to help me remember that this is not the end of the road, that God has not forgotten me, and that every promise God has made He will keep!

Have you misplaced your hope today? Let me remind you that hope is exactly where you last left it, in God's Word and in His presence.

Questions: *Have you ever misplaced something in your life? Does God seem far when you need Him to be near? How can you live in constant awareness of the presence of the Lord?*

Just Enough Faith

And without faith it is impossible to please Him, for whoever would draw near to God must believe that He exists and that He rewards those who seek Him.
Hebrews 11:6

Do you ever feel like you don't have enough faith no matter how hard you try? Consider this: The Israelites thought they were dead meat facing the Red Sea. But God still led them through it. They thought they would starve to death. But God still fed them. They thought they would never reach the promised land. But they did.

Hannah thought she'd never have a son. Yet along came Samuel. Elijah thought God had abandoned him, until he heard God's whisper. Mary and Martha thought their brother was dead. But God revived Lazarus. Thomas thought Jesus was buried until he put his hands in His side and in the palms of His hands. The disciples on the road to Emmaus thought Jesus was history until He walked right up to them. Peter thought his days in ministry were over until Jesus showed up. The early Church thought Peter was going to die in prison. But God delivered him.

But it all starts with faith. Without faith it's impossible to please God. The good news is that even when our faith fails us, God is still faithful.

Questions: *How is your faith? On a scale from 1 to 10, how strong is your faith in God? Now think about how strong and faithful God is. How does focusing on His goodness change everything?*

Holding on for More

These, though commended through their faith, did not receive what was promised, since God had provided something better for us....
Hebrews 11:39-40

Have you ever carefully read Hebrews 11:39-40? Hebrews 11 is the faith chapter in the Bible. It's the chapter where God gives us a list of all the great men and women of faith. When we finally get to the last two verses we read this: "These, though commended through their faith, did not receive what was promised, since God had provided something better for us."

Can you believe it? Despite having faith big enough to get them a mention in the faith chapter of the Bible, this small group of men and women never even got the things they were hoping for here on this earth. They waited and waited, and then eventually went to be with the Lord never having received the things they were waiting for. Yet they were not disappointed. They remained unafraid, undaunted, and unstoppable. Their secret was that they had found something, or rather Someone, far better than any hope they could find here on this earth.

They had found Jesus.

Do you know Jesus? Do you love Him? Or are you still holding out for someone else to fill the hole in your heart?

Questions: *What are you desperately still waiting for in your life? Have you found in Jesus your source of satisfaction?*

The Underdog

The stone that the builders rejected has become the cornerstone.
Psalm 118:22

For as far back as I can remember, I've been a sucker for the underdog. There's something so special about watching the least likely person rise through the ashes and take it all home. And the lower the underdog starts off, the more exciting it is when that underdog defeats all of the odds and becomes the hero.

While I'm not quite sure why God does what He does, I know that no one exemplifies the underdog better than Jesus Christ—God's Son. He left the splendor of heaven to be born in a manger. He lived a perfect life only to be brutally killed on a cross. He looked defeated. His story looked over. Until the underdog became the hero! When Jesus rose from the grave, He conquered death and became victorious.

Oh, how I love Jesus. Do you ever feel like the underdog? Take heart. Jesus knows exactly how you feel. And God has a track record of using underdogs for His glory.

Questions: *Have you ever felt like the underdog? How does knowing Jesus was an underdog encourage you to run to Him with your fears and doubts?*

Do Good

*Do good to everyone, and especially
to those who are of the household of faith.*
Galatians 6:10

It's easier not to get involved, isn't it? Think about it. You're running late for work when you see the old lady walking in the cold dragging a couple of grocery bags on her hips. Do you stop and give her a ride and risk being late for work? Or do you keep on driving and act like you didn't see her?

Or how about that neighbor, the single mom who can't keep up with the snow on her driveway? Do you offer to shovel her driveway, or do you mind your own business and get on with your day convincing yourself she wouldn't want your help anyway?

Every day we're given opportunities to show love to those around us. It's up to us to open our eyes and see the opportunities right before our eyes. It's up to us what we make of each fleeting moment.

In Galatians 6:10 Paul tells us to "do good to everyone, and especially to those who are of the household of faith." Are you doing good to those around you? To what extent will you go out of your way to show Christ's love to your world today?

Questions: *Who are the people you will run into today? How can you do intentional acts of love to reflect Jesus to them?*

DAY 141

Caught in Criticism

A good man out of the good treasure of his heart brings forth good;
and an evil man out of the evil treasure of his heart brings forth evil.
Luke 6:45

Do you ever catch yourself caught up in a cycle of criticism? I do and I hate it. The first step to break the cycle of criticism in your life is by examining your heart. Is your heart full of envy? The people I criticize are the ones who seem to be accomplishing things that I still long to accomplish in my life. The longer I fix my eyes on them and covet what they have, the more critical I become.

Or is your heart overflowing with ingratitude? Ingratitude makes me forget all the good things God has poured on my life and all the blessings He's filled my days with. When ingratitude takes over, it's easy to get critical.

Or perhaps your heart can't get out of the rut of discontent. Discontentment is driven by the feeling that God has given others what should have been mine. Contentment, on the other hand, rests in the truth that my Father knows what I need and will provide it in His perfect timing.

Jesus tells us that out of the abundance of the heart the mouth speaks, so when it comes to overcoming criticism, healing always begins in the heart.

Questions: *Are you a critical person? What do you see coming out of your heart when you tend to be critical? How might God be trying to change you in this area of your life?*

Still Waiting

From of old no one has heard or perceived by the ear, no eye has seen a God besides You, who acts for those who wait for Him.
Isaiah 64:4

Do you ever wonder if it's really worth it—this whole business of waiting on the Lord? Most followers of Jesus start out thinking the waiting is really worth it, but with each passing year, maybe you're starting to wonder. What's the point of waiting on God? And what if He doesn't show up like we hope He will? And what if the waiting goes on forever?

As a poster child for waiting, I have had my share of feeling frustrated with God in the waiting. I've waited too long in my singleness. I've waited too long for my dreams. I've waited too long for healing—which makes Isaiah 64:4 all the more encouraging. Here's what God promises those who wait: "From of old no one has heard or perceived by the ear, no eye has seen a God besides You, who acts for those who wait for Him." Whether you're waiting on God for marriage, or you're waiting on God in your marriage, or for any other area of your life, make it your resolve to hang on to this promise.

No one who has ever waited on the Lord has ever regretted it. He's a God who acts on behalf of those who wait for Him. He's a God who never lies.

Questions: *Are you tempted to give up in the waiting? What area of your life is hardest to wait on God for? Write down today's verse on a 3x5 card and memorize it.*

DAY 143

No Regrets

*Forgetting what lies behind and straining
forward to what lies ahead. I press on.*
Philippians 3:13-14

I regret to inform you that you did not get into the program you applied for. I regret to inform you that the wedding has been cancelled. I regret to inform you that we are letting you go due to budget cuts. No matter how you look at it, regret is painful and generally unwelcome. Even when we try to make the best of it, regret has a way of gutting the dreams out of our hearts.

If only things had turned out differently. If only we had said this or done that. We waste so much time on regret, don't we? We cry over spilled milk and can't seem to stop the tears from flowing.

When it comes to regret, here's God's take on it: "Forgetting what lies behind and straining forward to what lies ahead. I press on." In other words, learn from your mistakes and move forward. God has a better plan for your life.

Today is a new day. God loves you and is always for you. There's no place for regret when you're living for His glory, and there's always room for redemption at the foot of the cross.

Questions: *What do you regret most in your life? Will you give that regret over to God and get ready to move onward and forward?*

Raging Storm

*Who stills the roaring of the seas,
the roaring of their waves, the tumult of the peoples.*
Psalm 65:7

I was at the ocean recently and noticed that the waves were high. I went into the water anyway. Admittedly I was a bit nervous. I worried I might be sucked in, but you know what they say—all for the thrill of a challenge.

The very next day I walked by that very same ocean, and it was still as glass. I couldn't believe the contrast. The same ocean that was churning one day was crystal clear the next. Isn't it the exact same way in our lives? One day everything feels like it's going to fall apart, chaos reigns, you're anxious and worked up, and the very next day you have peace like a river, you're unshakeable and untouchable.

There comes a point where we must understand that the same God who rules over the noisy waves of the ocean is the God who gives us absolute peace in the storm. He's in control of the ocean on the good days and on the bad. So go ahead and jump in. You might actually enjoy the thrill of the challenge.

Question: *Are you walking through a restless storm right now, or is your life crystal clear? Meditate on God's presence reminding yourself that He is with you no matter what.*

Present Realities

*I want you to know, brothers, that what has happened
to me has really served to advance the gospel.*
Philippians 1:12

Do you ever wonder if there is a reason for what's happening to you? When bad things happen in your life, do you trust that God might be working things out for good somehow? When you're confused or feeling stuck, and when things don't pan out like you hoped they would, how do you react?

Truthfully, I'm not always pumped when I land in a prison of any kind, figuratively speaking. Yet that's exactly where Paul was when he wrote Philippians 1:12 where he said, "I want you to know, brothers, that what has happened to me has really served to advance the gospel." Paul understood what you and I often forget. That God uses every difficulty we face to advance His kingdom. That God is not threatened by our present realities or prison cells.

With this truth in mind, might you consider the challenges that you're facing as a blessing that God is going to use for His glory? As you do that, you'll find the strength you need to make it through this day.

Questions: *What is your present reality right now? How could God be using it for His glory?*

DAY 146

Who You Are

*For this reason I, Paul, a prisoner of
Christ Jesus on behalf of you Gentiles.*
Ephesians 3:1

How do you see yourself these days? When you look at yourself in the mirror, what do you see? Do you see brown hair, blue eyes, or do you look past the outside? When you look even closer, do you see your dating status or your profession? How closely is your vision compared to who you really are?

Paul found himself in prison, not once but multiple times. In his letter to the Ephesian church, Paul teaches us an important lesson about how we ought to see ourselves. Though he was a prisoner for preaching the gospel, Paul never looked at himself as a victim, or a guy with bad luck. No. Paul looked at his reality and saw so much more. Over and over again Paul described himself as a "prisoner for the Lord." While Paul's circumstances might have looked dire, his outlook was so focused on Christ that the result was an abiding joy and a life of powerful impact.

So let me ask you again: When you look at yourself today, what do you see?

Questions: Most of us believe what we tell ourselves about ourselves. Are the words you tell yourself about who you are consistent with the truth? Who does God say you are?

Run to Jesus

Therefore, as you received Christ Jesus the Lord, so walk in Him.
Colossians 2:6

Do you ever wonder if you've pushed God too far? Every so often, we all sheepishly wonder if we've pushed God too far. "What if I've crossed the line this time?" We wonder, "Will God find me if I've run too far away from Him?" The question actually reveals the heart of someone who longs to be back in communion with the Lord but doesn't know how.

The answer to this question is nowhere better seen than in the life of Jonah. Here was a guy—a prophet at that—who knew what God wanted and ran as far away from God as possible. He ran as far as his feet could take him and landed in the belly of a fish. It was as he finally landed in the dark that God finally showed up.

As much as you long to be with God, God longs for you even more. And when you don't know where to find Him, He'll always find you. No matter how far you've drifted from God's side, this very moment could be God's reminder to you that He knows exactly where you are at, and He still loves you. Won't you come running back home to Him?

Questions: *Is it hard for you to believe that God still wants an intimate relationship with you? What are the barriers that stand in the way of a closer walk with Jesus for you?*

Hard Stuff

Ah, Lord God! It is You who have made the heavens and the earth by Your great power and by Your outstretched arm! Nothing is too hard for You.
Jeremiah 32:17

Do you ever wonder if God could do it? If God could actually do something about your need? If you're walking through a trial today, you've probably had that thought—if God could do something about my trial, why hasn't He? That's a great question and one that deserves an answer.

In fact, the prophet Jeremiah wrote these words in Jeremiah 32:17: "Ah, Lord God! It is You who have made the heavens and the earth by Your great power and by Your outstretched arm! Nothing is too hard for You." Jeremiah hit the nail on the head when it comes to God's ways.

See, God *can* do anything. Even your problem is not beyond His ability to fix. If you truly believe God's Word, then the logical conclusion is that if God hasn't solved your present problem, there must be a really good reason for it.

It's time to believe that God is not only able, but He's also good. Nothing is too hard for Him, not even your present trial.

Questions: *Do you believe God can do anything? Do you believe God is good? How will your answer change the way you pray about your trials today?*

Don't Sweat It

*Many are the plans in the mind of a man,
but it is the purpose of the Lord that will stand.*
Proverbs 19:21

Are you a planner? What's your agenda for today? Do you have a plan set up already? Many of us obsess about the plans that we make. We've got Daytimers and apps. We've got five-year and ten-year plans. When it comes to planning, some of us have a Ph.D. in it and that's okay. I'm a planner too.

But every so often, an unexpected event puts a dent in my plans. When that happens I'm reminded of Proverbs 19:21. In that verse, the wisest man in the world concluded this: "Many are the plans in the mind of a man, but it is the purpose of the Lord that will stand."

If you're not a planner, you're probably ecstatic, and even if you are, you can be so encouraged. Your plans don't have to be perfect. Your plans don't have to include every single little detail. When push comes to shove, God's got your back. His purposes for you are sure and nothing, not even your perfect planning, will ever stand in the way of what He has planned for you!

Questions: Do you have five- and ten-year plans? Are you willing to hold them loosely in case God changes His plans for you, or are you more attached to your plans than your God?

DAY 150

Voice Recognition

And as soon as you heard the voice out of the midst of the darkness, while the mountain was burning with fire, you came near to me.
Deuteronomy 5:23

I've always been a fan of technology, but I had never understood its radical ability to change my life until two years ago. I began practicing telemedicine where, instead of always having to go into the ER, I now spend a large portion of my time treating patients via phone and video consults.

You can imagine my surprise when after uttering a few words of introduction, the patient on the other end recently exclaimed: "Hey, you're that lady from the radio." She was right! I was that lady, and she had recognized my voice simply by hearing it. Nothing that I could say would have convinced her otherwise.

When it comes to recognizing God's voice in our lives, many of us make it far too complicated. John, the beloved disciple, wrote these words quoting Jesus: "My sheep hear my voice, and I know them, and they follow me" (John 10:27).

Like my patient, you and I have a God-given ability to recognize God's voice even when we can't see Him. As we listen to Him enough, it won't be hard. We'll know it's Him as soon as He calls our name.

Questions: *How carefully do you recognize God's voice in your life? What are some ways you can become more familiar with God's voice in your life?*

DAY 151

Be Happy

Why are you cast down, O my soul, and why are you in turmoil within me? Hope in God; for I shall again praise Him, my salvation and my God.
Psalm 42:5-6

Do you ever feel down no matter how hard you try to be happy? We're living in tough times. Every day brings news of fresh disaster. People are hurting, and it's overwhelming to think about it, not to mention our own troubles and woes.

Every so often, even when I try to fight it off, I get the blues. Like David in Psalm 42, I start asking the Question: "Why are you cast down, O my soul, and why are you in turmoil within me?" Are you familiar with the question?

What's so amazing about God's love is that He never chided David for asking the question. In His goodness, God gently guided David to the answer. David would go on to write: "Hope in God; for I shall again praise Him, my salvation and my God." David practiced preaching good news to himself. Instead of wallowing in self-pity and despair, David turned his eyes upward and found his hope in God.

That hope is yours as well if you'll stop long enough to seek God's face no matter how you're feeling and no matter what you're facing.

Question: *Have you ever felt like David did, weighed down by your troubles? Spend 90 seconds preaching the good news of God's goodness over you, then write down how that made you feel.*

DAY 152

Step into the Unknown

And when He had finished speaking, He said to Simon, "Put out into the deep and let down your nets for a catch."
Luke 5:4

I like to be comfortable. As long as I have my Startbucks and some clean sheets when I'm out of town, life is good. But the longer I walk with Jesus, the more I'm learning that all the really good is unfamiliar.

In Luke 5, the disciples, who were expert fishermen, had just finished fishing for the day. It had been a horrible day for fishing. No one had caught any fish. I bet they were more than ready for a nap when Jesus challenged them to step out of their comfort zone and into the unknown. "Put out into the deep," Jesus said, "and let down your nets for a catch." It sounded hard. It sounded ridiculous. It must have felt uncomfortable, but it's only when the disciples were willing to step out of their comfort that their nets became full.

Jesus had so much more waiting for them than they had ever imagined. All He asked is that they trust Him and do what He asked.

Are you willing to throw your nets into the deep today, even if it means stepping out of your comfort zone? Who knows what might happen if you're willing to follow God's leading.

Questions: *Why is it scary to step into the unknown? In what areas of your life might God be asking you to take a step of faith? Will you do it?*

DAY 153

Letting Go of Perfect

And God is able to make all grace abound to you, so that having all sufficiency in all things at all times, you may abound in every good work.
2 Corinthians 9:8

Are you a perfectionist? Maybe it's time to stop. When it comes to most things in our personal lives, many of us tend to be perfectionists. We think we're still single because we can't get past that wretched first date. We assume our dream job is just out of our reach because we have fallen short of perfect one time too many. We are convinced our marriages are shaky because our weight is too high. We're convinced that if we tried harder and just did everything right, we might finally find the happiness that's just out of our reach.

In 2 Corinthians 9:8 Paul wrote, "And God is able to make all grace abound to you, so that having all sufficiency in all things at all times, you may abound in every good work." What Paul reminds us is that it really doesn't hinge on us. The things we long for don't depend on how good we are, but on how good our God is.

And when it comes to God, He's always full of grace. He always gives us way more than we deserve. He is always sovereign over the details of our lives. So don't wear yourself out trying to be perfect. God is perfect enough to provide for every one of your needs.

Questions: *In what areas of your life have you set a standard that's too high for you to reach? How does understanding God's sovereignty free you from needing to be perfect?*

DAY 154

Don't Despair

*The L%%ORD%% is good to those who wait for Him,
to the soul who seeks Him.*
Lamentations 3:25

One of my favorite things to do is to pick up my three-year-old nephew Sam from school. I was a few seconds late to pick him up one day, but what I saw when I walked into Sam's classroom filled my heart with joy. Instead of being worried and upset by my delay, Sam sat on the mat looking toward the door with joyful expectation. It never occurred to Sam that I might not show up. Certain that I would soon come, all he could do was wait with joy and expectation.

When I got a glimpse of his face, it occurred to me that that's how every one of us ought to wait for our Father. Are you constantly anxious, worried God might have forgotten you, crying your way to despair each day? Just because God has not given you what you're asking for yet doesn't mean He's forgotten you. You are precious in His sight. He knows what you need and when you need it. He knows what you need before you even ask for it.

Before you know it, you'll be on your way to your next adventure. In the meantime, just sit back and smile. If Sam isn't worried, neither should you be.

Question: *Why do you think God sometimes makes us wait even for the good things we ask Him for?*

DAY 155

Prayer Works

*You ask and do not receive, because you
ask wrongly, to spend it on your passions.*
James 4:3

One of my favorite authors is A.W. Tozer. He was a pastor in Chicago and wrote prolifically. Here's what he once said about prayer: "God answers our prayers, not because we are good, but because He is good." I always need this reminder.

Despite my best intentions, I never seem to pray enough or to say the right things when I do pray. The older I get, the more I recognize that even when I do pray, my motives in prayer are usually self-centered. Why in the world would God ever answer my intermittent and self-focused prayers?

Tozer reminds us that it's not because we are so great at praying, and it's not because of our own goodness. No, grace is the undeserved favor God pours on our life. Because of His goodness, God hears our prayers and answers. He's a Father who loves us so deeply.

Have you stopped to take note of God's goodness today? Make a list of the ways He's been good to you, and share it with someone.

Question: *Make a list of ten ways God has been good to you today. Examine what you're praying about and why you're praying about those things. Now pray about those things.*

DAY 156

God Hears

*And if we know that He hears us in whatever we ask,
we know that we have the requests that we have asked of Him.*
1 John 5:15

Do you ever feel like you pray and God isn't listening? Does it frustrate you? One of the hardest disciplines of the Christian life is when we pray and God doesn't seem to answer. It's happened to me before, and it doesn't always feel good. When that happens and our frustration grows, it's because we've forgotten a precious truth. It's the truth that there is a greater gift than the gift of answered prayers, and it is the gift of closer communion with God through unanswered prayers.

Every single time God delays in answering our prayers it forces us to our knees seeking His face more deeply. Every time we're frustrated by His silence, it causes us to listen more attentively.

God always hears us. He's not oblivious to our prayers. He is near to the brokenhearted. He's always closer than we think. What looks unanswered in your life right now is your chance to get to know God more deeply. So don't waste your waiting. God longs to draw you nearer to Him through the longings of your heart.

Questions: *What do you long for more than anything? Would you take two minutes and tell God about it right now?*

Full Attention

Everyone then who hears these words of Mine and does them will be like a wise man who built his house on the rock.
Matthew 7:24

How much of your attention does God have? We are all so easily distracted. When my nephews come over, I'll ask them to do something once, twice, five times later; and they still don't seem to be hearing me. Distracted by their phones, unable to focus on my words, they look like they're listening, but their reactions tell me a completely different story. The only way for me to know that they are listening to me is by whether they do what I ask them to or not.

It's the same with God. Many of us claim we hear Him, but until we start doing what He asks, He's only got part of our attention. Our obedience to God's words is the first sign that we're giving Him our attention.

The foolish man who builds his house on the sand is the man who hears God's words, but does not put them into practice. When the storm comes, that man's house will crash. The wise man listens and does. He is like a man whose house is built on a rock, unshaken by the storm.

Do you long to stand strong no matter what? Ask yourself if you're giving God your full attention. You'll be able to tell by how you're responding to what He tells you.

Questions: *Does God have your full attention? Is there something He's asked you to do that you're not doing?*

Starve Your Sin

*Those who belong to Christ Jesus have
crucified the flesh with its passions and desires.*
Galatians 5:24

Do you want to know how to kill a plant? Just stop watering it. Though I don't have a bright green thumb, even I know that there is one sure way to kill a plant. Stop watering it. It will surely die.

So many of us struggle with patterns of sin in our lives. We don't understand why we can't overcome our lust. We struggle with feeling stuck in our besetting sins. Yet the solution is easier than we think. When it comes to our sin, God has given us the ability to overcome it in Christ. We are dead to our sin. Yet many of us still struggle with sin because we're feeding it.

The surest way to overcome indwelling sin is to simply starve it. Stop watering it. Kill it by refusing to cultivate it.

Instead of creating an environment in your life where sin will grow, cultivate your life in Christ, and sin will slowly starve to death. It's easier than you think once you set your mind to it.

Is there a sin area that is growing out of control in your life? Resolve to starve it. It's your first step toward victory.

Questions: *What will it look like to starve a sin area in your life? Be specific. You might have to find an accountability partner to make it happen. Are you willing to do it?*

No More Fear

Fear not, for I am with you; be not dismayed, for I am your God;
I will strengthen you, I will help you, I will uphold you with My righteous right hand.
Isaiah 41:10

What makes you afraid? There are so many things that make me afraid. I'm afraid of spiders and of wasted potential. I'm afraid of unfulfilled dreams and awkward first dates. I'm even afraid of failing.

It's been said that 365 times in His Word God has told us not to be afraid. We can safely conclude that when it comes to fear, God knew we would struggle with it. But I'm learning the secret to overcoming fear in my life. When it comes to overcoming fear, the key is to set my mind and my heart on the pillars of God's promises. His Word never fails. He never lies. When I stop relying on my emotions and quit following my feelings, and when I start resting on all God has promised me, well, even first dates lose their tentacles, and I find the courage to go on.

So what makes you afraid? Can you find a promise in God's Word to fight off that fear? It's there. You simply have to look for it; then hang on to it no matter what. While we can't trust our feelings, we can always trust God's promises for our future.

Question: *What makes you afraid? Start memorizing today's Scripture and use it in your fight against fear.*

DAY 160

Hide Under the Banner of His Name

*The name of the Lord is a strong tower;
the righteous man runs into it and is safe.*
Proverbs 18:10

Where do you run to when you're under attack? If you're a follower of Jesus Christ, you can be sure that sooner or later you will be attacked. I don't mean to sound melodramatic, but it's biblical.

In 1 Peter 5:8 we're reminded that Satan is like a roaring lion, walking about, seeking whom he may devour—and he's focused on anyone who calls himself a follower of Jesus Christ.

Paul, in his letter to Timothy, wrote that those who desire to live a godly life will suffer persecution. So make no mistake about it, you and I will be attacked if we are pursuing a life of greater Christlikeness and holy obedience.

The question is not whether we will be attacked, but how, and more importantly, where will we run to when we are being attacked. In Proverbs 18:10 we're given the answer: "The name of the Lord is a strong tower; the righteous man runs into it and is safe."

There is a place of safety for us, and it's near to the heart of God. Let's hide under the banner of His name because even the enemy will flee at the mention of Jesus' name.

Questions: *What are some ways you might be under spiritual opposition these days? How can you make it a habit to run into the safety of Jesus?*

DAY 161

Through it All

God is our refuge and strength, a very present help in trouble.
Psalm 46:1

When it comes to God's promises, we don't often read them very carefully. For example, consider Psalm 46:1. It's one of the most encouraging verses ever written. It says, "God is our refuge and strength, a very present help in trouble." If you're like me, you assume God meant that He would help us stay away from trouble. But read the verse again and you'll see. You haven't read it very carefully. God doesn't say that He would help us from trouble, but that He is our help *in* trouble. That's a world of difference.

If you're walking through a tremendous storm right now, rest assured that God knows it, and He's promised to help you while you're in it. James alluded to the same thing. He wrote that the blessing for the Christian is in staying steadfast under trial, not in the absence of trial.

True joy is found in recognizing God's very presence even when we're smack dab in the middle of our fiery furnace. What trial are you going through right now? Won't you recognize God's presence with you and find the joy you need to make it through that trial?

Questions: *What are some sure and tried ways God has offered us to make it through our trials? Are you taking advantage of the weapons He's given you to remain strong no matter what?*

DAY 162

Don't Stop Yet

Moreover, it is required of stewards that they be found faithful.
1 Corinthians 4:2

Hey, how bold are you? Bold enough to step out of the boat and leap into the unknown? Have you ever felt God calling you to action? Did you leap out of the starting blocks without thinking twice? I've done that before and it feels great...until the road gets tough.

See, faith that leaps at the mere calling of the Savior is awesome, but consider this: Faith that steps out is of limited value without the faithfulness to stick it out. It's not that stepping out by faith isn't great, but there is more to be said about faithfulness over time.

In 1 Corinthians 4:2 Paul writes, "Moreover, it is required of stewards that they be found faithful." He doesn't tell us that it is required for stewards to be courageous or strong or focused. God merely asks that we remain faithful to the end. He wants us to continue to persevere no matter how we feel and no matter how hard the road gets.

The reason we can do it is simple: He who called us is faithful, and He's with us to the end. So go ahead, leap, but don't stop yet. The race is not over until it's done.

Question: *What makes faithfulness so hard? Write a note to someone you know who's on the verge of quitting, encouraging him/her to remain faithful to the end.*

Living by Faith

And without faith it is impossible to please Him, for whoever would draw near to God must believe that He exists and that He rewards those who seek Him.
Hebrews 11:6

Some days are hard. We wake up on the wrong side of the bed. We don't feel up to anything. I love drinking a cup of coffee in the morning, but some mornings, even after three cups of my favorite brew, I still don't feel "it." If you've ever felt like I sometimes do, you need to hear what I'm about to tell you.

Some things you don't have to feel. You just have to believe. In other words, you don't have to feel faith in order to have it. When it comes to believing God, our feelings have little to do with believing Him. Faith is holding on to God's promises no matter how we feel. It's doing what God asks us to do, knowing that God always promises a good result. How we act today, and how we respond to others around us, has less to do with how we feel and everything to do with what God has promised us.

Are you keeping track of God's promises? Are you walking by faith no matter how you feel? The Christian life is impossible without faith, and it becomes possible when we're resting on all God has promised us in His Word.

Question: *Praise is a great way to break the cycle of negativity if you've woken up on the wrong side of the bed! Will you spend three minutes praising God by faith this morning no matter how you feel?*

Be Content

I have learned in whatever situation I am to be content.
Philippians 4:11

What do you do when discontent engulfs you? No matter how hard I try to avoid it, there are times when discontent has a way of literally engulfing me. One minute I'm fine, and the next, like a forest fire, discontentment completely lights up my life. I hate it when that happens, but there is a better way.

In Philippians 4, Paul says, "I have learned in whatever situation I am to be content." It was no accident that Paul used the word "learned." He wasn't born with contentment. He didn't find a magic pill for contentment. Paul figured out that the way to be content is simply by learning to be content. And the only way to learn to be content is by finding yourself in situations where you might be prone to discontent.

Are you guilty of comparing yourself with others? Have you overlooked God's blessings in your life? Do you have uncontrolled selfish ambition? You're a setup for discontent. But when you choose to rest in God's goodness no matter what, like Paul, you'll slowly be learning the way of contentment.

Questions: *In what areas of your life do you struggle with discontent? What could be the cause for your discontent? Will you confess it to God, and ask Him to teach you contentment?*

DAY 165

True Grit

And do not be grieved, for the joy of the Lord is your strength.
Nehemiah 8:10

I recently heard a TED talk on the topic of grit. The speaker explained that grit is the reason why some people make it while others don't. The speaker had found that of all the factors that might predict success, grit was the one distinguishing feature.

A quick google search of the meaning of the word "grit" describes grit as a small, loose particle of stone or sand—for example, she had a bit of grit in her eyes. And while that's interesting, it's not the meaning the speaker was using. "Grit," you see, is also the courage and the resolve to do something. It's your strength of character. For example, he displayed the true grit of a Navy pilot. Or she displayed the true grit of a surrendered follower of Christ.

It takes grit to stay the road to holiness. It takes grit to remain committed to God and His ways. It takes grit to hold on to hope when life looks hopeless.

The good news is that you're not in it alone. God has given you His Spirit to make it. The resurrected Jesus is on your side. There's enough grit in the resurrection to help you overcome whatever it is you're facing!

Questions: *What are some ways God is building grit in your life? Have you been resisting Him, or are you submitted to His ways even when they don't make a lot of sense right now?*

Fatal Mistakes

My people are destroyed for lack of knowledge.
Hosea 4:6

I was talking with a friend recently who pointed out Hosea 4:6: "My people are destroyed for lack of knowledge." She went on to say that in a world where everything looked like it was falling apart, the prophet wrote these words to remind us that what will kill God's children is not immorality, or disobedience, or even rebellion, as harmful as these things are. But what will ultimately destroy us is our lack of knowledge.

We're living in a time where we think we know a lot because of our access to information. But all the access in the world won't save us if we don't know the things that matter the most. In other words, living in ignorance of God's character and His ways, and in ignorance of His Word is not just a bad idea. It's fatal.

So let me ask you an obvious Question: What are you doing to increase your knowledge of God's ways? How are you growing in your understanding of it? Where do you need to buckle down and get serious about God's purposes? There's no better time than right now to get learning.

Questions: *Are you growing in your knowledge of the truth? How can you prioritize your time better to make knowing God and His Word a priority in your life?*

He Delights in You

*The LORD your God is in your midst, a mighty one
who will save; He will rejoice over you with gladness;
He will quiet you by His love; He will exult over you with loud singing.*
Zephaniah 3:17

I picked up my three-year-old nephew Sam from school recently, and we started out on our usual post-school routine: First, we drove over to Menchies for frozen yogurt. He then begged to come to my house, his favorite hangout.

When we got out of the car, I grabbed some bags from the trunk, and that's when he saw the box of raspberries. His eyes lit up. "Those are my favorite!" he said. "I know," I answered, "it's why I bought them." The smile on his face was enough of a reward.

As I washed the raspberries, I thought about the Lord. Our heavenly Father takes delight in us in much the same way. In both big ways and in small, He pours His favor on us daily, knowing exactly what we love and how to surprise us with it. He takes pleasure in us, His people. He delights greatly in us. He even rejoices over us with singing. Sometimes He'll even go out of His way to make sure we get a bucket full of raspberries just because He knows how much we love them.

In what ways has God poured His delight on you today?

Question: *Make a list of the little things only God could have provided for you today. How does knowing He delights in you change your perspective on your day?*

DAY 168

Joy in Service

For we are His workmanship, created in Christ Jesus for good works, which God prepared beforehand, that we should walk in them.
Ephesians 2:10

One of my favorite things to do is to hang out with my nephews. When they come over, they can't stop asking for ways to help me. "Can we cut your grass?" they want to know. "Can we clean your gutters?" They've even offered to help clean out my closets for me!

Truthfully, I never really need their help. I can do most of those jobs on my own, but it gives me delight to hear them ask, and it fills them with joy to help me. It's how we're wired. We get satisfaction in serving one another.

When it comes to serving God, we often forget this important truth. God doesn't need our help. The gospel isn't a help wanted sign. Quite the opposite! God is here to help us! Yet He gives us the privilege to serve Him because He knows it fills us with joy. So go ahead and ask Him for ways to serve Him; then enjoy the jobs He gives you. Pretty soon you'll see, He's always there when you need His help to get it done!

Questions: *What sort of things do you enjoy doing? In what areas do you love to serve Him? Ask Him to open more doors for you to serve Him even more in those areas.*

DAY 169

Take a Shot

There is no fear in love, but perfect love casts out fear.
1 John 4:18

I once read this quote by hockey great, Wayne Gretzky: "You miss 100 percent of the shots you don't take." It's remarkably true. If you're looking to get a perfect score in this life, aim at playing it safe and you'll see. You'll score 100 percent.

So if you're single and never make an effort to go out on a date, you're gonna get a 100 percent score on datelessness. And if you don't apply for a job, well, there's a 100 percent chance you won't get that job. This even applies to serving the Lord. You'll miss 100 percent of the service opportunities you don't step up and take in your local church. You'll miss 100 percent of the evangelism opportunities you don't speak up in.

We were created to be brave. Because God loves us, we have no fear. We can take those shots unafraid of failure, knowing that God is able to redeem even our failure for good.

How are you doing today? Are you taking some shots for the kingdom, or do you need to try to make a few more shots for God's glory?

Questions: *Have you lacked the courage to take some shots in your life out of fear? If you knew you couldn't fail, what would you try to accomplish for God's kingdom and glory?*

Walk by Faith

For we walk by faith, not by sight.
2 Corinthians 5:7

When I was growing up, we had a Sunday school teacher who used to train us to stop, look, and listen. Ever heard that before? It was her way to get our attention and get us to settle down. It worked more or less depending on our moods.

Unfortunately, the pattern my old teacher taught doesn't apply as well to the life of faith. Most of us want our faith to be a matter of seeing first and then moving forward. But faith doesn't work this way at all. When it comes to faith, we must listen first, and then we see. If we wait until we see, we're not walking by faith at all. We're walking by sight.

Paul wrote in 2 Corinthians 5:7 that we are to walk by faith and not by sight. There is no reason to continue straining so hard to see. Instead, you must lean in with your ears and listen to God's voice in your life.

If you're looking for direction that never fails, get used to listening before seeing. Then resolve to act by faith no matter where God leads you.

Questions: *Are you living by faith or by sight? How can you tell? In what area in your life is God inviting you to step out and live by faith?*

Precious Grace

What shall we say then?
Are we to continue in sin that grace may abound?
Romans 6:1

There is no worse feeling than the feeling of being stuck in the same pattern of sin. When it comes to grace, many of us have a hard time understanding it. Grace is the undeserved favor God gives us. It doesn't depend on us, but on Him. It is a gift that every follower of Jesus Christ gladly receives at salvation.

But when it comes to the besetting sins in our lives, we mistake the meaning of grace. Some of us think grace is a get-out-of-prison free card that keeps us safe and secure no matter how we behave. That's cheap grace and an insult to the gospel. While God's grace is deep enough to cover our worst sins, God's grace is so much more than that. Grace is what gives us the power to overcome.

Because God loves us and because He has poured His favor on us in Christ, grace should propel us into victorious living. We *can* be free. We have been given the ability to overcome sin. Grace will always catch us when we fall, but let's refuse to continue in sin relying on grace.

Grace is much more than a net to catch us when we fall. Rather, grace ought to fuel us into the freedom that's already been granted us in Christ.

Questions: *Do you have a pattern of besetting sin in your life? How does understanding God's grace move you toward greater holiness?*

DAY 172

Patiently Waiting

Wait for the Lord; be strong,
and let your heart take courage; wait for the Lord!
Psalm 27:14

The other day I was in a hurry to get to wherever I was going. I got in my car and flew out the driveway. Everything was going smoothly until I hit the train tracks. Then, just like that, everything came to a halt. With a car in front of me, a car behind me, and the sound of the train in the horizon, I had nothing to do but wait.

I waited until the train unloaded its passengers and took off again. I waited until the light changed to green again. I waited for the car in front of me to move on. After I took off and got to where I was going, a thought crossed my mind. I had made it to my destination despite the waiting. I ran a couple minutes late for my next appointment, but everyone survived the ordeal. No one was hurt. The job still got done.

What I'm learning about the waiting is that it's not the waiting that kills us, but how we respond when we're stuck in the waiting that hurts us.

Are you running late in your life? Are you rushed to get to your next destination? Be still. Know that God is still God. You're going to make it in the end. Worship God in the waiting, and rest in knowing that everything is going to be all right.

Question: *What are some ways you can worship God in this season of waiting that you're stuck in? Think about a verse that encourages you in the waiting.*

Ask for Permission

Seek the Lord while He may be found; call upon Him while He is near.
Isaiah 55:6

It's easier to ask for forgiveness than to ask for permission. Have you ever heard that expression before? I wonder if David thought about that when he made the biggest mistake of his life.

David was a man after God's own heart. Things had gone very well for him. Then one day, he skipped the battle. Many suggest he got a little bored in that season of his life. He looked out his window and saw Bathsheba. He kept on looking. At that crossroad, it would have been wise for David to ask God for permission before proceeding. We all know what the answer would have been. But like many of us, David figured it would be just as well asking for forgiveness instead. So David moved forward, not seeking permission until it was too late.

Eventually, God used Nathan to stop David in his tracks, and he had to ask for forgiveness. And oh! The pain of it all. And oh! The consequences of his sin. If only he had stopped long enough to ask for permission instead of waiting to ask for forgiveness.

We all love to flirt with sin. We bend the rules and make exceptions for ourselves. Sooner or later God confronts us and gives us a choice to repent.

What if today we stopped and asked for permission before jumping into sin? We might spare ourselves a whole lot of pain.

Questions: *Have you ever waited to ask for forgiveness when asking for permission would have spared you a whole lot of pain? What can you learn moving forward?*

Friends Matter

Iron sharpens iron, and one man sharpens another.
Proverbs 27:17

I have the most unlikely friendship you can imagine. She's married, I'm not. She's got a house full of kids—I don't. She lives in the boondocks somewhere in Wisconsin while I live in the hustle and bustle of Chicago. She's German and I'm Lebanese. And did I mention, we've never even met? Yet at least once every week she'll call me to pray over the phone for me, or text me to encourage me to keep on going in the ministry.

Our friendship started when she found me through my blog and reached out to me to pray for me. That was five years ago, and our friendship has lasted through the months. The reason we have a deep and abiding friendship is because of the truth that we're more than just friends. We're sisters in the Lord. The strength of our connection in Christ breaks down every demographic and sociological barrier we could ever put up.

I wonder what sort of friends we might have if we were willing to look past the obvious and see in other brothers and sisters in Christ. I wonder what might happen if we chose to be to others the friends we always hoped we could have. That sort of friendship might be worth a try.

Questions: *Do you have a friend you might never be a friend with were it not for Jesus? What are you looking for in a friend? Could you be that person to someone today?*

Preach Truth

The steadfast love of the Lord never ceases; His mercies never come to an end; they are new every morning; great is Your faithfulness.
Lamentations 3:22-23

How much grace have you given yourself today? I'm great at giving grace...to others. I know how hard life can be and how human we all are.

When I hear that a friend blew it, and that friend calls me for support, I'm quick to encourage her and to remind her that God loves her. And when someone I know struggles with fear—I totally get it—and I'm there to remind that friend of God's presence with her helping her overcome every fear.

But then I take a long look in the mirror and hear myself tell a different story. I tell myself I'm a disappointment in my failures. I am way too hard on myself in my fears. I've noticed that preaching grace to others is great, but that same grace must be first received by me.

When it comes to God's grace, it's ours to embrace. It's ours to rejoice in. It's ours freely moment by moment and day after day. It's ours with each new rising of the sun. Imagine how much more free your life would be if you were willing to receive all of God's grace for you today.

Stop speaking lies to yourself. Preach God's truth to your hurting heart today, and receive His grace unending.

Questions: *What sort of lies are you believing about yourself? How does God's grace answer those lies with truth?*

DAY 176

Ball of Yarn

*He has made everything beautiful in its time.
Also, He has put eternity into man's heart, yet so that he cannot
find out what God has done from the beginning to the end.*
Ecclesiastes 3:11

There's a girl I work with who likes to knit. Anytime it's quiet in the ER, she whips out her knitting bag and gets to work. It's infuriating and fascinating at the same time. For days, it looks like she's wasting her time one wrist flick at a time. Then suddenly she's got a blanket or a hat or something equally wonderful to hold in those same hands.

I have a habit of getting aggravated with the Lord. I watch Him weave my life one stitch at a time, one day at a time, too slow for my liking. It doesn't feel like He's making any strides. I'm tempted to complain and want to give up. But then suddenly, He takes me by surprise when I finally see the finished product and stand amazed. I stand amazed that God created something wonderful out of a big ball of yarn like myself! I'm amazed at the ashes God uses to make beauty.

Our days are fashioned in the hands of our Creator God. While it might feel like a whole lot of nothing right now, He sees the end and won't stop until He's satisfied with the work in His hands. He won't stop until He sees something wonderful take shape.

Trust Him completely. He'll never let you down.

Question: *Has God ever used your ashes to make something beautiful? Think about that time and thank Him for His faithfulness.*

DAY 177

True Joy

*The L*ORD *appeared to him from far away. I have loved you with an everlasting love; therefore I have continued My faithfulness to you.*
Jeremiah 31:3

Do you ever ask yourself what your purpose here on this earth is? To watch popular culture one might think the reason for our being is to fall in love and live happily ever after. But a look at God's Word tells a different story. While marriage is a wonderful picture of the gospel, it is not the primary reason we were created. Furthermore, God didn't create us because He needed us.

In fact, in Acts 17:25 we're told, "Nor is He [God] served by human hands, as though He needed anything." It's in Jeremiah 31:3 that we're given a deeper glimpse into God's heart for us: "I have loved you with an everlasting love." In one of the most baffling moves of all, God created us simply because of love. He wants to be in relationship with us.

John Piper has said it this way: "God is most glorified in us when we are most satisfied in Him." When we receive God's love and find our joy in Him, we glorify Him the most. That's the purpose we've been created for!

Are you living God's purpose for your life, or are you distracted by lesser goals? Do you know what God's love for you is? The only way to understand it is to fix your eyes on Jesus.

Question: *Write down your purpose in this life as you understand it. What are some intentional ways you can choose to be satisfied in God alone today?*

DAY 178

Overcoming Expectations

*Though the fig tree should not blossom, nor fruit be on the vines...
yet I will rejoice in the Lord; I will take joy in the God of my salvation.*
Habakkuk 3:17-18

Ask any Christian what the best thing that's ever happened to him/her is, and they'll exclaim: the day we received Jesus into our life! But we so quickly lose sight of the preciousness of the gift.

In Habakkuk 3:17-18 we read these awesome words: "Though the fig tree should not blossom, nor fruit be on the vines, the produce of the olive fail and the fields yield no food, the flock be cut off from the fold and there be no herd in the stalls, yet I will rejoice in the Lord; I will take joy in the God of my salvation."

Some words are easier read than lived. Technically speaking, every Christian should nod in agreement with Habakkuk. His words should make any of our hearts soar in truth. But the longer we stare at our unfulfilled expectations, and heavier our burdens become. Would you still rejoice in the Lord if you didn't get that answer to prayer you've been waiting so long for? Would you still find happiness if your dreams don't come true?

The more you rejoice in the Savior, the more you'll find that to be true.

Questions: *How do you respond when God says no to your prayers? What makes the words of Habakkuk so difficult for us to live?*

God Outside Your Box

Now to Him who is able to do far more abundantly than all that we ask or think, according to the power at work within us.
Ephesians 3:20

Do you leave room for God to be God in your life? Most of us are control freaks. While we say that we're leaving room for God to be God in our lives, an inventory of our days reflects a different story. That's probably why we're so tired all the time.

There isn't a situation in our lives that we haven't considered from every angle. We've covered all our bases. We've got not just Plan A and Plan B, but we're down to Plan Q and running. No matter how much you say you want God to move, it's only when you step back and leave room for Him to work that you'll start seeing the miraculous.

When you consider Christians all over the world, you'll find that many of them are experiencing God in more awesome ways than we do in the West. The reason is that they are living circumstances that are beyond their control. Their only option is to turn to God and allow Him to be God in their lives. They don't have the luxury of putting God in a box.

Are you worn out trying to fix your life? Instead, why don't you start to pray? Give God room to be God, and watch Him do what you simply cannot do.

Questions: *Do you tend to be a control freak? How can you let go of the control of your life and turn it over to Jesus? Take time to pray about the challenges you're facing.*

Rely on God

*Indeed, we felt that we had received the sentence of death.
But that was to make us rely not on ourselves but on God who raises the dead.*
2 Corinthians 1:9

I like things to run smoothly, don't you? I don't like trials and obstacles as a general rule. But if I'm going to have to deal with a problem, it might as well be a fixable one. Yet God allows us to come across overwhelming and life-shaking trials from time to time, and He does it for a reason.

In 2 Corinthians 1 Paul recounts a harrowing time in his Christian life. Things got so bad that Paul thought he was going to die. But Paul understood what many of us don't. There's purpose in the trial. There is a reason for the pressure. God specializes in helping us overcome the impossible and loves it when we turn to Him for help. Sadly, most of us don't turn to God until our circumstances become really impossible. Yet no matter when we do turn our faces to God and ask for help, He's waiting with open arms to help us.

Stop trying to fix everything on your own. Look to Jesus and find all the help that you need to make it to the end.

Questions: *Have you ever been under such trying circumstances that you could do nothing but pray? How did that affect your spiritual life?*

DAY 181

In the Gap

Every word of God proves true;
He is a shield to those who take refuge in Him.
Proverbs 30:5

Do you ever wonder whether God's promises will ever come to pass? Perhaps you're living in the gap. Every promise God gives us is typically followed by a time of waiting. I call it the gap.

Life in the gap can be challenging. You might be tempted to give up in the gap. You might be prone to doubt God's Word and to question your decisions that led you to where you are now. Yet God's Word is clear.

The wisest man in the world wrote this verse to remind us that no matter how we feel today, our confidence is not in our feelings, but in God's promises. In time, every Word God has spoken will come to pass. The only thing you must do in the meantime is to learn to take refuge in Him.

Run to Him when you're afraid. Reach out to Him in your waiting. God is faithful, and in time you'll learn that indeed every Word of God will prove true for you too.

Questions: What promises has God given you in the past that you need to hang on to right now? What circumstances in your life might be causing you to doubt God's promises?

Battling Unbelief

And we know that for those who love God all things work together for good, for those who are called according to His purpose.
Romans 8:28

How do you battle unbelief? Have you ever noticed that fear has a way of choking us when we need to be able to breathe the most? Whether it's in your personal life or in the face of a new venture, fear can play a trick with the mind. But when you stop and think about it, fear is nothing more than unbelief. Fear forgets that God is always for us. Fear neglects to remember that God is good. Fear overlooks the cross of Christ and relies solely on self.

You might wonder what we should do when we're paralyzed with fear. Living by faith requires that we hold on to God's promises no matter how we feel, to fix our feet on the solid ground of His Word. When you're anxious and struggling with fear, the only way to fight unbelief is by hanging on to one of God's promises and standing firmly on it.

For example, Romans 8:28 is a great go to in battling unbelief. All things will work together for good for those who love God. No amount of fear can suffocate God's promises in your life. It's time you believe it!

Question: *What's your go-to promise from God's Word to battle fear and unbelief?*

Even More Awesome

No, in all these things we are more than conquerors through Him who loved us.
Romans 8:37

Have you ever been tempted to use God and His Word for personal motivation? It's easy for us to quote our favorite Bible passages in an effort to pump ourselves up and get the job done. But God's truth is even greater than that. God is indeed greater. He can do even more.

Most of us have never begun to taste the awesome power of who God really is. Ephesians 3:20 is far from a motivational verse. It's the honest to goodness truth. God inspired the apostle Paul to remind us that He is able to do far more abundantly than all we ever ask or think, according to His power at work within us. He also inspired Paul to write that we are more than conquerors in Christ.

While words like that do indeed motivate us to get stronger, they should convict us too. God is bigger than our dreams, stronger than our fears, and more understanding than we could ever imagine. He knows us so well and still loves us so much. He's always waiting for us with open arms.

Just think. If God didn't long to show us more of His power, would He have ever included these awe-inspiring promises for us?

Questions: *Do you ever underestimate God's promises in your life? Do you assume they were written for someone else? How can you personalize His promises for you today?*

God First

*But seek first the kingdom of God and His righteousness,
and all these things will be added to you.*
Matthew 6:33

If you're like me, your life is down to five-minute increments— and mornings are even crazier. Some mornings, no matter how hard I try, I simply run out of time. On those days even my best intentions fail me. If I intend to squeeze in a run, but run out of time, the run must be skipped.

The preciousness of each moment has forced me to prioritize my mornings better. If something needs to be done, it has to be done first. When it comes to spending time with God, most of us miss it because it's simply not a priority. We figure we could do without it. When time runs out, and it always will, we're out the door. We might feel bad about it, but there's nothing we can do about it.

Given enough time, compromising your time with God will kill your soul. Before you know it, your soul will slowly starve to death without a regular intake of God's Word. Corrie ten Boom is known to have said, "Don't pray when you feel like it. Have an appointment with the Lord and keep it. A man is powerful on his knees."

Question: *How is your relationship with God? If you don't feel an intimacy with God, check your priorities and see how much time you're spending on your knees with Him each day.*

God Goals

As for me, I shall behold Your face in righteousness;
when I awake, I shall be satisfied with Your likeness.
Psalm 17:15

We are living in a goal-oriented culture. We all make goals and try to keep them. Even spiritually, many of us get caught up in making journaling goals, and Bible reading and memorization goals.

I was flipping through my Bible recently when I came across Psalm 17:15. David wrote, "As for me, I shall behold Your face in righteousness; when I awake, I shall be satisfied with Your likeness." That sounds pretty radical for a king. That sounds pretty radical for anyone. Instead of asking for riches and power, or fame and position, David knew the secret to the contented heart: "Satisfy me with Your likeness," he prayed.

I wonder how our days would look differently if you and I made this our goal. Single or married, young or old, what would it look like to make every day's goal focused on becoming more Christlike? Are you willing to pray this prayer with David? "God, make us satisfied in Your likeness." Then watch what happens as God answers the sincere desires of your heart.

Questions: *What are some of your goals right now? How would your life look differently if becoming like Christ became your #1 goal?*

Taste and See

Oh, taste and see that the Lord is good!
Blessed is the man who takes refuge in Him!
Psalm 34:8

What's the best thing you've ever tasted? Was it an exotic fruit or an unbelievable dessert? Who doesn't love to taste good stuff? Whether it's a memorable meal or something your mom made over the holidays, you and I can spend the next ten years reminiscing over something great we tasted.

God understands the reality of taste so much, because in Psalm 34:8 he used the analogy of taste to remind us of His goodness. He inspired David to write: "Oh, taste and see that the Lord is good! Blessed is the man who takes refuge in Him!"

Like a great meal you can't forget that makes your mouth water even thinking about it right now, God's goodness is something to yearn for, to dream about, and to experience fully over and over again. The only way to taste God's goodness is by taking refuge in Him. That's where true peace is found—in His presence is fullness of joy.

Questions: *In what practical ways are you taking refuge in God's presence today? As you reminisce over God's ways, how have you tasted of His goodness in this season of life?*

God Is Your Helper

And I will ask the Father, and He will give you another Helper, to be with you forever, even the Spirit of truth.
John 14:16-17

Sooner or later we'll all experience it: the struggle with loneliness. It's a part of life whether you live alone or have a household full of kids. You wonder who will help you and why the ache deep in your heart. You wonder if anyone really knows you.

Jesus understood exactly how we would feel. In fact, He talked about it while here on this earth. In John 14:16-17, Jesus made a promise to His disciples. He promised to send them a Helper. He said: "And I will ask the Father, and He will give you another Helper, to be with you forever, even the Spirit of truth."

Jesus made provision for us even in our loneliness. Perhaps especially for our loneliness. He saw before we did just how much we would need Him. He provided an answer for our trouble before we were even born. We do have Someone who will never leave us nor forsake us. We do have a Helper always with us even when we don't feel His presence. We don't have to be afraid. We don't have to wonder. We are never alone.

We simply must recognize the Spirit's presence, and ask Him to help us in our time of need. It's what He does best.

Questions: *When do you feel most alone? Where do you need the most help? Would you get in the habit of talking out loud to the Holy Spirit when you need Him the most?*

More Grace

*But He gives more grace. Therefore it says,
"God opposes the proud but gives grace to the humble."*
James 4:6

I was teaching through James recently when I stumbled into James 4:6. I'd read the verse many times before but never felt its impact as deeply. There were just five words, but they seemed to wash over me like never before. These five words are what you need to hang on to today like a lifeline.

Here they are: The five words that will change your day if you'll let them: "But He gives more grace." Five words that will free you from worry. Five words that will help you live victoriously. Five words that will set you free from guilt and shame. God promises us more grace. God doesn't just promise us grace. He promises us more grace. So if you need just a little bit of grace for the day, God promises you more. And if you feel you need a whole lot of grace today, the promise is for more.

God didn't promise much grace. He promises more grace. If you're feeling the weight of your sin, rest reassured that where sin abounds, grace abounds even more. More grace. Isn't that exactly what the doctor ordered?

Question: *What makes it hard for you to receive God's grace? Think about the worst failure in your life; then grab on to more of God's grace to help you live like an overcomer there!*

DAY 189

Steadfast Waiting

See how the farmer waits for the precious fruit of the earth, being patient about it, until it receives the early and the late rains.
James 5:7

Have you ever thought about how a farmer works? God often used farmers as examples for us because we can learn so much from them. One of my favorite examples God gives us is in James 5:7. We're told, "Be patient, therefore, brothers, until the coming of the Lord. See how the farmer waits for the precious fruit of the earth, being patient about it, until it receives the early and the late rains."

Have you ever watched a farmer work? Most of us know about farming from watching TV. But here's what you need to know about farming: It takes time. It's not easy. It puts up with weather challenges and unexpected circumstances and disasters. It demands early mornings and late nights. It brings out tears and a heart that bleeds over the condition of the land. But eventually, a farmer who waits long enough will see—fruit is coming. Fruit is on the way.

Are you about to give up? Take a tip from the farmer and don't give up. Keep on waiting. The rain is coming.

Questions: *What makes you want to give up? Does knowing fruit is on the way give you what you need to keep on going?*

DAY 190

In-Between

According to His great mercy, He has caused us to be born again to a living hope through the resurrection of Jesus Christ from the dead.
1 Peter 1:3

I've always been fascinated by Saturday. What happened on Saturday? Everyone knows that Friday was about the crucifixion, and Sunday brought about the good news of the resurrection. But what about Saturday in between? Most of us get sidetracked by Saturday. We don't like living in the gap.

Most of us get antsy living between the promise and the miracle. We'd rather know *right now*. We'd rather see the answers *now*. But Saturday is part of every story, that day in between. It's hard to live in the in between. But if you long to see the resurrection, you'll have to make it past Saturday and then you'll see. Sunday is coming. The miracle will happen if you're willing to make it past Saturday.

Today might be your Saturday. You've stepped out in faith, you've done what was asked, but still you're waiting, not sure how your story will end. Take heart. Sunday's coming. The resurrection is real! Jesus has overcome. Deliverance is ours in Christ.

Don't give up before Sunday, the day where you'll finally see that it was worth every moment we waited on that Saturday in between.

Questions: What are some things you can do while you're living in the gap? How can you hold on to hope until Sunday finally comes?

Holding on to Hope

*Let us hold fast the confession of our hope
without wavering, for He who promised is faithful.*
Hebrews 10:23

What are some of the things you hope for? On any given day, I hope for a whole lot of things. I hope the weather is sunny and my ER shift is easy. I hope I get an unexpected bonus, and I hope I fall in love.

We all have hopes and dreams and subconsciously wake up with a list of things to hang our hope on. While there is absolutely nothing wrong with many of the goals we hope for, the truth is that if we rest our hopes on them, they're going to lead us down a disappointed path.

I mean, seriously, when was the last time you fell in love on any given Monday? But if you're looking for unshakable joy in your life, you must learn to put your hopes in things that cannot fail you—like the Person of Jesus Christ and the truth of His promises, or the presence of the Holy Spirit with you no matter what you're up against.

Hope is the confident expectation that God will do what He promised He will do. While He hasn't promised that you'll fall in love today, He has surely promised that He will be with you if and when you do!

Question: *Make a list of all you are hoping for today. Now make a new list of what God has promised you for today. How do the two lists line up against each other?*

No More Selfies

If anyone would come after Me, let him deny himself and take up his cross and follow Me.
Matthew 16:24

Do you ever wonder what God thinks about selfies? God actually tells us what He thinks about selfies in His Word.

First, God tells us to examine our selfies. In 2 Corinthians 13:5 He said, "Examine yourselves, to see whether you are in the faith." Second, God tells us to die to our selfies. In Matthew 16:25, we're told, "If anyone would come after Me, let him deny himself and take up his cross and follow Me." And third, God tells us not to compare our selfies. In 2 Corinthians 10:12 Paul reminds us that comparing ourselves with others is not wise! Ouch! The problem with selfies is that they are based on making ourselves look better than we really are.

In a world obsessed with selfies, we have been given a better way. There's nothing more defeating than living life fixated on your "self" or on someone else's best version of their "selves." Instead, we must learn to become free of selfies by fixing our eyes on Jesus.

Questions: *How has social media affected your identity and obscured God's purpose for your life? What are some practical changes you can do to die to selfies?*

In Due Season

And let us not grow weary of doing good,
for in due season we will reap, if we do not give up.
Galatians 6:9

Do you ever get discouraged and want to give up? I do and more often than I care to admit. Whenever I've hit a wall and feel like nothing will ever work out like I thought it would, I'm reminded of three words that I desperately need. Just three little words with so much power to propel me forward. They're not "I love you," even though those are great little words. But the three words I'm talking about are even more powerful for you today. They are words that will fuel you to endure. Here they are: "In due season."

In due season. Are you familiar with these words? They pop up over and over again in God's Word. They're words we need to be reminded of regularly. God is at work in your life right now, even though you don't see it clearly. But in due season, you will see clearly. In due season, what confuses you right now will finally make sense. In due season, what you're praying for right now will be answered. In due season, God will make a way where there seems to be no way.

So instead of giving in to despair, let these three little words fill you with hope. In due season, anything is possible!

Questions: *To what area in your life are you going to apply these three words today? What will you do today as a result of the encouragement you've been given?*

Old-fashioned

They are not of the world, just as I am not of the world.
John 17:16

Do you consider yourself old-fashioned? Let me give you a quick test: If you dress modestly, you're probably old-fashioned. If you refuse to live with your boyfriend before you get married, you're old-fashioned. If you have your driver's license and are still a virgin, you're old-fashioned. If you go to church on Sundays, you're old-fashioned.

Come to think of it, in today's world, anyone who is a follower of Jesus Christ and obedient to His Word is considered old-fashioned. Come to think of it some more, anyone who loves Jesus and is obedient to His Word considers it an honor to be called old-fashioned. So whether you still write checks or stop at holding hands, don't let the world intimidate you when it comes to being old-fashioned.

God's love is old-fashioned, and I'm old-fashioned too. As you continue to make Jesus the center of your life, take joy in His old-fashioned ways.

Questions: *In what ways do you feel old-fashioned in today's culture? How can you connect with others around you while still hanging on to old-fashioned ways?*

Out of the Pit

He drew me up from the pit of destruction, out of the miry bog, and set my feet upon a rock, making my steps secure.
Psalm 40:2

I once had a skunk trip into one of my window wells. It was an interesting experience. The skunk tried to jump out for hours until he finally gave up. I simply avoided walking anywhere near that well. What I did do was call 911. I knew I needed help.

The next day two guys in armored suits showed up to retrieve the skunk who was still snuggled against the side of the well. They literally had to draw him out of the pit of destruction, out of the miry clay, and set him back free to go on.

There are times and seasons in our lives where we simply tumble into a pit so deep we can't pull ourselves out of it. No one likes to be stuck in a pit. Whether it's a pit of bitterness or a pit of self-pity or a pit of bad decisions, as long as you call to the Lord for help, He won't keep you stuck in the pit for long. God specializes in pulling us out of the pits we've stumbled into.

Do you feel stuck in a pit today? Whether you hopped in on purpose or just can't seem to get unstuck, God's grace will pull you out the minute you cry out for help.

Questions: *What pit are you stuck in right now? How did you get here? Are you willing to cry out to the Lord for help?*

For Us

Have I not commanded you? Be strong and courageous. Do not be frightened, and do not be dismayed, for the Lord your God is with you wherever you go.
Joshua 1:9

Do you ever feel stuck in uncomfortable places you dislike so much? Whenever I get stuck in a bad place, I'm tempted to ask why...Why is this happening to me? While asking why might help ease my pain in the short run, the more important question to ask is—what does God want me to learn in this place?

There are generally four reasons why God allows us to stay in uncomfortable places. First, God wants us to learn to trust Him. Will we depend on Him even in this place? Second, God is preparing us for what's coming. God never wastes the waiting. He is always at work preparing us for what He has prepared for us. Third, God is purifying our motives. Think about why you so desperately want out of this place. Is it all about God, or is it really still all about you? The answer is sometimes hard to admit. Lastly, God is teaching us to glorify Him even in difficult places. The harder it is to praise God where we are, the more glory He gets when we do rejoice in our discomfort.

Seasons of pain can often endure longer than we want them to. But rest assured, God is always for us, and He is closer than you think.

Questions: *As you consider the reasons God allows us to stay in uncomfortable places, which applies to you the most? How can you glorify God in your life even if nothing ever changes?*

Finding Solutions

Continue steadfastly in prayer, being watchful in it with thanksgiving.
Colossians 4:2

When it comes to the problems we face, the answer is often much more obvious than we make it.

Hannah was a woman who desperately wanted a son but couldn't have one. She prayed and prayed and nothing happened. Then one day, the story goes on to say, "As she *continued* praying before the Lord" (1 Samuel 1:12), she had an encounter that changed her life. Hannah prayed. And she prayed. And she kept on praying. Hannah's big secret was that she didn't give up. She continued to pray. And eventually God answered.

For most of us, our problem is that we give in to despair. We stop praying too soon. We assume that because God hasn't answered us yet, He never will. What if, like Hannah, we continue to pray for the problems that we face? I wonder how many more answers to prayers we would see if only we would continue to pray like Hannah did.

What if there might be a Samuel waiting to be born if only we refuse to give up? May God give you the strength that you need to continue to pray if you're on the verge of giving up.

Questions: *What have you prayed for, for years without answers? Would you be willing to go on praying like Hannah did until God gives you the answer?*

DAY 198

Redeeming God

Get Mark and bring him with you, for he is very useful to me for ministry.
2 Timothy 4:11

I love second chances, don't you? If you've ever felt the weight of failure, I have a feeling you agree. Thankfully, our God is a God of second chances and new beginnings.

In Paul's letter to Timothy, Paul penned these words toward the end of his life from a prison cell: "Get Mark and bring him with you, for he is very useful to me for ministry." Paul's words can easily choke me up. See, I know the background of the story. I remember exactly who Mark was. As a young man, Mark had messed up badly. He had been given a chance to travel with his uncle, Barnabas, and Paul, but under the strain of the challenges they faced, Mark chickened out and quit. It was awful. It eventually cost Paul's friendship with Mark's uncle, Barnabas.

And yet…God gave Mark a second chance. It was Mark, you see, who wrote one of the Gospels and that same Mark whom Paul asked for on his deathbed. Mark's ashes had been turned to beauty by our redeeming God.

I don't know about you, but I praise God that He's a redemptive God and the God of do-overs.

Questions: *Have you ever felt like you desperately needed a second chance? How does understanding God's heart encourage you no matter what you've done in the past?*

Not a Hair

Are not two sparrows sold for a penny? And not one of them will fall to the ground apart from your Father.
Matthew 10:29

Every couple of days I notice that my hairbrush needs cleaning. The amount of hair I remove from that brush is mind-boggling. Where does all that hair come from? And yet it keeps growing back on my head somehow!

Have you ever considered how crazy some things in life are and wondered why? When it comes to hair, it would be impossible for us to count the hair on our heads if we tried, which makes the words of Jesus even more stunning when He says, "Are not two sparrows sold for a penny? And not one of them will fall to the ground apart from your Father. But even the hairs of your head are all numbered. Fear not, therefore; you are of more value than many sparrows" (vv. 29-30).

You are of more value than the sparrows. You don't ever need to fear. God knows you so well that not even a hair on your head will go missing without His knowing exactly where it went! He knows you so well, and He still loves you so much. How amazing is our God!

Questions: *Do you ever feel forgotten by God? How does knowing He knows the number of your hairs encourage you to run toward Him in your fears?*

Free to Run

Jesus said to him, "If it is My will that he remain until I come, what is that to you? You follow Me!"
John 21:22

Do you ever look at the world and assume that everyone's life is better than yours? We're all guilty of thinking everyone else's life is better than ours. Everyone's vacations have better views than ours. Everyone's dating lives exceed ours. Everyone's job pays more than ours. It's easy to feel disillusioned and empty when our focus is on what everyone else has that we want.

Peter once looked over at his buddy, then turned to Jesus and asked the inevitable question: "What about him?" Peter's question came right after an awesome encounter between Peter and Jesus where Jesus had just restored Peter from failure back into mission. The last thing that should have been on Peter's mind was everybody else, but he couldn't help himself. And neither can we.

It's easy to let envy creep in and assume that others are getting a better deal than we are. Yet Jesus didn't coddle Peter. He looked straight at Peter and said, "What is that to you? You follow Me!" In other words, "Stop worrying about everybody else, and focus your eyes on Me."

The only way to become free of envy and discontent is to fix your eyes on Jesus. When you become satisfied in Him, everything and everyone else fades into the background.

Questions: *Who do you have a tendency to compare yourself to? How can you cultivate your relationship with Jesus so that everyone else becomes secondary?*

God's Peace

Do not be anxious about anything, but in everything by prayer and supplication with thanksgiving let your requests be made known to God.
Philippians 4:6

There are two sorts of people in the world. Those who worry and those who worry more. Are you a worrier? I tend to be. I like to blame my worry on my genes, but I'm afraid it's much less complicated than that!

I worry simply because I'm a control freak. I worry because I want everything to work out exactly like I want it to. I worry because I stop believing God. The minute I feel that God isn't cooperating with my plan, I worry even more.

Wherever you live and whoever you are, worry seems to be a fixture in our lives, but it doesn't have to be. God's solution to our worry problem is not complicated: "Do not be anxious about anything, but in everything by prayer and supplication with thanksgiving let your requests be made known to God."

God promises that prayer is the antidote to worry. The reward when we do pray, it goes on to say, is a peace that passes all understanding (see v. 7).

What are you worried about? Will you stop long enough to pray about your worry, and watch God's peace wash over you today?

Questions: *How badly do you want to overcome the worry in your life? Badly enough to pray? Spend the next five minutes praying through your problems. Ask God to give you His peace instead.*

DAY 202

Daily Bread

I fed you with milk, not solid food, for you were not ready for it. And even now you are not yet ready.
1 Corinthians 3:2

When I started med school, someone wisely told me that I'll only get out of it what I put into it. I found it to be true. To make the most of any experience, we have to be intentional about it.

The same applies to our Christian life. What are you doing to get stronger? Who are you in relationship with? What sort of books are you reading? How much time are you spending in God's Word each day? You can call yourself an artist, but if you never pick up a paintbrush, your talent will never grow. You can call yourself a runner, but if you never put on your running shoes and step out on the pavement, you're kidding yourself.

So many Christians call themselves Christians, but a life void of communion with the Lord will leave those Christians empty and weak. No wonder so many are so easily shaken at the mere mention of a storm.

If you long to grow stronger, it's time to cut your teeth on the meat of God's Word.

Questions: *How can you tell if you're drinking milk or eating solid food in your walk with the Lord? How can you tell if you're getting stronger?*

Life Change

For the word of God is living and active, sharper than any two-edged sword, piercing to the division of soul and of spirit, of joints and of marrow, and discerning the thoughts and intentions of the heart.
Hebrews 4:12

Hey, what's the current state of your Bible? Charles Spurgeon once said that "a Bible that's falling apart usually belongs to someone who isn't." So let me ask you again, what's the current state of your Bible? You don't need to rip up the pages to prove that you're okay. But it is important for you to consider how deeply imbedded your life is to God's Word.

If you're going through pain, God's Word will give you the comfort that you need. If you're dealing with sin, His Word will convict you where you need it. If you're in need of a friend, God's Word is your companion anytime, anywhere. There's not a question in your life that God's Word won't answer. God's Word will give you rest when you need it. His Word will propel you forward when you feel stuck. His Word will direct you when you're feeling confused. The first step is to open it up, and humbly expect it to change you.

Question: *In what specific ways has God's Word changed you since you gave your life to Jesus?*

No Fear

God gave us a spirit not of fear but of power and love and self-control.
2 Timothy 1:7

If you've been a Christian longer than a day, you probably know and love this verse. You might even have a tattoo of it on your arm, and that's understandable. It is an amazing verse.

I've used it right before any big exam, and I still recite it when I pull into my detached garage at 2:00 in the morning and get a case of the nerves. I say the verse like it's a mantra, and wait for its magic to take effect. Too often we do that with verses. We find one we love and we put it on repeat. We listen to it like it's a mantra and miss the awesomeness of the God behind the verse.

Our God is powerful. He has defeated the enemy. He loves us deeply. And in a moving letter to his protege, the Spirit of God inspired Paul to write these words of encouragement to remind him of his God. This verse moves us past letters on a page to a reality so astounding about a God so awesome.

It is our God, and not the mere words we recite, who has given us power over evil. It cost Him His Son to do it, but because of love He'd do it again in a heartbeat. So go ahead and recite the words, but worship the God behind the words with every syllable.

Questions: *What are you afraid of? How does thinking about God—His character and His love for you—bring this verse to life for you?*

DAY 205

His Eye on You

Behold, the eye of the Lord is on those who fear Him, on those who hope in His steadfast love.
Psalm 33:18

Have you ever taken a child to the playground? Whether the child is yours or your friend's is indifferent. Most of us who have ever taken on the responsibility of taking a kid to the playground or to the mall develop eyes around the back of our heads.

We don't get distracted by our phones. We don't take a nap while we're watching. We are too aware of the dangers around. We know things that make us pretty vigilant. We won't let anything happen to that kid on our watch if we can help it.

When I read Psalm 33:18, the same picture comes to mind. I think about God watching us, His beloved children, undistracted, completely focused, His eyes never leaving our every movement. He knows where you are right now. He sees you in your joys and in your pain. His eye is on you.

Tragically, even those with the best of intentions sometimes fail to keep bad things from happening to those we love, yet God in His awesome power can keep bad things from happening to us. Even when we walk through what feels like the valley of the shadow of death, His eye is still on us as we hope in His love.

Questions: *Have you ever been tempted to stop hoping in the Lord because of the size of your valley? Does knowing that God's eye is still on you encourage you to keep on walking?*

DAY 206

Live to Please Him

And without faith it is impossible to please Him, for whoever would draw near to God must believe that He exists and that He rewards those who seek Him.
Hebrews 11:6

Do you long to please God? We all do. You can't know God without having a deep heartfelt desire to please Him.

When it comes to pleasing God, I have this tendency to think that if I do more I'll somehow impress Him. So I buy that new journal, and I start that Bible reading plan. I look for ways to serve more and give more and do more until I'm worn out and bitter. For all the more I do, I can't feel Him any closer. I get so easily caught up in this performance trap that I miss the essence of faith—which is what drew me to God in the first place.

In Hebrews God makes it clear what pleases Him. It turns out that belief, not behavior, is the way to God's heart. Doing simply wears us out. Believing God renews us. Believing God entails believing in His character, His goodness, even when life is hard. Believing God rests in God's strength and love. Believing God means letting go of self and hiding in Him, certain that He will help you through it. Believing God rests from work and hangs on to hope, not because I am strong enough, but because I know my God and have come to know that He is indeed strong enough to carry me in my weakness.

Do you believe God?

Questions: *In what ways do you get caught up in a performance cycle? Think about the most difficult circumstance in your life right now. Are you believing God in it?*

More than You Can Handle

Indeed, we felt that we had received the sentence of death. But that was to make us rely not on ourselves but on God who raises the dead.
2 Corinthians 1:9

Do you ever roll your eyes when people say things like, "God won't give you more than you can handle?" You feel every bit of the weight of your present trial, and right now it *feels* so much heavier than you can handle. I know what you mean. I've been there too.

In 2 Corinthians 1:9 Paul gives us a hint of how to handle the trials that seem too heavy for us to bear. He says, "Indeed, we felt that we had received the sentence of death. But that was to make us rely not on ourselves but on God who raises the dead." Paul was walking through a trial that felt way too hard to bear. But instead of feeling discouraged, Paul saw an opportunity, a chance to trust.

Has your trial gotten you to the place where there's nothing left to do but trust? That's the perfect place to be. Like Paul, it's only when we get to the place where there's nothing for us to do but trust that we're finally ready to say, "On Him we have set our hope that He will deliver us again."

If you're facing a trial that only God can see you through, don't despair. You might be closer to a breakthrough than you can imagine.

Questions: *Will you speak today's truth into your present life situation? Will you choose to hope in God even if your trial feels too heavy for you to handle?*

Alone and Isolated

*No temptation has overtaken you that is not common to man.
God is faithful, and He will not let you be tempted beyond your ability.*
1 Corinthians 10:13

Have you ever thought about Jesus' beloved disciple, John? Did you know that John, the disciple whom Jesus loved, did his best work in exile on an island called Patmos, completely isolated and alone? Though John was the only one of the disciples not to be martyred for the faith, he was banished into exile for a large portion of his life.

This might sound exotic to you if you're dreaming of a vacation on a remote island, but let me assure you that there was nothing exotic about his exile. John was being persecuted by the Roman emperor, and his exile was hard. After years of faithfully serving God, this disciple, whom Jesus loved, spent his later years in life alone and isolated from any fellowship with other Christians. But it was on the island of Patmos that John was given visions of God and wrote the book of Revelation.

What an encouragement for every one of us to remember that God can use even seasons of isolation and loneliness in our lives to accomplish His purposes for us. What we see as present punishment might just turn to blessing in the hand of our good and sovereign Lord.

Questions: *What part of your life right now feels like exile on an isolated island? How does knowing God redeems your pain encourage you to keep on going?*

Don't Compare

But when they measure themselves by one another and compare themselves with one another, they are without understanding.
2 Corinthians 10:12

No matter how hard I try to avoid it, self-pity has a way of visiting me more often than I care to admit it. Over time I've noticed that I know the exact cause that leads me down the road to self-pity. It always seems to happen the very moment my eyes wander from all the blessings God has given me and become fixed on what others have that I want. Suddenly discontentment sets in, and my entire self-worth becomes at stake.

"Does God really love me?" I begin to ask myself. "Is He fair?" You'd think I'd have learned by now. Comparison is indeed the thief of all joy. And the test of contentment is how we react when others get what we want.

Are you content with what God has given you? Do you believe that your loving Father is behind every good and perfect gift in your life? It's time to let go of our expectations and hang on to the truth of God's Word and see Him guide us out of the pit of self-pity with His grace.

Only God's love is strong enough to bail us out. Only His love is strong enough to shield us from ourselves.

Questions: What are some steps you can take to avoid making it down the road of comparison leading to self-pity? Are there some apps you need to better control or habits you need to adjust?

Immovable

Be steadfast, immovable, always abounding in the work of the Lord, knowing that in the Lord your labor is not in vain.
1 Corinthians 15:58

Do you ever feel like giving up? Sometimes I do. I want to give up when things don't go my way, and I don't see the results I want, I want to give up.

I recently read about Frances Perkins who was the longest serving U.S. Secretary of Labor and the first woman to be appointed to the U.S. cabinet under FDR. She was the brains behind the new deal of FDR's administration. This woman got the job done. But her life was far from easy. She was misunderstood, maligned, and had a tough home life. Throughout her life she hung on to this truth that gave her strength: "Be steadfast, immovable, always abounding in the work of the Lord, knowing that in the Lord your labor is not in vain."

The words of Paul in 1 Corinthians 15:58 were her motto. No matter how much she felt like quitting, Frances chose to remain steadfast, immovable, abounding in the work of the Lord.

Can the same be said of you? Will you remain steadfast, unshaken, even when the winds of trial beat down on you? Because of Christ's power in you, you can do it. You can stay strong even when you feel like giving up.

Question: *What are some of the things that you will commit to keep on doing knowing that they are not in vain in the Lord?*

Vine Science

Abide in Me, and I in you. As the branch cannot bear fruit by itself, unless it abides in the vine, neither can you, unless you abide in Me.
John 15:4

When it comes to God and His ways, it's not rocket science. It's vine science. Think about trees. If a tree doesn't bear fruit, you eventually chop it down. If it does, it must be pruned until it gets stronger and fuller and eventually bears more fruit.

It doesn't matter how you look at it, the cutting will always hurt. Pruning is not fun. At first, it's counterintuitive. The tree gets smaller and smaller, and looks weaker and less robust to the casual observer. But anyone who has grown lasting fruit on trees knows that you must not judge the tree too soon. If you've grown lasting fruit, you know that eventually the tree will become even more fruitful.

The most interesting thing about vine science is that the vine does none of the actual work. It simply sits there. The gardener is the one who holds the sheers and decides what goes. The gardener is the one who trims, cuts, and uses his experience to make sure that just the right amount of foliage is removed. The vine simply abides.

See? It's not rocket science. It's vine science.

Question: *Think about the painful seasons in your life. What might God have been trying to accomplish in those pruning seasons?*

DAY 212

Overcoming Insecurities

Be still before the LORD and wait patiently for Him.
Psalm 37:7

Sometimes when I look at others I'm tempted to feel like a loser, like I'm not doing enough, and I don't measure up. When I'm in that place, I force myself to do what Psalm 37 tells me to do: I try to keep my eyes firmly fixed on the Lord.

Nothing will steal our joy faster than a horizontal focus on what others are doing. We must choose to look up instead of around. Next, we must learn to avoid the temptation to *do more.* Instead, God tells us, "Be still before the LORD." Sitting still in God's presence brings rest while working harder will only lead to exhausted frustration. Third, I force myself to keep on waiting patiently. I remind myself that as long as I'm not dead, my story's not over yet. And finally, I ask the Lord to help me keep a close watch over my emotions. I ask Him to help me "refrain from anger and forsake wrath!" (v. 8).

Fixing our eyes on others will always lead to frustration, anger, and anxiety. While we won't always get it right, by God's grace we will overcome our insecurities more and more each day.

Question: *How can you practice focused stillness today? Meditate on today's verse as you apply it to an area of insecurity that has caused you discouragement.*

Refuse Bitterness

*For my father and my mother have forsaken me, but the L*ORD *will take me in.*
Psalm 27:10

Rejection is not easy and it's hard to deal with no matter how old you are. If you have a pulse right now, you've probably experienced rejection before. When I think about the pain that rejection has caused me, I see patterns of bitterness and anger settling in my heart in response to the pain of rejection. Once in a while, when the pain is very deep, I turn my frustration to the Lord.

Why does God allow us to feel rejection so deeply? But there is a way to escape the negative emotions of rejection. First is to recognize that the battle starts in our minds. Stop rehearsing the pain of your rejection over and over again. Stop planning your revenge and disliking everything related to the source of your rejection. Instead, choose to walk in the Spirit and refuse to gratify the desires of your flesh. Even in the most painful rejection, God is at work sanctifying you and producing in you the fruit of His Spirit—love, joy, peace, and self-control.

Knowing how much our Father loves us and rehearsing His faithfulness is one of the best ways to renew our minds and find the joy that is unshakeable.

Questions: *Is there anyone in your life right now who has hurt you deeply? Are you harboring bitterness toward that person? Will you choose to let go of your anger and forgive instead?*

DAY 214

Can't Please Everyone

I, I am He who comforts you; who are you that you are afraid of man who dies, of the son of man who is made like grass, and have forgotten the Lord, your Maker?
Isaiah 51:12-13

Have you ever noticed that no matter how hard you try, you'll never be able to please everyone? If you're a parent, I am sure you are nodding your head in agreement. You get it. You stopped worrying about pleasing everyone the moment after kid number two was born. But even if you have no kids like me, we get it too.

It's hard to please everyone. It's impossible to please everyone. There will always be someone who thinks we should be doing it differently. The sooner we learn this lesson that we can't please everyone, the happier we will be.

I love how God frames it for us in Isaiah 51:12-13. He says, "I, I am He who comforts you; who are you that you are afraid of man who dies, of the son of man who is made like grass, and have forgotten the Lord, your Maker?"

Behind our desire to please everyone is a deathly fear of man. The only cure for the fear of man is absolute trust in the Lord.

If you're feeling stretched in one thousand different directions, stop and ask yourself, who am I really trying to please?

Questions: *Who do you struggle with wanting to please? Why does that person have so much power over your actions and desires? Ask God to free you of that burden.*

DAY 215

Don't Fear

*Even though I walk through the valley of the shadow of death,
I will fear no evil, for You are with me; Your rod and Your staff, they comfort me.*
Psalm 23:4

Have you ever thought about what the most frequent command in the Bible is? You might think that the most frequent command in the Bible is to be holy. Or maybe you would have guessed it's the command to stop sinning, or to tell others about Jesus. Or maybe you'd guess it's to love one another.

While all of these commands are indeed awesome and an integral part of God's Word, they don't constitute the most frequent command in the Bible. If you're looking for the most frequently spoken command that God gives us, it's this one: Do not fear. That's right! God commands us over and over again not to be afraid. "Fear not," He says. Don't ever give in to fear.

Aren't you glad that God knows us so well that He made sure we wouldn't miss this? He knows how easily moved by our circumstances we can become and how quickly we forget that He is in control of every detail of our lives.

There's nothing to fear when God is at the helm of our lives. So whatever you're facing today, make sure you remember that you don't have to be afraid. God is with you always. He's a whisper away.

Questions: *What makes you afraid? How can you practice the presence of God and overcome your fears more consistently?*

DAY 216

Out of My Funk

We destroy arguments and every lofty opinion raised against the knowledge of God, and take every thought captive to obey Christ.
2 Corinthians 10:5

Once in a while, even when I don't want to, I end up in a funk. I'm referring to the place where I get too tired to care about anything and where nothing exciting is really happening in my life.

There are two great dangers to pay attention to if you're prone to land in a funk every so often. First is the danger of quitting, and then there's the danger of comparing. While it might be easy to run away under pressure, I've learned that running only lands me in a place where I'm still stuck with myself. There's no escaping me no matter how far I run. And when it comes to comparing my story to others, nothing will deepen my funk more than the lie that "they" have it better than I do.

God has a plan for each of our lives. Comparing your story to others' will only veer you off God's course for your life. What I'm learning is that when I'm in a funk, the only God-honoring solution is to take every thought captive to the obedience of Christ until He tells me it's time to move on.

Question: *What are some of the thoughts you need to start taking captive to the obedience of Christ? Write them down and replace them with the truth of God's words.*

Still Waiting

And in the fourth watch of the night He came to them.
Matthew 14:25

Why does it sometimes feel like God is taking so long to show up when we're in trouble? In Matthew 14, Jesus had sent His disciples in a boat to the other side of the sea when suddenly "the boat by this time was a long way from the land, beaten by the waves, for the wind was against them. And in the fourth watch of the night He came to them." (vv. 24-25). What took Jesus so long to show up? Why didn't He spare the disciples the anxiety of waiting? Why didn't He just stop the storm before it even started?

What takes me by surprise in my walk with Jesus isn't the fact that we face storms, but it's the reality of how long my storms seem to last. Why doesn't God show up before I become desperate and hopeless? Why does it always feel as if I'm fighting the waves on my own?

It wasn't an accident that Jesus waited to reveal Himself to the disciples, and it's no accident that He waits with us today. His goal is to get us stronger in faith. His aim is to make us more Christlike and strong.

He wants us to learn to trust Him no matter how strong the storm feels. His delays are a time for us to learn that God is faithful and will always show up in His perfect timing.

Question: *Will you take a moment and tell God you trust Him even though you don't feel His presence in your storm?*

Stronger

If we are faithless, He remains faithful— for He cannot deny Himself.
2 Timothy 2:13

Do you ever feel like you don't have enough faith no matter how hard you try?

Consider this: The Israelites thought they were dead meat facing the Red Sea. But God still led them through it. They thought they would starve to death. But God still fed them. They thought they would never reach the promised land. But they eventually did. And they're not the only ones to experience God this way.

Hannah thought she'd never have a son. And then along came Samuel. Elijah thought God had abandoned him, until he heard God's whisper. Mary and Martha thought their brother was dead. But God eventually revived him. Thomas thought Jesus was buried until he put his hands in His side. The disciples on the road to Emmaus thought Jesus had failed them until He walked right beside them. Peter thought his days in ministry were over. Then Jesus showed up. The early Church thought Peter was going to die in prison. But God freed him of his shackles.

What we see in all these examples is that without faith it's impossible to please God. The good news is that even when our faith fails us, God is still faithful.

Questions: *How strong is your faith today? How do you think God is working to make your faith even stronger?*

Satisfied

These, though commended through their faith, did not receive what was promised, since God had provided something better for us.
Hebrews 11:39-40

There are some things I just can't shake. Take for example Hebrews 11:39-40. Hebrews 11 is the faith chapter in the Bible. It's the chapter where God gives us a list of all the great men and women of faith. When we finally get to the last two verses we read this: "These, though commended through their faith, did not receive what was promised, since God had provided something better for us."

These verses blow my mind away! Despite having faith big enough to get them a mention in the faith chapter of the Bible, this small group of men and women never even got the thing they had hoped for. They waited and waited, then eventually went to be with the Lord in eternity. Yet their lives were full. They were not disappointed. They remained unafraid, undaunted, and unstoppable. Their secret was that they had found something far better than any hope they could have here on this earth. They had found Someone far more satisfying than the thing they had longed for. They had found Jesus.

How well do you know Jesus? How much do you love Him? Or are you still holding out for someone else or something else to fill the hole in your heart?

Question: *What do you feel will make you happy if only you had it? Ask the Lord to show you if that desire has become an idol in your life and if so, confess it to Him.*

DAY 220

Choose God

But as for me and my house, we will serve the Lord.
Joshua 24:15

One of the greatest Christians of all times is Dwight L. Moody. He once said: "The Bible will keep you from sin, or sin will keep you from the Bible." In today's world, Moody's words sound archaic and old-fashioned. They seem completely transposed from another era, and maybe they are. Moody lived and died in the 1800s after all.

Most people today don't like thinking about sin. We've learned to excuse it and minimize it. When we can't overcome it, we just ignore it. We've forgotten that we have everything we need to live victoriously in Christ. We assume that we have no option but to sin. Yet no matter how many times you've tried to defeat sin in your life and failed, God's promise to us is that we can still live the powerful Christian life God intends for us.

God promises to give us all we need for victory, and it starts when we open God's Word and submit to His Spirit. Are you doing what He has asked you to do? In reality, Moody had it right. When we give sin free reign in our lives, the last place we turn to is God's Word. But when we make God's Word our priority, sin becomes an afterthought.

Today, will you choose to sin, or will you submit to God? The two cannot coexist.

Questions: *Are your choices honoring to God and His Word? How can you tell?*

Spiritual Disciplines

*But I discipline my body and keep it under control,
lest after preaching to others I myself should be disqualified.*
1 Corinthians 9:27

Have you ever noticed that most things in life that are good for you don't always feel good? It's the most uncanny thing— but consider your health: Exercising regularly doesn't always feel good—but it is good for you. Skipping that slice of cake after dinner doesn't give me the warm fuzzies, but it is good for you and me. Going to bed on time instead of watching an extra episode of your favorite show might be hard, but you'll be thankful in the morning. The list goes on and on.

We all know it and we accept it. Yet when it comes to living out the Christian life, we resist the idea that the spiritual disciplines might not always feel good, but they are both good and necessary for us. Whether it's reading your Bible daily, or learning to pray consistently, or fasting, or gathering together with other believers regularly, it is not until you commit to doing what does not always feel good that you'll find the strength to live the life that is good in Christ.

And just like with exercising, the more you practice the disciplines, the more they actually start to feel good.

Questions: *What spiritual disciplines do you struggle with? How can you resolve to bring your mind under control to God's disciplines until they start to feel good?*

Stay the Course

*In a little while you will see Me no more,
and then after a little while you will see Me.*
John 16:16

Do you ever grow impatient in the waiting? More often than I care to admit it, I do. I get tired in the waiting. To know me is to know that I don't love to wait. It doesn't matter if it's in the line at Starbucks or on the phone for a customer service representative, I'm as impatient as they come.

The truth is most of us don't love to wait, and our culture is only reinforcing our impatience. We're living in the age of Amazon Prime and insta-shopping. We're being trained to expect our best dreams to come to pass at the mere click of a finger. God's way is not the same. God's way is in the waiting.

Whenever I get impatient in the waiting, I think of the words of Jesus in John 16:16: "In a little while you will see Me no more, and then after a little while you will see Me." Jesus understood our frustration in the waiting and wanted to make sure that we knew that no matter how long the waiting seems, it would only be a little while before the waiting would end.

Do you need to be encouraged in the waiting today? Jesus promises that in a little while, your waiting will end too. In a little while, God will accomplish His purposes for your life. In a little while, you'll hardly remember the frustration of today's waiting. In a little while doesn't seem so bad after all, now, does it?

Questions: *In what area of your life have you felt disappointed that God hasn't answered? How does today's perspective encourage you to keep on going in your place of waiting?*

Secrets

"I did not speak in secret, in a land of darkness; I did not say to the offspring of Jacob, 'Seek Me in vain.' I the Lord speak the truth; I declare what is right."

Isaiah 45:19

Do you remember playing telephone when you were a child? I loved that game, and it never ceased to amaze me how much we all wanted to hear what was being said at the beginning of the line. We all long to know the words that are being spoken.

In Isaiah 45 God says, "I did not speak in secret, in a land of darkness; I did not say to the offspring of Jacob, 'Seek Me in vain.' I the Lord speak the truth; I declare what is right." The truth is that God speaks, and He longs for us to hear Him. The real question is: Are you listening?

One of the hardest ways God speaks to us is through detours and delays. Most of us get mad when our plans are stalled. We get frustrated when we face delays. Yet God uses detours and delays to reveal our hearts and to show us where we need to rely on Him more. He's not interested in our destination as much as He's interested in how we get there. He's not interested in our performance as much as He's interested in our hearts, and He uses delays to reveal to us where our hearts are.

Are you longing to hear God more? Stop and listen. He's promised to speak in your darkness.

Question: *Are you facing a detour in your life right now? Stop and ask God to speak to you through this unexpected delay.*

DAY 224

Call for Help

And call upon Me in the day of trouble; I will deliver you, and you shall glorify Me.
Psalm 50:15

Who do you call when you need help? As a single woman who lives alone, I often run into situations that require help. Like, for example, the day my garage door got stuck, and I couldn't figure out how to fix it. Or the time the water in my shower wasn't draining smoothly, and no amount of Drano did the trick.

What starts like little irritations can become big obstacles in the course of my day. My knee jerk response is to panic. I wonder: Who do I call for help in this situation? It shouldn't sound as complicated as I probably make it, but it quickly can turn into a crisis if I'm not careful.

I've been reading in the Psalms lately and have noticed that over and over again the writer says, "I call on the Lord who will help me." It seems to me that the psalmist knew that no matter how complicated his problems were and how big the obstacles he was facing felt, he knew that God would always come through for him the moment he cried out to Him. If calling out to God worked for the king of Israel thousands of years ago, surely it should work for us today.

Instead of fretting and worrying about how to fix your problem today, won't you stop and call on the name of the Lord first?

Questions: *What areas in your life do you need the most help with? Where do you turn to when you need help?*

DAY 225

Unshakeable Hope

*Let us hold fast the confession of our hope
without wavering, for He who promised is faithful.*
Hebrews 10:23

Hope is what keeps us going on when we don't feel like taking another step. The reason we lose hope so quickly is that we place all of our hopes on our dreams and our circumstances. When things run smoothly, our hope explodes. We feel unstoppable. Then when the going gets tough, and our dreams delay or worse yet die, we fall in a funk and accuse God of forgetting us.

Hope that rests in your circumstances is always going to fail you. But when it comes to developing the kind of hope that will take you through life's storms, you must learn to anchor your hope on the unconditional love of God and the surety of His presence. This kind of unshakeable hope is established in God's promises which never fail us. This kind of hope rests in God's character which never changes. This kind of hope expands in the light of God's goodness which never stops.

What kind of challenges are you facing today? Will you resolve to put your hope in God no matter what you're going through? Will you bank your all on His love for you? His love will never let you down. He is good. His faithfulness endures forever. That's the truth you can build your life on.

Questions: *Do you trust that God is good even when life is hard? How can you tell you're trusting in Him in this season of your life?*

Grace Unending

Your steadfast love, O Lord, extends to the heavens, Your faithfulness to the clouds.
Psalm 36:5

Do you like gifts? Did you know that you've been given a gift today? It's a gift that you desperately need and a gift you might not even notice. And the one mistake that will ruin your life today is to refuse to receive this gift. I'm talking about the gift of God's grace. It's yours today if you'll receive it.

No matter what happened yesterday, God promises new grace for you today. No matter how badly you screwed things up, today you get to start fresh. You might have been too rushed to notice the gift this morning. Maybe you stumbled out of bed and ran right past it. You barely noticed it. Your mistake will cost you your peace and your joy. It might even affect everyone around you.

The responsibilities ahead of you today are huge. The expectations are massive. The demands are beyond your ability to cope. You can try doing it on your own...or you can stop for a moment and simply receive God's grace.

This gift of God's grace is unending. It's undeserved. It's life changing. And it's the one thing that will make the difference in your life today.

Question: *Hold your palms out and tell God you'll receive His grace today no matter what. Picture God's grace washing over you as you think through the obstacles ahead of you today.*

Soul Health

The people who survived the sword found grace in the wilderness...I have loved you with an everlasting love; therefore I have continued My faithfulness to you.
Jeremiah 31:2-3

How's your soul today? Is it at peace? Are you resting in the Lord, or are you churning with worry and chaos? It's not always easy for me to find true rest. I've got way too many burdens, way too many responsibilities, and way too many dreams and things I still need to do to rest. Even after reading my Bible and trying to pray, I catch myself still weighed down by the noise in my life. I desperately need soul rest.

Jeremiah tells us that "the people who survived the sword found grace in the wilderness; when Israel sought for rest, the Lord appeared to him from far away. I have loved you with an everlasting love; therefore I have continued My faithfulness to you."

The one thing you need to know if you're looking for rest is that God will always love you. His love is the key to your freedom and your rest. His love is the stability that will help you make it when your life feels unstable. His love is steadfast. His love is solid ground on shifting sand.

If you're looking for rest in the midst of chaos, don't go anywhere, don't do anything, and don't talk to anyone, until you receive God's perfect love for you in Christ.

Questions: How can you experience God's love for you today? In what ways are you trying to make it on your own without God's love sustaining you?

Divine Perspective

*For now we see in a mirror dimly, but then face to face.
Now I know in part; then I shall know fully, even as I have been fully known.*
1 Corinthians 13:12

Have you ever taken a moment to look in the rearview mirror today? Maybe you shouldn't! The rearview mirror effect is one of the most dangerous objects you'll face.

You might have had a perfectly decent morning until you get in your car and start driving. You barely make it to the first stoplight when you accidentally look into the rearview mirror. Suddenly that tiny blemish on your face becomes the center of your universe. It's ridiculous how magnified everything looks in the rearview mirror!

Everybody knows that what you see in the rearview mirror isn't your reality. The rearview mirror has a way of making small things look big. The rearview mirror blows things out of proportion in your life and will literally kill you if you let it. Satan loves the rearview mirror. He takes joy in making small things look big and big things look small. Don't fall for his trap.

Refuse to look into the rearview mirror of regret and retrospection, and start seeing things clearly from God's point of view. His perspective will never leave you defeated. His view overflows with His love.

Questions: *What do you see when you look in your rearview mirror? How would your life look from God's perspective?*

Dismantling Lies

For I am sure that neither death nor life, nor angels nor rulers, nor things present nor things to come, nor powers, nor height, nor depth, nor anything else in all creation, will be able to separate us from the love of God in Christ Jesus our Lord.

Romans 8:38-39

We all believe lies about God. They seep into your thinking without your noticing, but they'll kill your hope if you don't recognize them.

There are two very common lies we believe about God. The first is the lie that if God loves me He won't let me suffer. Yet suffering exists in our broken world. It's inevitable even for the Christian. The amazing truth about God's love is that it will reach you and sustain you *through* your suffering. Someday we will live in a place without suffering, but until then we hold on to the truth that God has overcome suffering in His resurrection, and He takes great joy in helping us through our pain.

The second lie we believe is the lie that if God gives me what I want, I'll finally be happy. The truth is that God knows what we want, but also what we need.

Our joy begins the minute we surrender our needs to God and thank Him for all He's given us. Happiness is a choice we make when we boldly affirm that our Father loves us and knows what's best for us.

Questions: Which of these two lies are you more prone to believe? How will dismantling the lie free you and restore your joy?

DAY 230

Truth to Live By

For the L<small>ORD</small> is good; His steadfast love endures forever, and His faithfulness to all generations.
Psalm 100:5

There are many things that will go wrong today. Some of your plans will fall through. Some of your dreams will hit dead ends. Some of your people will let you down.

In the midst of all of your impending messes, here are three truths you will be able to count on no matter what: First of all is that God's love will never fail you. The steadfast love of the Lord does endure forever. The world might fall apart, but God's love will endure forever. Second, God's mercy will not run out on you no matter how much of it you will need. As sure as the sun rises, God's mercies are new toward you today. They will never come to an end. There's such hope in this truth. Third is that God's presence will never leave you. No matter what you do today and no matter where you go, the one thing you can be sure of is that God's presence will be right there with you.

I can't tell you how often I need to be reminded of these truths daily. I need solid promises to hang onto when everything around me feels like it's shifting. Don't you?

Question: *Write down today's three truths on a 3x5 card, and carry it in your pocket today, a reminder of who God is and how much He cares about you.*

Your True Worth

Indeed, I count everything as loss because of the surpassing worth of knowing Christ Jesus my Lord.
Philippians 3:8

Where do you find your significance? What makes you feel important? Is it your accomplishments or your position? Is it your reputation or your possessions? Or is it your husband or wife or the essence of your dating status?

Paul understood the rightful place to find his true significance. In Philippians 3:8 he said, "Indeed, I count everything as loss because of the surpassing worth of knowing Christ Jesus my Lord." Paul understood that even good things can become bad things when they stand in the way of God things.

One of the biggest ways to know what matters most to you is by seeing how you react when you don't get the thing you desperately want. Do you get mad at God because of it? Do you feel disappointed and discouraged and full of despair? Do you feel angry when someone else gets what you want? Perhaps God is trying to show you what's in your heart. You don't need "it" to be complete. All you really need is Him!

You are worth far more to God than your stuff. It's time to start believing who God says you are.

Questions: *Where do you find your worth? How would you react if you lost your job or your reputation? How can finding your worth in God be your pathway to greater freedom?*

DAY 232

God of Glory

In hope he believed against hope, that he should become the father of many nations, as he had been told, "So shall your offspring be."
Romans 4:18

When was the last time you faced a problem you couldn't fix on your own? I am not a fan of problems in general, but I'm learning a lesson that God has been trying to show me: that our problems are the platforms that propel us to our purpose.

The primary way we can glorify God is by finding joy and rejoicing in our suffering. When we go through an insurmountable problem and still see God as our good, good Father, we give Him the glory. When we point to His faithfulness, even when life looks grim, we glorify His name.

Abraham waited *forever* to see God's faithfulness, *always* holding on to God's promises and character, never losing hope that God would show up for him. And eventually, God did show up. In Romans 4 it says that Abraham believed against hope, giving glory to God.

The very thing that is causing you the greatest pain right now is your chance to stand strong in faith, giving glory to His name. As you do that, others will see in our God a God worthy of our worship. And when we do that, we will be living out our God-given purpose for our life.

Questions: What kinds of reactions have you had to the problems in your life? How can you practically start glorifying God in the midst of your problems?

A Closer Walk

Draw near to God, and He will draw near to you.
James 4:8

A friend recently confided in me: "I wish I knew God better, but He just seems so far away." Here's what I asked her in response: "How much time do you spend with the Lord and His Word each day?" She couldn't look me in the eyes with her answer.

See, most of us want a closer walk with Jesus. We long for more intimacy. We are desperate for growth. Yet few of us are willing to pay the price for an intimate relationship with the Lord. We will never know God more intimately without making His Word our priority. We will never grow stronger until we seek God's presence as a treasure worth finding.

If you don't have a plan for reading God's Word regularly, you can start right now. This is one habit that will change your life. When you open God's Word and ask the Spirit to change you, He will! When you submit your life to what He tells you in His Word, everything changes. You become more Christlike, and victory becomes yours.

Questions: *How much time are you spending with the Lord each day? Are you willing to make time with God your priority in order to deepen your walk with Him?*

No More Pretending

But you are a chosen race, a royal priesthood,
a holy nation, a people for His own possession.
1 Peter 2:9

Do you know the greatest temptations you will face today? It won't be a temptation related to food or lust or speeding. It won't be a temptation that's as obvious as you might think. The greatest temptation you face today is the temptation to pretend to be something you're not. Today you'll be tempted to pretend you're richer than you really are. Or holier, or nicer, or more generous than you are.

The reason we all pretend is simple: We long to be liked. We long for the approval of others. We'll do anything to be accepted and well liked by others. But the truth is that God already knows exactly who we are, and He still loves us. He sees us. And He died for us.

If you're looking to become more Christlike, the fastest way to do it is to stop pretending to be something or someone you're not. Look for it today, this temptation to pretend. Watch your Facebook update and the list of updates you'll like. Think about it as you choose the best filter on your most flattering pic.

Simply stop and ask yourself: Am I telling the truth in this situation, or am I merely pretending?

Questions: *In what specific areas in your life do you tend to pretend the most? How can you practice honesty in that area today?*

God of Hope

Casting all your anxieties on Him, because He cares for you.
1 Peter 5:7

There are days when I can easily be my own worst enemy. Instead of hoping for a good outcome, I expect the worst. Instead of holding on to hope, I get caught up in a cycle of negativity.

Slowly but surely I'm learning to identify some of the thought patterns in my life that stand in the way of my hope in God. One of the most common obstacles that defeat me is my past disappointments. Those are the times when I've prayed and waited, but instead of seeing the answer I want, the opposite of what I pray for happens. So I wonder: Can God be trusted? Of course He can! He is trustworthy no matter the outcome of my prayers.

Romans 15:13 is a great reminder helping me to overcome the obstacle of hopelessness: "May the God of hope fill you with all joy and peace in believing so that by the power of the Holy Spirit you may abound in hope."

Do you struggle with your past disappointments? Do you wonder if God cares about you? He does. He cares. He's the God of all hope. Turn to Him today, and find in Him all the joy and peace you need to rise above your fears.

Questions: *In what specific areas in your life do you become your own worst enemy? Does knowing God cares deeply about you help you overcome your negativity?*

Happiness and Money

The rich and poor have this in common, the Lord is the maker of them all.
Proverbs 22:2

When it comes to money, most of us think we need more of it. We complain that we never have enough of it. Deep down we secretly think that money will surely enhance our happiness.

We're wrong about money. Watch most rich people, and you'll find they're no happier than the rest of us. In fact, some are plain miserable. Money, you see, doesn't buy happiness. Money never delivers what we assume it promises. Proverbs 22:2 tells us that "the rich and poor have this in common, the Lord is the maker of them all."

It turns out that some things are more important than money—like your faith in God and everything that pertains to Him. Jesus believed it so much that He told us to seek first the kingdom of God, and all these things would be added unto us.

If you've already started your day worried about money, stop and consider God and His ways. He's promised to meet your needs as you seek to find your joy in His presence.

Questions: Are you seeking God first in your life, or are you chasing after riches? How can you tell the difference?

DAY 237

Beauty from Ashes

To grant to those who mourn in Zion—to give them a beautiful headdress instead of ashes, the oil of gladness instead of mourning, the garment of praise instead of a faint spirit.
Isaiah 61:3

Do you ever feel broken and beyond repair? To be completely honest with you, sometimes I feel broken, even beyond repair. No matter how well I've tried to live my life, I've made some decisions I've lived to regret which is why reading verses like Isaiah 61:3 makes me so happy.

Isaiah writes to tell us that God makes beauty out of ashes. He specializes in redeeming what's broken and making the most of our messes. He is near to the brokenhearted. Jesus made a habit of healing broken people and surrounding Himself with those who were sick.

While I don't want to stay broken, my heart longs to remain near to the One who can take my broken pieces and make something beautiful out of them. There is no brokenness too shattered for God's healing touch.

Whether it's your past with your broken choices that fill you with shame, or your present messes that keep you from hope, God promises to make something beautiful out of your brokenness if you'll let Him.

Question: *What area in your life fills you with shame? Turn it over to the Lord, and ask Him to make something beautiful out of your broken pieces.*

DAY 238

Happy

This is the day that the L<small>ORD</small> has made; let us rejoice and be glad in it.
Psalm 118:24

Do you ever get stuck in the trap of feeling like you're waiting for something better to happen in your life? Like what's happening in your life right now may be okay, but that there must be something better right around the corner?

There is a dangerous flaw with this sort of thinking. While it sounds hopeful, it can soon turn into a test we give to God. Will God come through for us in the way we want Him to? If He does, we deem Him good and we feel happy. If He doesn't, we give in to disappointment. This kind of thinking is not undergirded by God's love but by our own expectations.

In Psalm 118 the writer reminds us that "*this* is the day that the L<small>ORD</small> has made. Let us rejoice and be glad in it." While the best is still yet to come, today we live right here and right now. This is indeed the day we've been given. We have this life. We hold these relationships dear to us. We have this job that helps sustain us, and this church to edify us.

Let Jesus be our hope. Let Him be our joy and our stability. Let this life He has given us be the starting point of our rejoicing.

Questions: *Are you happy? If not, can you trace the source of your unhappiness to unmet expectations? How can you align yourself with God's will to find happiness right now?*

DAY 239

For Good

*As for you, you meant evil against me, but God meant it for good,
to bring it about that many people should be kept alive, as they are today.*
Genesis 50:20

Every so often I get sucked into the land of "what ifs" and "if only's." While it might sound benign, this line of thinking can eventually emotionally derail us.

"If only I had worn a different outfit." "If only I hadn't mentioned my past." "If only I hadn't ended that relationship so quickly." If I don't pay attention, before I know it, I'm living in a pit of regret, a place that will keep me stuck forever if I let it.

God wants more for us than to live in regret. He longs for us to live in His freedom He purchased for us and to rest in His love. When it comes to the "what ifs" in your life, nothing will encourage you more than the truth that God is sovereign. He is in control. Joseph understood it in Genesis 50:20 when he said: "As for you, you meant evil against me, but God meant it for good, to bring it about that many people should be kept alive, as they are today."

No matter what part of your past threatens to derail you, remember that God can and will use it for good!

Questions: *In what areas in your life do you tend to revert to an "if only" mentality? How does Joseph's example encourage you to live at peace no matter what's happened to you?*

DAY 240

Happy Christians

I appeal to you therefore, brothers, by the mercies of God, to present your bodies as a living sacrifice, holy and acceptable to God, which is your spiritual worship.
Romans 12:1

Who's the happiest Christian you know? Have you ever stopped long enough to ask yourself, "what makes some Christians so happy?"

Whenever I meet a man or woman of God who radiates pure joy, not an ounce of worry on their faces, I am tempted to ask myself if they are faking it. But the more you get to know those happy Christians, the more you realize they have just one thing in common: They're fully surrendered to God. They have submitted their wills completely to the Savior's, and the result is an abiding peace.

True joy is impossible without absolute surrender to our Father's loving ways. It is impossible to have lasting joy if we're constantly fighting for our way over God's. We can fool ourselves into believing that we can be happy without surrender, but eventually, if we are true children of God, He promises to correct us and discipline us until we yield to Him completely.

The best part is that when we do surrender everything to Jesus, joy will flood our lives. It's that simple.

Questions: *Are you a happy Christian? What is the last thing you surrendered to the Lord? Is there anything He's asking you to still surrender to Him right now?*

Not Done Yet

I believe that I shall look upon the goodness of the L<small>ORD</small> in the land of the living!
Psalm 27:13

Do you ever stop reading before the end of the story? I have the bad habit of starting a story and stopping halfway, and I've found it to be a horrible idea. Let me illustrate why.

If you don't read all the way to the end of the story, you might think that Abraham never had any children, Jacob and his brother never spoke again, Joseph spent the rest of his life in prison, Moses was banished to the wilderness forever, and that David's highest moment was the day he killed Goliath.

But...Abraham did have a son named Isaac, and Jacob did eventually reconcile with his brother Esau, Joseph eventually became the ruler of Egypt, Moses lived out his dream of leading his people out of Egypt; and David, well, David lived well past defeating Goliath! David became the strongest king of Israel.

And then there was Jesus hanging on a tree. Everyone thought His story was over on the night of His crucifixion. Today Jesus is alive and reigning over everything. His story was far from over at Calvary.

Stop believing the lie that your story is over, and resolve to persevere no matter what. God has a plan for your life, and nothing's going to stand in His way.

Questions: *Have you ever been tempted to feel like your story is already over, like your best days are behind you? What would you change in your life today if you knew there was still more to come?*

DAY 242

Waiting Is Hard

Wait for the Lord; be strong, and let your heart take courage; wait for the Lord!
Psalm 27:14

They say the hardest part of a marathon is the last mile. Though I've never run a marathon, they might be right.

Think about it: The hardest part about waiting is that we never know when we're in the final lap. Early on, everyone is very excited about the project. Our dreams fuel us to jump out of the starting blocks with much vigor. Then we hit the flats where the scenery is monotonous and everything starts looking very much the same. That's when most people are tempted to give up.

But what if somewhere in the flats is actually the final lap? What if that last stretch where you desperately want to quit is the final week in prison before Pharaoh calls you out to freedom? What if right when your muscles start burning is the bend before the burning bush lights up? What if your breakthrough is right around the corner? Wouldn't it be worth the extra push?

If you've ever felt like selling it all and moving to Tahiti for the rest of your life, stop for a minute and consider that though waiting is hard, and the road to victory seems endless, the end might be coming sooner than you think.

Don't stop your race before it's done. You're almost there. You might be a lot closer to the finish line than you think!

Questions: *Have you ever felt like quitting? How does knowing breakthrough is coming help you go on? Would you take some time and thank God for what He's doing in you in the waiting?*

Even More

That you, being rooted and grounded in love, may have strength to comprehend with all the saints what is the breadth and length and height and depth.
Ephesians 3:17-18

It surprises me how forgetful I can be about the things that matter in life. Though I don't mean to forget, sometimes I simply lose track of all God has done. I get so focused on what I still want God to do in my life that I forget all He's already done.

There was a time in my life when I dreamed of becoming a doctor. And a time in my life I dreamed of writing a book. And a time when I dreamed that more than twenty people might read anything I'd written. And a time when being on the radio sounded too good to even dream up. But in His goodness, God opened doors and beat the odds in my life to show me over and over again that He can be trusted. He moved past my failures. He overcame my disappointments. He did what only He could do. In my desire to see Him do even more, it's easy to lose sight of the wonder of His love and His wonder-working power.

Instead of whining about what God hasn't done for us yet, let's feast on His grace and remember all He has done for us today. Let's remember His goodness and give thanks for what He's still going to do.

Mostly, though, let's rejoice in Him. He's the reason we exist and the One who makes it all worth living!

Question: *What do you long to see God still do in your life? Take a moment and reflect on all the impossible things He's already done in your life to get you this far.*

DAY 244

Rest in Him

For God alone my soul waits in silence; from Him comes my salvation.
Psalm 62:1

We're living in a Xanax culture. Have you ever noticed how stressed everyone is these days? It's like everyone needs a chill pill to turn it down a notch. People are stressed and mad all of the time. It's like they need a Xanax. But if you scratch past the surface, you might quickly figure out why. If you look past the facades, you'll see why everyone is so mad and frustrated.

Today's culture is a culture of distraction and demand. People all over are tired and overworked. They feel under-recognized and unappreciated. They are frustrated and alone. Most people are living lives they thought would look different. They are in a state of constant disappointment and feeling like they are not enough.

St. Augustine once famously said that "our hearts will not rest until they find their rest in God." Perhaps the reason everyone acts like they need a Xanax is that we're trying to find our rest everywhere but in the only One who will give us true peace.

When it comes to finding your rest, Jesus is the answer. No matter how hard you look, ultimately, it's Jesus your heart craves.

Question: *How can you fill yourself with Christ and find the rest your heart longs for?*

DAY 245

Need to Pray

*Then He said to them, "My soul is very sorrowful,
even to death; remain here, and watch with Me."*
Matthew 26:38

If I have a problem, I need to fix it, stat! I suppose that's a hazard of a couple of decades in the ER. I like getting things done, don't you? So if you're single and want to get married, I'll likely have you join a dating site to find your match. Married and not happy? I'll point you to a florist or a chocolate shop. I like action and I like it now.

But if you've ever taken a good look at Jesus, it seems He speaks a completely different language. On the night before His crucifixion, Jesus took His three closest friends apart, looked them straight in the eyes, and asked them to do one thing for Him. He asked them to watch and pray. That's all He asked—that they watch and pray. Instead, you probably know what they did: they slept. They couldn't even watch and pray for one hour.

Most of us can understand the disciples' predicament. Prayer and waiting sounds ridiculous in the face of impending danger and pain. Prayer sounds like inertia in a moving culture. Yet on the night before He was crucified, Jesus asked the disciples to do the only thing that would ultimately make a difference in their lives. He asked them to pray.

Prayer, you see, is the only strategy that will make a difference when you're facing the unknown. Will you do it? Will you watch and pray?

Questions: Are you facing a difficult circumstance in your life right now? How much time are you spending in prayer about the things that overwhelm you the most?

Trust in His Heart

Trust in the L<small>ORD</small> with all your heart, and lean not on your own understanding; in all your ways acknowledge Him and He will direct your paths.
Proverbs 3:5-6

As a doctor, I've noticed that people are typically happy when they get what they want from me. They come to me with a pretty good idea of what they need. If I agree with their medical assessment, they're happy. If I present a different concept, they're disappointed and underwhelmed. Sometimes they tell me why I'm wrong. Lucky for me, I tend to have thick skin.

I've noticed that when it comes to my prayer life, I approach God with the same attitude. I come to Him with my own personal agenda. If He cooperates and does what I want, I'm happy. If He doesn't, my joy meter plummets.

Almost every Christian is familiar with Proverbs 3:5-6: "Trust in the L<small>ORD</small> with all your heart, and lean not on your own understanding; in all your ways acknowledge Him and He will direct your paths." These are verses that are easier said than lived. Most of us rely way too much on our own understanding and only want God to step in when we need a troubleshooter.

I'm learning that the only path to lasting peace is complete trust in the Father. When it comes to our happiness, He knows what's best and simply needs our trust.

Questions: *Do you believe that God is good and wants what's best for your life? Are you living your life in such a way to reflect your belief in His goodness?*

Pray Boldly

Oh that You would bless me indeed and enlarge my border, and that Your hand might be with me, and that You would keep me from harm.
1 Chronicles 4:10

Do you remember the prayer of Jabez? It was big in the 80s. Everyone memorized it and prayed it at least once a day.

I remember the season in my life when I first read the prayer of Jabez in 1 Chronicles 4: "Oh that You would bless me indeed and enlarge my border, and that Your hand might be with me, and that You would keep me from harm." How desperately I wanted this to be my prayer too.

What continues to amaze me isn't just that God *can* bless us, but that He wants to! And do you know who God blesses? He blesses the one who asks! On any given day God blesses us in ways we recognize and in many ways we don't. But there is a blessing for the one who approaches His throne boldly like Jabez did and actually asks for God's favor.

Over and over again in His Word, God tells us of men and women who asked Him to intercede on their behalf, and in His mercy God did. He's that faithful and good. God is waiting to bless us in ways above and beyond what we can imagine if only we'd ask Him to.

Are you humble enough to ask Him to bless you, and are you dependent enough to rest in His care?

Question: *Think about what you pray about. Are you boldly grabbing on to God's promises in prayer, or are you too timid and proud to admit your need?*

DAY 248

Impossibly Good

You have turned for me my mourning into dancing;
You have loosed my sackcloth and clothed me with gladness.
Psalm 30:11

Who doesn't love a good lemon? They're unique and with just enough sugar, irresistible to drink. Sometimes, no matter how hard we try to avoid them, life hands us lemons. But you know what they say about lemons—they're great for making lemonade! The thing about lemons, though, is that when you're chewing on them, it's hard to think about much past the sour feeling in your mouth. It's hard to see the beauty in the pain.

I'm learning that some things in life are best learned when life is sour. It's easier to believe that God is in control when we walk through the valley and come out of it stronger. It's confidence building to hang on to God's promises when failure feels imminent. It's only then that we truly understand that God's promises are trustworthy. If you're looking for a miracle, it helps to land in a situation where a miracle is desperately needed!

It's only when circumstances look impossible to man that God's power becomes evident. And it is as you learn who God really is that your bitter lemon suddenly becomes sweet.

Questions: *What situation in your life feels sour and impossible? What aspect of God's character might He be trying to teach you in order to transform your pain into joy?*

DAY 249

God Sees You

Their cry for rescue from slavery came up to God. And God heard their groaning, and God remembered His covenant with Abraham, with Isaac, and with Jacob.
Exodus 2:23-24

Did you know that God is not daunted by the length or breadth or depth of your trial? The hardest part of any ongoing trial is the feeling that things will never go back to normal, that time is standing still forever.

Whenever I face a trial of epic proportion, deep down in my heart is the fear that life as I know it has ended and that no one is truly paying attention to my pain. Nothing will lead to despair faster than the notion that we are alone in our pain.

In Exodus 2, the people of Israel felt forgotten, but they were wrong. They felt alone, but they were not. We're told, "During that long period, the king of Egypt died. The Israelites groaned in their slavery and cried out, and their cry for help because of their slavery went up to God. God heard their groaning and He remembered His covenant with Abraham, with Isaac and with Jacob. So God looked on the Israelites and was concerned about them" (vv. 23-25).

Though they felt forgotten, God had not forgotten them. Though they felt overlooked, God had never lost sight of them. God saw them. God heard them. God knew them. And God delivered them. And He'll do the same for you.

Questions: *When do you feel forgotten by God? How does knowing God sees you right now encourage you to draw closer to Him?*

DAY 250

Born for a Purpose

Before I formed you in the womb I knew you, and before you were born I consecrated you; I appointed you a prophet to the nations.
Jeremiah 1:5

Every day each one of us buys into a whole lot of lies. Like the lie that we'll be happy if we buy more stuff. Or the lie that a relationship will be the answer to our deepest loneliness. The biggest lie we buy into is the lie that our part in the story doesn't really matter.

God created you for a purpose. All He asks is that you do what you can, and give Him room to work out His purposes for your life. You are part of His story.

Remember the little boy with the two pieces of fish and five pieces of bread?

God used the little that he had and turned it into much, and He'll do the same in your life when you give Him your all. It's never about how much you have, but what you do with what you have that matters.

What *are* you doing with what you have? Are you believing the lie that you're not going to put a dent in the world, or will you rest in the truth that God will take what you have and explode it for His glory? Your part really does matter. It's time to start living like it, holding nothing back!

Questions: *Do you know God's purpose for your life? Are you holding back what He's given you and missing all He could do in your total surrender?*

All to Jesus

I beseech you therefore, brothren, by the mercies of God, that you present your bodies a living sacrifice, holy, acceptable to God, which is your reasonable service.
Romans 12:1

We're living in a post-Christian world where everyone claims to be a Christian, but few really live like it. When I browse Facebook, I start to feel like everyone is a Christian. Yet I can't help but also notice that our culture is more morally corrupt than ever, our families are more in shambles than ever, our society is hurting more than ever.

Why aren't Christ's followers making a dent in this world? Could it be that some who say they're Christians aren't truly following Jesus? Romans 12:1 says, "I beseech you therefore, brothren, by the mercies of God, that you present your bodies a living sacrifice, holy, acceptable to God, which is your reasonable service. And do not be conformed to this world, but be transformed by the renewing of your mind" (vv. 1-2).

The true test of discipleship is our willingness to surrender everything to Jesus all of the time. Surrender simply means that we give all that we are and all that we have to the One who gave all that He is for us.

Now it's time to do some personal housekeeping. Are you a true disciple? Would we be able to tell if we spent the day with you? Or do you just claim to be a Christian on Facebook? You'll be able to tell by your surrender to God and His ways.

Questions: What area in your life is the hardest for you to surrender to God? Why is it so hard?

DAY 252

Refuse Self-pity

Give thanks in all circumstances; for this is the will of God in Christ Jesus for you.
1 Thessalonians 5:18

Do you ever get stuck in the pit of self-pity? No matter how hard I try to avoid it, I have a tendency to fall into the bottomless pit of self-pity. Like a pig in his sty, living in self-pity can become comfortable and soothing. Yet self-pity is the bane of every Christian's existence.

Elizabeth Elliott wrote, "Refuse self-pity. Refuse it absolutely. It is a deadly thing with power to destroy you." See, self-pity makes you the center of your universe. While that might sound logical—you are after all the main ingredients in your own world—it is a far cry from the way God created us to live.

God created us to live beyond ourselves. He created us to live for Him. Self-pity paralyzes you from God's plans and purposes for your life. Self-pity says that you deserve more. Self-pity claims that others have been given what should have been rightfully yours. Self-pity forgets that there is a sovereign God overseeing the affairs of your life and who will make a way through your pain.

The only way out of self-pity is to fix your eyes on God's goodness and keep them on the cross!

Question: *Are you prone to self-pity? Make a list of ten things you're grateful to God for, and ask Him to help you get out of the pit of self-pity today.*

Stop Fishing

And God is able to make all grace abound to you, so that having all sufficiency in all things at all times, you may abound in every good work.
2 Corinthians 9:8

Do you want to know what my least favorite expression in the world is? I'll tell you what it is. It's the expression that goes, "There's plenty of fish in the sea." Typically, it's an expression that is used to console someone who is disappointed. It's an expression to help keep our hopes up. But if you've ever felt the sting of failure or rejection or disappointment, the last thing you want to hear is that there's plenty of other fish in the sea besides the very one you longed for.

Instead of framing our disappointment with trying harder next time, we should direct our focus on the Lord. What matters the most in life is that God knows the exact fish that every one of us needs for every circumstance in our life. Not only does He know the exact fish, He knows the best time to fish and the best time to catch that fish He has purposed for our life.

He alone is able to bring your fish to you in His perfect timing. You don't have to work so hard. You don't have to try harder next time. You simply have to trust God's goodness and His timing and do what He's called you to do today.

Cannot the Creator of the fish figure out which fish is your fish? Of course He can. So today, let go of your fishing rod, and grab your Bible instead. Let God do the fishing for you.

Questions: *What are you working so hard to accomplish in your life? Will you let go and trust God to do your fishing for you?*

DAY 254

Don't Overindulge

*And those who belong to Christ Jesus have
crucified the flesh with its passions and desires.*
Galatians 5:24

Do you ever overindulge? While I try not to overindulge daily, it's a temptation I face on a daily basis. Just about the time I finish dinner, my sweet tooth kicks in. One piece of pie becomes two and the rest as they say is history. You know how this story ends and it's not pretty. Before long my stomach is bloated, and I'm living in a land of regret and the land of should have.

When it comes to self-control, we all mean well, but sooner or later our actions betray our true desires. Our appetites are generally untrained. In Galatians 5 Paul reminds us that self-control is a fruit of the Holy Spirit. "Those who belong to Christ Jesus have crucified the flesh with its passions and desires."

We are no longer living for self. We don't call the shots. He does. We are dead to sin. We don't have to overindulge. Whether it's in your eating or your thought life, or any other area of self-control, you and I have the power by God's Spirit to stand strong and refuse the desires of our flesh.

The more we give in to the Spirit, the easier it is to stand strong.

Question: *In what areas of your life is it easiest to overindulge? Take a moment and confess your sin to God, and ask Him to give you the strength you need to live in victory over that area!*

Too Good to Be True

*Fear not, for I am with you; be not dismayed,
for I am your God; I will strengthen you, I will help you,
I will uphold you with My righteous right hand.*
Isaiah 41:10

There are some things in life that sound too good to be true, but they are true indeed. For example, ice cream and Netflix and anything by the beach. But far better than the material things we deem too good to be true are the promises God gives us in His Word. His promises sometimes do sound too good to be true, but they are true indeed!

Like, for example, consider Isaiah 41:10 which says, "Fear not, for I am with you; be not dismayed, for I am your God; I will strengthen you, I will help you, I will uphold you with My righteous right hand."

Can you even believe it? The Creator God who spoke the entire universe into existence promises to be with us always. He encourages us not to be afraid. He promises to help us, to give us strength, to hold us up with His very strong arm.

No matter what you're facing today, you can hang on to God's promises knowing that they are true. God longs for you to believe Him. Do you believe His promises? Are you resting your all in His Word?

Question: *What aspect of God's character sounds too good to be true? Choose one of God's promises that sounds too good to be true, and hang on to it today.*

DAY 256

Step Out of Yourself

*And we urge you, brothers, admonish the idle,
encourage the fainthearted,
help the weak, be patient with them all.*
1 Thessalonians 5:14

I attended a conference on my own not long ago and didn't think much about it until I got there. When I arrived, I looked around and felt like a fish out of water. I didn't belong. I thought about leaving but stayed. I took a deep breath, gulped down my fears, then went home and tweeted about it.

The next day I showed up to the sessions and listened with the others. Eventually I mustered enough courage to step out of my shell and talk to the others. I soon realized something I had chosen to ignore: that every one of the others felt as much out of water as I did.

Do you ever feel like you don't belong? No matter how much we try to avoid it, we feel like outsiders and it can last well past high school. Yet it only takes a little bit of courage to step out of our comfort zone to get to know someone.

If you're feeling like a fish out of water in your life, try what I did: Take a deep breath and gulp down your fears; then start talking to the others. You'll find exactly what I did—you're not as alone as you think.

Questions: *God created us for community. How is your life in community in this season of your life? What can you do to be more engaged with the people in your life?*

Find Rest in Him

So then, there remains a Sabbath rest for the people of God, for whoever has entered God's rest has also rested from his works as God did from His.
Hebrews 4:9-10

I have a lot of bad habits, but there is one that sticks out. No matter how hard I try to avoid it, every so often I will look down on my dashboard and see the empty light blinking at me. Over and over I forget to fill up. I end up scrambling for the next closest gas station to avoid a disaster. It's the worst feeling in the world.

I tend to do the same with the Lord. I run myself ragged until I absolutely am forced to rest. God gave us seven days in the week, and one of them He meant for rest. Yet over and over, if you're like me, you'll catch yourself trying to make the most of every moment of every day, including the Sabbath—that is, until you're running on nothing but fumes.

But the Sabbath, you see, was meant to remind us that we can't do it on our own. It's meant to remind us to trust God with our lives.

Are you guilty, like me, of running on fumes? Perhaps it's time to pull over and rest. God's peace will sustain you when you're too empty to go on. His grace is sufficient when you feel like you can't go on another mile.

Questions: *How faithful are you to rest in the Lord when your life gets hectic? What are some ways you can carve out times of rest in the course of your day today?*

DAY 258

Be Healed

*The woman said to Him, "I know that Messiah is coming
(He who is called Christ). When He comes, He will tell us all things."
Jesus said to her, "I who speak to you am He."*
John 4:25-26

One of the main observations I've made as an ER doctor is the observation that everyone is looking for healing or for something to medicate their pain. People come in to the ER all the time with pain. They want something to stop the pain. Anything will do. They are looking for healing, but if I can't heal them completely, most folks will settle for anything to numb the pain.

There was a woman in Samaria once who hung out by a well. She was looking to be healed and didn't even realize it. Broken and hurting, she longed for acceptance. On most days, though, she simply settled for whatever would numb her pain. For the Samaritan woman, that meant a lifestyle of jumping from guy to guy in a lifestyle of empty lust. Then one day Jesus showed up, and everything changed for her.

On that day Jesus offered the Samaritan woman healing, and she received it. She quit numbing the pain with empty relationships. She'd finally found true belonging and victory over shame.

How about you? Have you found healing, or are you still numbing your pain with whatever feels good? Christ came to heal you. Won't you turn to Him for wholeness and stop settling for less?

Questions: *Where do you turn to numb your pain? In what ways can you fill your soul with Christ and find healing for your pain?*

DAY 259

Pleasing God

For am I now seeking the approval of man, or of God? Or am I trying to please man? If I were still trying to please man, I would not be a servant of Christ.
Galatians 1:10

Do you want to know the hardest thing about breaking off an engagement two weeks before the wedding? Don't worry. I'm about to tell you. I remember it like it was yesterday.

By the time I figured out that I needed to end the engagement, it was two weeks before the wedding. The hardest obstacle to overcome? By far and above my greatest fear was, "What would people say? What will everyone in my life think?"

In Galatians 1:10 Paul wrote, "For am I now seeking the approval of man, or of God? Or am I trying to please man? If I were still trying to please man, I would not be a servant of Christ."

The secret to your freedom in the Christian life is to learn to live for the audience of one. You and I will never please everyone. We will never make decisions that are unanimously accepted by all the people in our lives. What matters the most isn't what other people will think, but rather, it's what God thinks about you and me.

Do you find yourself paralyzed with fear today? Stop and ask, who am I trying to please?

Questions: *How can you tell if you're living for an audience of one or for the eyes of everyone else? Who do you long to please the most?*

Don't Fret

Do not be anxious about anything, but in everything by prayer and supplication with thanksgiving let your requests be made known to God.
Philippians 4:6

I once got a call from a patient's father worried that his kid might have stepped on an open needle at the beach, but he wasn't sure. He wanted to know what could happen and what he should do. We spent over thirty minutes belaboring all of the options. Eventually I hung up the phone and chuckled to myself. Have I not done the same thing in my life? Have I not thought up scenarios that might happen and lost sleep over them only to see that no negative outcome took place?

No wonder God tells us over and over again in His Word to stop fretting. No wonder God reminds us again and again not to worry. Philippians 4:6 says, "Do not be anxious about anything, but in everything by prayer and supplication with thanksgiving let your requests be made known to God."

Every day we are given ample opportunity to run into danger. I suppose you could say we're given a million chances to possibly step on an open needle at a beach. And every day in a thousand different ways God protects us from ourselves and all the dangers around us. God cares for us and hides us under the shadow of His wings.

Instead of worrying about what could happen today, let's spend our time rejoicing in all God is doing to protect us.

Question: *What do you fret most about? Set your clock for five minutes, and use the time to pray about what it is that worries you the most.*

Through the Storm

Then they cried to the L<small>ORD</small> in their trouble, and He delivered them from their distress. He made the storm be still, and the waves of the sea were hushed.
Psalm 107:28-29

Have you ever been caught in the middle of a storm? It's a scary place to be. Yet over and over again in the Gospels, we get a glimpse of Jesus sending His disciples into the middle of the storm. Jesus does it intentionally and persistently. Over and over again, the disciples seem to miss the point. Instead of seeing a pattern emerge, they keep on freaking out when they catch themselves tossed by the strength of each wave.

It's not hard to wonder why Jesus consistently did that. Why did He intentionally send His friends into the storm over and over again? The reason is not as obscure as we might imagine. In each and every occasion, after the storm stilled, as it always did, Jesus revealed Himself to His disciples a little bit more clearly. In other words, it was the storm that allowed the disciples to know Jesus more deeply.

Do you hunger to know the Lord more intimately? Don't be surprised if you're facing a storm. God longs to reveal Himself to you through your storms, and that's how your faith will grow just a little bit stronger. Will you trust Him to help you make it through the storm?

Questions: *How can you stand strong in the middle of the storm? How can you become more aware of Christ's presence in the midst of your trial?*

DAY 262

Glorify God in the Waiting

*No unbelief made him waver concerning the promise of God,
but he grew strong in his faith as he gave glory to God.*
Romans 4:20

Do you ever feel like you're waiting for God and nothing is happening? When that happens there are a lot of ways we can respond. Most of us, when we're waiting for God and nothing happens, are tempted to do what Abraham did. We're tempted to *make* something happen. But the worst thing we can do when we're waiting for God and nothing is happening is to try to make something happen.

Just ask Hagar. She was the product of Abraham and Sarah trying to make something happen in their life. You could say it backfired big time. Are you guilty of trying to make something happen in your life? Do you believe that if you don't act, then nothing will change? You couldn't be more wrong.

Biblical hope rests in the knowledge that God can make something happen anytime He chooses to. The burden does not rest on you. The outcome of every circumstance in your life rests on the Lord, even if it looks like you're still waiting and nothing is happening.

Instead of trying to make something happen, let's learn to use the time in the waiting to glorify God with our words and our actions.

Question: *What are some practical ways to glorify God when your waiting gets too long?*

Clay Pots

But we have this treasure in jars of clay, to show that the surpassing power belongs to God and not to us.
2 Corinthians 4:7

Have you ever taken a good look at a clay pot? Have you ever wondered about it? If you've ever stopped at the local hardware store for a flower pot, you'll find plenty of choices. Some people buy ceramic pots while others settle for clay. Clay pots aren't much to look at, but they seem to get the job done.

Most of us intuitively understand that it's not the pot that makes the plant beautiful, but what grows in the pot that makes it lovely. The pot simply serves to hold the beauty of the plant.

In 2 Corinthians 4:7 Paul compares us to clay pots. He said, "We ourselves are like fragile clay jars containing this great treasure. This makes it clear that our great power is from God, not from ourselves." What that means is that if you're a follower of Jesus Christ, you're nothing but a clay pot.

No matter how you feel today, it is Christ in you that makes you beautiful. You're simply the vessel that God uses to highlight who He is. He's the One worth looking at. The more you allow Him to fill your life, the more like Him you'll look and the more beautiful you'll be.

Question: *What are some decisions you can make today that will allow Jesus to shine through your clay pots?*

His Perfect Timing

My times are in Your hand; rescue me from the hand of my enemies and from my persecutors!
Psalm 31:15

I heard an interesting expression the other day, and it's quickly becoming a favorite: "Moving the hands of the clock to suit you doesn't change the time." If I'm being honest, I have been guilty of trying to manipulate the clock of my life. Haven't you? You and I tend to forget that our times are in God's hand. No matter how hard we try to speed things up, the clock doesn't change just because we try to force it to!

God's timing is perfect. In Ecclesiastes 3 we're told that God makes everything beautiful in its time. God knows the pace we can keep, and there's no need to turn the hands of the clock any faster.

Are you pushing things forward in your life right now? Are you rushing through the season God has you in? Are you pushing to move when you should stay put? No matter how hard you try to speed God's timetable, He's not going to move until it's time.

There is great freedom when you simply let go and trust God.

Questions: *In what ways do you try to rush God? How can you tell if you're fully trusting Him or trying to control your life?*

Facing the Future

Therefore do not be anxious about tomorrow, for tomorrow will be anxious for itself. Sufficient for the day is its own trouble
Matthew 6:34

What do you feel when you think about your future? Do you feel excited and upbeat or worried and overwhelmed? Whether you're a recent graduate of high school or just retired, in truth, most of us feel some level of fear when we think about our future. Will I have enough money to retire? Will my kids keep following Jesus? Will I be healthy and able to move around on my own? Will I still have a job this time next year? Will I ever find someone to marry?

God's Word is clear. When it comes to the future, over and over again God tells us not to worry about tomorrow. Tomorrow will worry about itself. The only way to fight worry is to grow our faith muscles, and the only way to do that is with practice.

Paul reminds us that faith comes by hearing and hearing through the Word of God. So we must spend time in God's Word to stay strong. Peter tells us to *grow* in grace and in the knowledge of our Lord. This process takes time. It takes discipline. As we spend time with God we learn His character and in time, learn to trust Him more and more. Slowly, our faith muscles grow.

Now think about your life. What do you feel when you think about your future? If you're burdened with fear, it might be time to start working on those faith muscles.

Question: *What sort of feelings cloud your thinking about the future? Write down each worry, and next to it write down one of God's character attributes to help you overcome your fear.*

DAY 266

Fix Your Eyes on Jesus

*Looking to Jesus, the founder and perfecter of our faith,
who for the joy that was set before Him endured the cross,
despising the shame, and is seated at the right hand of the throne of God.*
Hebrews 12:2

What image is on your home screen? Go ahead and check your phone. What do you see? I came across an article recently that said that you can tell a lot about a person from their home screen. Do you want to know what's on my home screen? My home screen consists of a whole lot of nothing. I prefer a clean blue background that never changes reinforcing the fact that I am a minimalist creature of habit. I bet you can make up your own conclusions about me from that too. The truth is that you can tell a lot about a person by where they fix their eyes.

In Hebrews 12:2 we're told to fix our eyes on Jesus, the founder and perfecter of our faith. The writer of Hebrews helps us to understand that fixing our eyes on Jesus is the key to our endurance.

Are you facing a trial today? Fix your eyes on Jesus. Are you struggling with a decision to make? Fix your eyes on Jesus. The more you fix your eyes on Christ, the more clearly you will see.

Where are your eyes fixed today? What image are you gazing at throughout the day? Remember—you can tell a lot about yourself by what you're looking at today.

Questions: *What's on your home screen? What do you spend most of your day staring at? What does where you fix your eyes say about your heart?*

Stop Sinning

*Whoever conceals his transgressions will not prosper,
but he who confesses and forsakes them will obtain mercy.*
Proverbs 28:13

My mom is one of those people who hears random facts and worries about me, especially as it relates to my driving. "Did you hear about the bus crash where fourteen people died?" she recently asked. "The guilty driver was texting and driving." I knew what she was trying to say. She was simply trying to warn me not to text and drive. I rolled my eyes, but deep down, she'd hit a nerve.

More often than I care to admit, I do things that I say I'd never do. And even after hearing the ramifications of other people's bad decisions, I assume I'll be the exception to the rule. Why is it that we think we can get away with what everyone else gets caught for? Whether it's texting and driving or indulging our eyes on what we have no business seeing, sooner or later we all know that continuing down a path of sin will only lead to suffering.

Listen to the warnings before it's too late. If you're caught up in a cycle of sin, turn around. Repent. Be humble enough to admit, "Yes, I did what I thought I'd never do, but with God's grace and power I have all I need to stop doing it."

Questions: *Has anyone ever given you a warning that you refused to heed? What was the result? Is there something you're involved in right now that needs to change?*

Beautifully Made

*I praise You, for I am fearfully and wonderfully made.
Wonderful are Your works; my soul knows it very well.*
Psalm 139:14

How did you feel when you looked at yourself in the mirror today? I hate looking in the mirror. When it comes to correctly interpreting what I see, I'm usually left to my own devices when I look in the mirror. Because no one is around to tell me I look okay, I can become super critical about the way that I look. I don't like my hair, my face, or my waist; and depending on the day, you won't convince me otherwise.

In Genesis 1:26 God said, "Let Us make man in Our image, after Our likeness." God created us to be His image bearers. What an awesome thought. In Psalm 139 the psalmist reiterated the beauty of God's creation when he reminded us that we are fearfully and wonderfully made. Whether you're tall or short, big or small, black or white, Western or Asian, God created you in His image.

Even on the days when you don't see your own value clearly, God's Word reminds us that God loves what He sees as He looks at us. See, when God looks at us, He sees His image. That ought to change the way you think about yourself and everyone around you today.

We have value, not because of the way we look, but because we are made in the image of God. So go ahead and rejoice as you look into the mirror!

Questions: *Do you tend to be critical of the way you look? How does knowing God finds you beautiful change the way you feel today?*

Quit Comparing

But when they measure themselves by one another and compare themselves with one another, they are without understanding.
2 Corinthians 10:12

Do you ever go to a restaurant and order something only to immediately regret it when you see what the person next to you ordered? It happens to me all the time, even when I like what I ordered myself!

It shouldn't come as a surprise. We're constantly caught in a cycle of comparisons and deflated expectations when it comes to most things in our life, including but not limited to the meals we eat! Sadly, even the most delicious dish loses its flavor when my eyes get focused on what's on the table next to me.

The moment we start looking around at what others are eating or doing in their lives is the moment we lose the battle for joy. How come their fish looks better than mine? Why didn't my meal come with fries? Instead of appreciating the meal right in front of our faces, we nurse our wounded expectations that will never live up to what everyone else is eating.

The fight for joy begins when we stop looking around at others and trust that God in His goodness has given us exactly what we need today. It's only as we let go of our expectations that God can fill our hearts with joy.

Questions: *In what areas of your life do you tend to compare yourself with others? How can you build parameters to keep your eyes grateful and content on what God has given you?*

DAY 270

Listen to the Truth

Do not be conformed to this world, but be transformed by the renewal of your mind.
Romans 12:2

There's a voice in my head, and I'm constantly listening to it. We all have one. It speaks to us when no one else is listening. It tells us the things we've already programmed it to say. Sometimes the voice in my head tells me I'm single and that is never going to change. Other times the voice in my head hollers that I'm not good enough, pretty enough, or rich enough to live out my dreams. Perhaps the voice in your head reminds you of your sin and tells you you're a loser. Sadly, most of us have heard that voice for so long we don't even pay attention to it anymore.

In Romans 12:2 Paul instructs us to be transformed by the renewing of our minds. In other words, it's time to change the voice we hear in our heads. It's time to start listening to the voice of truth. Instead of condemnation, God speaks words of love to us. Instead of hearing that we're not enough, God's voice reminds us that it is in our weaknesses that He is our strength.

God longs to wash over us with His Word if we'll let Him. Won't you start listening to His voice in your head? It's the only way to peace.

Questions: *Whose voice is loudest in your head and why? How can you get better at listening to God's voice of truth instead of the lies you've grown accustomed to?*

Hope Is Alive

Why are you cast down, O my soul, and why are you in turmoil within me?
Hope in God; for I shall again praise Him, my salvation and my God.
Psalm 42:11

There are some things we can live without—like cable television and dessert. We can even live without food for a few days if we absolutely had to. But there is one thing we cannot live without. I'm talking about hope. No matter where you live and what you do for a living, you and I need hope in order to survive. We need hope to get up in the morning. We need hope to make it through the darkest nights. Hope is what every Christian needs to keep on keeping on.

The hope we need is not an optimistic, everything is gonna be all right kind of mushy feeling. No. Hope is the confident expectation that God will do what He has promised to do. This hope is rooted in the Person of Christ and His finished work on the cross.

We might not be able to change our circumstances, but we can rest in a God who can change our circumstances and who promises to help us make it through any trial we're facing. Hope is the belief that change is possible. It hinges on the power of the resurrected Jesus. This hope is yours in Christ if you'll receive it.

No wonder the psalmist said, "Why are you cast down, O my soul?...Hope in God; for I shall again praise Him, my salvation and my God." This hope will never disappoint you!

Question: *Practically speaking, how does the resurrection of Jesus restore your hope no matter how hard your trial is right now?*

More than Conquerors

No, in all these things we are more than conquerors through Him who loved us.
Romans 8:37

I'm a huge Green Bay Packers fan. Sometimes when I'm watching the game and my team is up by three, or even seven points, my friends will ask, "Aren't you happy that they're winning?" After years of watching the Packers, my answer is a definite "no." I don't love it when my team is up just by three points. I want them to be destroying the other team in order to feel joy. I'm only comfortable when we're two or three touchdowns ahead.

When it comes to feeling unstoppable and confident, nothing reflects that truth like Romans 8:37. Paul writes, "We are more than conquerors through Him who loved us." See, when it comes to our position in Christ and the victory we have in Him, we are not just conquerors. We are *more* than conquerors. We're not just a measly three points ahead, eke by the skin of our teeth victorious. No—we are destroying the enemy by God's grace and then some.

So you can breathe. You can smile. You can enjoy the ride because you've been given the outcome, and you are more than a conqueror in Christ Jesus. You can face anything today because of what Christ has accomplished!

Questions: *Do you feel like a conqueror in your Christian life? In what specific areas in your life are you living less than victoriously? What's your plan to change?*

Bearing Much Fruit

By this My Father is glorified, that you bear much fruit and so prove to be My disciples.
John 15:8

Are you thriving in your Christian life? Are you bearing fruit in abundance? Does your life feel full and complete in Christ? We all long to thrive. We all long to more than just survive. God created us to be fruit-bearing Christians no matter where we live.

I was recently looking through some old teaching notes of mine and saw a great definition for thriving. "Thriving" is the ability to bear fruit in all seasons including winter and maybe even in a drought. The life that thrives is unaffected by circumstances. It rests not on the external pressures in life, but on the internal assurance that God is in control, and that fruit will eventually come no matter how things look right now.

Thriving is less about my present comfort, and more about my future assurance that fruit is coming because I'm rooted in good soil and cared for by the best vinedresser. Thriving is what God longs for us.

Are you a thriving Christian? Would you like to be? As you abide in Christ His promise to you is that you will keep on bearing much fruit. Don't stop believing it. God's Word will always prove true in time.

Questions: *Think about your life today compared to a year ago. What fruit is present now that wasn't there this time last year? What fruit do you long to see more of?*

Stop Negotiating

And he believed the Lord, and He counted it to him as righteousness
Genesis 15:6

I've noticed that there's nothing more exhausting than endless negotiations. I hang around my nephews a lot, and recently heard one of my nephews ask my sister if he could go over to his friend's house. She said no. She had good reasons for saying no. Instead of agreeing with her and letting it go, my nephew then spent the better part of an hour trying to negotiate his way over to his friend's house. The answer remained no. I was merely listening in and felt utterly exhausted.

There's nothing more exhausting than endless negotiations, especially when we're clearly told that the answer is no. Yet over and over again I have found myself exhausted negotiating with God over what He should or shouldn't allow in my life. I argue that His timing is off, that my circumstances should be different. As much as God loves me, His answer is loving enough to remain—no.

God makes no mistakes. He has His reasons for allowing us to remain in our present circumstances. The longer you fight God and His ways, the harder you resist submitting to His ways, and the more elusive your peace will be.

Stop negotiating with God for what you want. As you trust Him more deeply, you'll see. His way is best and His love never ends.

Questions: *In what area in your life are you trying to convince God to change His mind about you? How does meditating on God's goodness allow you to rest in the answer He's giving you?*

Pray with Confidence

Likewise the Spirit helps us in our weakness. For we do not know what to pray for as we ought, but the Spirit Himself intercedes for us with groanings too deep for words.
Romans 8:26

Do you ever struggle to pray? Sometimes I do. Every Christian intuitively knows that we should be praying. God's Word tells us that we should pray. Luther once said that to be a Christian without prayer is no more possible than to be alive without breathing. Deep down most of us wonder if we haven't received because we haven't asked.

I'm in the middle of reading several books on prayer right now and have been blessed by them, but nothing has encouraged me as much as Romans 8:26 when it comes to prayer. Paul writes, "Likewise the Spirit helps us in our weakness. For we do not know what to pray for as we ought, but the Spirit Himself intercedes for us with groanings too deep for words."

Often in life I don't know exactly how to pray. I want to but words fail me. Paul reminds us that when we don't know how to pray, God's Spirit prays on our behalf. When we don't have words to express the longing of our hearts, the Holy Spirit steps right in where we need Him the most.

I don't know about you, but when I think about the Spirit praying on my behalf, it gives me the courage to fight past the struggle to pray.

Questions: *How is your prayer life? Where in your life do you long for more of God's Spirit praying on your behalf?*

Not Alone

I, I am He who comforts you; who are you that you are afraid of man who dies, of the son of man who is made like grass, and have forgotten the Lord *your Maker.*
Isaiah 51:12-13

Do you ever struggle with loneliness? I was at a large conference not long ago with over nine thousand other people attending, and yet I never felt more alone. It felt like the darkness was closing in on me. Would my life ever change? Would I ever feel a sense of belonging on this earth?

I walked to my hotel room feeling despondent and did the only thing I knew to do. I opened God's Word to Isaiah and read the following words: "I, I am He who comforts you; who are you that you are afraid of man who dies; of the son of man who is made like grass, and have forgotten the Lord your Maker." Deep into my aching heart God had found a way to remind me that though man may not care about me and though I may feel insignificant, the Creator of heaven and earth, God Almighty, didn't just know me but had taken the effort to comfort me.

Are you weighed down and alone today? Do you feel misunderstood, a stranger in your own home or church? Turn to the Lord and find comfort in His Word. His presence is real.

Questions: *When do you feel most alone? How does the knowledge of God's presence give you the comfort you need to make it when you feel most alone?*

DAY 277

Hold on to Hope

Therefore, behold, I will allure her, and bring her into the wilderness, and speak tenderly to her. And there I will give her her vineyards and make the Valley of Achor a door of hope.
Hosea 2:14-15

I remember a turning point in my life. I'd just ended an engagement and my heart was broken. I couldn't understand how a God who claimed to be so good and to whom I'd surrendered my life years before could have treated me this way. Though He hadn't caused my engagement, surely He could have stopped me sooner. I was at a crossroads with a decision to make. Would I surrender to God, trusting in His goodness, or would I insist on doing things my way?

I still don't know how I landed in Hosea in my Bible reading plan, but by God's grace I did. The Lord reached down and whispered His words to me: "Therefore, behold, I will allure her, and bring her into the wilderness, and speak tenderly to her. And there I will give her her vineyards and make the Valley of Achor a door of hope." It dawned on me that God in His goodness had allowed me to feel pain in order to find a deeper hope, a hope that rests in Him alone.

Are you struggling with pain? Do you feel disappointed? Perhaps God has called you to the wilderness for a reason too.

Question: *Think about the last time you found yourself in the wilderness. What did you learn about God during that season?*

DAY 278

Be Kind

Let no corrupting talk come out of your mouths, but only such as is good for building up, as fits the occasion, that it may give grace to those who hear.
Ephesians 4:29

I called the cable guy recently with a quick question about setting up a new service. I'd worked all day and was tired. I was being extra nice. Instead of a pleasant response in return, the cable guy sounded mad. I gave him a chance to change his tone, but it was an epic fail. I finally confronted him: "Why are you so mad at me?" I asked. "I'm not mad," he responded.

Whether or not he was mad remains a mystery to be solved, but I did learn one thing: When it comes to speaking with others, we are as mad as we sound. We might think that we're being kind, but our words and our tone will always betray us. You might think you're being patient, but ask the one who's listening to you, and you'll get a straight answer. You're only as kind as your words are.

No matter what you've got on your plate today, remember the power of your tongue. Wield it wisely. Use it for God's glory. Be kind. Who knows who might be listening when you speak. Give them Jesus instead of your anger.

Questions: *If you asked your closest friends and acquaintances what tone and words you tend to use the most, what answer would you get? In what ways do you need to change?*

Safe in His Arms

*He who dwells in the shelter of the Most High
will abide in the shadow of the Almighty.*
Psalm 91:1

Do you know where the safest place on earth for you is? I grew up in Beirut, Lebanon, in the 70s and 80s, and trust me when I tell you this: It wasn't very safe. People ask why my family moved from Beirut, Lebanon, to Green Bay, Wisconsin. I suppose the most honest answer is that we were looking for a safer place.

But the older I get, the more I realize that the safest place on earth isn't a quiet town in the middle of nowhere. No...the safest place on earth is right in the center of God's will for you.

In Psalm 91:1 we read, "He who dwells in the secret shelter of the Most High shall abide in the shadow of the Almighty." In other words, whether you're in the trenches of a war-torn town or in the middle of a quiet farmland, you're only as safe as you are safely sheltered in the arms of Jesus.

No matter where you're headed right now, abide in the shelter of the Almighty. Make His shadow your home, and you'll find all the rest that your heart so desperately longs for.

Questions: *Are you living in the center of God's will for your life? If not, why not? How can you abide in God's shadow today?*

DAY 280

Don't Doubt

For I know whom I have believed, and I am convinced that He is able to guard until that day what has been entrusted to me.
2 Timothy 1:12

One of my favorite Christian authors of all times is Elizabeth Elliott. She was a giant of the faith. While Elizabeth Elliott said many great things, this one quote of hers sticks out: "Don't dig up in doubt what you planted in faith." Are you ever tempted do that?

One day you find yourself strong, standing on one of God's sure promises for you. You circle that promise and date it in your Bible. You're hopeful and waiting. Then the waiting drags on and on. Doubt creeps in. Did God really mean His promise? Will God prove faithful? Will He show Himself good?

When I'm tempted to doubt, I go to 2 Timothy 1:12: "For I know whom I have believed, and I am convinced that He is able to guard until that day what has been entrusted to me." In the face of my doubt, I remind myself who God is. When I'm tempted to wonder if God is going to come through for me, I refuse to give in.

You and I can stand strong in faith no matter what. We can remain unshaken, not because we are strong, but because God is true to His Word always. And the good news is that when we are faithless, He remains faithful!

Questions: *Which promise of God are you hanging on to today? Will you proclaim it afresh telling God you trust Him no matter what?*

Satisfied

Jesus said to her, "Everyone who drinks of this water will be thirsty again, but whoever drinks of the water that I will give him will never be thirsty again. The water that I will give him will become in him a spring of water welling up to eternal life."
John 4:13-14

When I wake up in the morning, I'm usually dying of thirst. But instead of grabbing a glass of water, I make the same mistake every single morning: I press the brew button on my coffeemaker and take a sip of the dark brew. You might think this is perfectly normal, and at first, all seems well. But it doesn't take long for my body to remind me that I'm still thirsty and nothing but water will do.

In John 4 when Jesus met the Samaritan woman by the well, He recognized that she was thirsty. She had tried to quench her thirst with human relationships and physical pleasure and had failed miserably. She had tried to ignore her thirst, but Jesus saw right through her. He recognized her need and offered her the only water that could satisfy her forever. He offered her Himself.

Are you dying of thirst today? Do you feel defeated by your wants and your needs? You don't have to be. Your thirst is simply God's cry to your heart. Turn to Him and find all that you need. He's the fountain that will never run dry. He's the water that will satisfy you forever.

Questions: *In what ways are you trying to quench your thirst outside of Jesus today? How can you find your complete satisfaction in Him today?*

Don't Judge

Behold, how good and pleasant it is when brothers dwell in unity!
Psalm 133:1

I'm from Chicago which automatically means that I love pizza. Don't you? When it comes to pizzas, there are so many choices. Do you like pineapple on your pizza? I have found that there are two kinds of people in the world: those who like pineapple on their pizza and those who do not. The minute you find out a person's answer, you automatically place that person in a box. We react this way all the time. We have categories and we lump people into one bucket or the other and refuse to budge.

Do you hate animated movies? All right, me too. Baptism by immersion? You pass. ESV only? All right. All right. You're in. See how this goes? No wonder the Church is so divided. We do it with our education, country of origin, race, and income status. We do it with singles on one side, marrieds on the other. No wonder the psalmist said, "How good and how pleasant it is for brothren to dwell together in unity" (v. 1). It's hard but critical to be united. God loves it when His children are one. Jesus prayed that we be one with Him.

Are you judging people too harshly simply because they like pineapple on their pizza? Maybe it's time to stop.

Questions: *In what ways do you tend to categorize people and put them in boxes? Would you confess your sin to God and ask Him for unity with someone you don't quite understand?*

DAY 283

Love the Church

And I tell you, you are Peter, and on this rock I will build My church, and the gates of hell shall not prevail against it.
Matthew 16:18

Have you ever considered that when it comes to most things in life, it always boils down to one thing: Jesus?

When I was growing up, we used to sing an old hymn that went like this: "The Church's one foundation is Jesus Christ her Lord; she is His new creation by water and the Word. From heaven He came and sought her to be His holy bride; with His own blood He bought her and for her life He died."

What an awesome reminder of what the Church should be today. The Church isn't about finding the right program for your kids, or connecting to the right group of people to help your social life grow. The Church isn't even about finding something to do on a Sunday morning or filling in the time until we get to heaven. No. The main goal of the Church is to be Christ's bride. Jesus shed His blood for His Church. The Church is much more than just a place to plug in. The Church is the Body of Christ. It's where we belong as followers of Jesus Christ. The Church has one foundation—it's Jesus Christ her Lord.

If Jesus gave His life for the Church, shouldn't we value it too?

Questions: *Are you part of a local body of believers? Why is it hard for you to love the Church like Jesus did?*

Power of a Moment

And He said to him, "Truly, I say to you, today you will be with Me in paradise."
Luke 23:43

Do you ever think about the power of one moment? Anything can happen in a moment.

Consider the man who has spent his whole life making bad decisions. The day came for him to pay up and the price was high, higher than he was able to pay. The plan was to crucify him on a cross. On that particular day, two other men would be crucified too. One was another thief, and the other was Jesus of Nazareth.

You might say the thief on the side of Jesus earned the punishment for his sin, but still...it would only take one moment for everything to change. In one moment the thief on the cross looked toward Jesus and asked for forgiveness. In one moment the thief on the cross was granted freedom. "Today you will be with Me in paradise," Jesus promised the thief on His side.

One moment is all it takes to change your destiny. All you need is Christ's mercy and grace.

What are you carrying today that feels too heavy to bear? Whether it's the weight of your sin or an unresolved problem in your life, all it takes is one moment of turning to Jesus in simple faith for everything to change. Will you do it right now? One moment. That's all it takes to change.

Questions: *What do you wish you could change about your past? What if you could find freedom in a moment? Would you be willing to look to Jesus right now and ask for mercy?*

DAY 285

One Thing

One thing have I asked of the Lord, that will I seek after:
that I may dwell in the house of the Lord all the days of my life,
to gaze upon the beauty of the Lord and to inquire in His temple.
Psalm 27:4

What is it that gets you up every morning? If you polled the people you know, you'd find a variety of answers. Some people get up in the morning and want to make it their goal to have a lot of fun. Others are simply trying to be good parents. Still others are hungry to get rich. They're saving like crazy with the hopes of making even more someday and buying a bigger house.

And then there are some who are wearing themselves out for Jesus. While there is some value in each of those things, none of them should be the main thing that gets us up in the morning. In Psalm 27:4 David nailed it. He summarized his daily goal like this: "One thing I ask from the Lord, this only do I seek: that I may dwell in the house of the Lord all the days of my life, to gaze on the beauty of the Lord and to seek Him in His temple."

When you make this your goal, you'll hear the Father whisper the same words He said over Jesus: "You are My beloved Son; with You I am well pleased" (Luke 2:22).

Do you long for God's pleasure? Make it your goal to seek Him above all else.

Questions: *What is your main goal when you get up each morning? How does it measure up with Psalm 27:4?*

DAY 286

Clear Vision

*Then Elisha prayed and said, "O Lord, please open his eyes that he may see."
So the Lord opened the eyes of the young man, and he saw, and behold,
the mountain was full of horses and chariots of fire all around Elisha.*
2 Kings 6:17

How good are your eyes? Or maybe I should ask about your vision first. Do you ever feel blind as a bat?

I was driving the other day looking for a church and must have driven around the block seven times when I finally cried out to God to help me find the place. Suddenly I saw it. The church had been right in front of me the whole time. I just hadn't been able to see it.

In 2 Kings 6 the exact same thing happens to Elisha's servant. He was looking around at the enemy surrounding him and became terribly afraid. The army of the enemy looked massive. He felt so small and weak. Elisha looked at his servant and could tell what was going on. So Elisha cried out to God: "O Lord, please open his eyes that he may see." Suddenly, the servant's vision was restored, and he saw what had been there all along. God's army was right there, closer than he believed. He just hadn't been able to see it clearly.

Maybe you're staring at your enemy today shaking in fear. Ask God to open your eyes so that you too can see—God is closer than you feel. He's right here beside you, and no enemy stands a chance in His presence.

Questions: *How would your day change today if you could see God's mighty army fighting on your behalf? Would you ask God to open your eyes and give you clearer vision to make it?*

Be Strong

The Lord your God is the One who goes with you to fight for you against your enemies to give you victory.
Deuteronomy 20:4

I'm not much of a war story sort of person, but I heard an interesting fact recently: A discouraged army enters a battle with a certainty of defeat. If defeat is part of an army's mind-set, the odds are against that army no matter how big or how well armed it is.

No wonder Satan is constantly pushing us toward discouragement and despair. No wonder Satan tries so hard to dismantle our faith. He knows that if we feel like all courage is gone, we're done for. And the place where Satan will attack us always begins in our minds. Yet God's Word is clear. We have been given the ability to be strong in the Lord and in the power of His might.

In Deuteronomy 20:4 God tells us, "The Lord your God is the One who goes with you to fight for you against your enemies to give you victory." Victory is ours in Christ. We never have to give in to despair. Because God is at our right hand, we will never be shaken.

As we enter our battles today, let's not be discouraged. Let's have the mind-set of victory. That victory is already ours in Christ today.

Questions: *What mind-set do you revert to the most? Are you more prone to Satan's attacks than you care to admit? How can you develop a mind-set of victory?*

DAY 288

Eyes Wide Open

It is for discipline that you have to endure. God is treating you as sons. For what son is there whom his father does not discipline?
Hebrews 12:7

My sister was correcting her two-year-old toddler when she spoke a stern word to him, but he didn't look like he had heard her. I glanced over to where he was sitting and suddenly saw what he was actually doing. I couldn't help but laugh. Without turning his head one bit toward my sister, my nephew had just shut his eyes tightly. It was a stare down contest. My sister's stern look on one side and his tightly closed eyes on the other.

It was such a vivid picture of how we try to manage our Lord. We do wrong—sometimes intentionally and other times innocently. When God corrects us, instead of submitting in agreement, we shut our eyes tightly ignoring His warning. Yet just like my two-year-old nephew knew deep down in his bones, no amount of shutting our eyes will push our Father away from us. See, only a loving Father will correct His child, and a truly loving one will do it even when it hurts.

Has God spoken a word of correction to you? Is He giving you the look? Are you responding with eyes tightly shut hoping He'll leave you alone, or are you quick to confess you've been wrong?

God loves you too much to leave you alone. Open your eyes, repent, and find the freedom your heart longs for.

Questions: *Could God be correcting you right now regarding an area of sin in your life? How are you responding? In what ways can you show that you are indeed repentant?*

DAY 289

In Your Need

Trust in the Lord with all your heart, and do not lean on your own understanding. In all your ways acknowledge Him, and He will make straight your paths.
Proverbs 3:5-6

My bathroom has ceramic tiles for a wall. On one particular day I decided to hang a shelf on that wall. I figured if I just got a hammer and banged on that nail hard enough, I'd be able to shove the nail into the wall. I was wrong. So I got a screw driver and tried harder. I was wrong again. I even tried to get the job done using my never-used-before electrical drill, but even that strategy failed me. So after much striving, I finally did what I should have done in the first place. I called someone who knew what they were doing and asked for help.

Have you ever noticed how we do the same thing in our lives? We have a plan and figure that if we try really hard, and hustle just a little bit more than everyone else, we'll finally make it work. But all the striving in the world leaves us simply tired and empty. It's in those moments when you've tried your best and still can't see the results you long for that you must stop and do the only thing that will work. It will demand humility and admitting your need.

You've got to simply call on Jesus. He's the only One who knows where you're going and how to get you there. He's the One with the answers you're looking for.

Questions: *In what areas in your life do you feel tired and worn out? Where do you long to see more results? Take some time and pray over these areas right now asking God to answer.*

DAY 290

Don't Stop Now

So that you are not lacking in any gift, as you wait for the revealing of our Lord Jesus Christ, who will sustain you to the end, guiltless in the day of our Lord Jesus Christ.
1 Corinthians 1:7-8

Some days are harder than others. We wonder if we'll even make it. I was feeling a bit like that recently when I opened my Bible and came across 1 Corinthians 1:7-8. Paul's words were like healing over my soul. He wrote, "As you wait for the revealing of our Lord Jesus Christ, who will sustain you to the end." Sustainer God, that's who our God is. He will keep us to the end. No matter how tired and worn out you might feel right now, you have a God who promised to sustain you to the end.

Paul's focus was always on God's faithfulness. He never lost sight of the One who had called him into the fellowship of His Son, Jesus Christ our Lord.

No matter what you're going through right now, rest assured in the faithfulness of our God. He doesn't give up on us. He knows us so well and still loves us so much.

Tim Keller explains the gospel like this: "We are more sinful and flawed in ourselves than we ever dared believe, yet at the very same time we are more loved and accepted in Jesus Christ than we ever dared hope." *(The Meaning of Marriage)*

No matter what you're facing right now, God is faithful and with Him by your side, you're going to make it to the end.

Questions: *Why do you think God loves us so much? How does knowing that nothing can separate you from the love of God give you what you need to make it through today?*

Grow Up

The eyes of all look to You, and You give them their food in due season.
Psalm 145:15

I have an amazing nephew who will remain nameless. He only has one vice: He loves to shop, especially with his single aunt Lina.

Every time we go to a store, he is on mission. He knows that if he asks persistently enough, I'll get him what he asks for. Lately I've noticed that he's developed a habit of asking for stuff he doesn't even need. After talking to my sister about it, I've started to say no to my nephew.

The reason I've started to say no is not because I don't love my nephew. It's also not because I can't afford to get him what he wants. I'm learning to say no because my nephew needs to learn a few things, like the value of money and the importance of waiting. He needs to learn self-control and self-sacrifice. He needs to learn things that are necessary for his long-term success in life. So because I love my nephew so deeply, I'm saying no to him for his own good.

Do you get easily frustrated with God when He says no to the things you ask of Him? Perhaps He's simply teaching you to become mature. In due season He'll give you all that you need and more.

Question: *Think about a couple of the things God has held back from you recently. What could He be teaching you in these refusals?*

DAY 292

Don't Look Back

*Say not, "Why were the former days better than these?"
For it is not from wisdom that you ask this.*
Ecclesiastes 7:10

Are you guilty of looking back on your life in regret? I'm afraid I am sometimes guilty of that too. I've got a lot in my past that I don't love, don't you?

I was looking through my Facebook feed the other day and came across a picture of an old friend. I started walking down memory lane and came up with at least thirty-five scenarios of what my life could have been like if I had made different choices. Pretty soon I felt burdened and heavy-laden. I felt miserable and alone. I found myself sinking into self-pity. I should have known better.

In Ecclesiastes 7:10 God tells us, "Say not, 'Why were the former days better than these?' For it is not from wisdom that you ask this." Wisdom is understanding God's heart. It is knowing that God has a plan for your life because He loves you and knows what's best for you. While what's past is over, God still has a plan for your welfare, to give you a future and a hope.

They say it's hard to see your future when you're staring at your past. They are correct. Learn to look with God's eyes at both your past and your future, and rest in knowing that He is still in control of every detail of your life.

Question: *What's your biggest regret in life? Write it down on a piece of paper. Now look at that regret from God's perspective; then rip up that piece of paper to shreds and rejoice.*

Plan for Thriving

But in your hearts honor Christ the Lord as holy, always being prepared to make a defense to anyone who asks you for a reason for the hope that is in you; yet do it with gentleness and respect.
1 Peter 3:15

I took care of an asthmatic recently and reviewed the obvious plan with the family. See, every asthmatic has both a maintenance plan and a rescue plan for their treatment. Both are necessary for thriving. Both are important. Both serve different functions.

The same principle is true in our Christian walk. In order to thrive, we need a maintenance regimen when it comes to our relationship with God and with others. Our maintenance disciplines include the daily habits that we do simply in order to stay healthy—like reading our Bibles and praying and gathering with other believers regularly.

But we've also got to establish a specific rescue plan. The rescue plan includes steps we turn to when we're hit with a sudden trial or feel the weight of despair crush us. These are actions that we take on the spot to avert crisis. For me, that includes a text to a friend to pray for me right then and there. Or a Bible teaching podcast or radio show that I tune in to just because I really need it. Or it may be my favorite Scripture memory verse that I remind myself of.

We need both a maintenance plan and a rescue plan to stay healthy. Have you established a strategy for victorious living in Christ?

Questions: *Where do you turn to when you're hit with a sudden crisis? What Scripture encourages your heart to stay strong no matter what?*

DAY 294

Burned Down Houses

I will restore to you the years that the swarming locust has eaten, the hopper, the destroyer, and the cutter, My great army, which I sent among you.
Joel 2:25

My pastor once taught me a great lesson about a house that burned down. One day my pastor was walking by a house he'd walked by a million times before. Except this time, the house he'd seen a million times before had completely burned down. A truth hit him like never before, and it is the reality that sometimes houses burn down and that's okay. Bad things happen, and there's nothing we can do about it. Disasters are part of life. Tragedies exist this side of heaven.

Do you ever look at your life in disappointment? Do your dreams feel dead? Like a house that burned down, there comes a point where you've simply got to accept it.

But there is good news. One day my pastor was walking on the street by the burned-down house, but this time he saw something new. This time my pastor saw that the house was being rebuilt. And it hit him again. See, what we need to remember is that God is in the business of rebuilding burned-down houses. He uses our disappointments as the launching pads for what's to come.

If you're looking at your burned-down house, won't you trust Him enough to let Him start rebuilding you again?

Questions: *What specific areas in your life need rebuilding? Would you ask God to rebuild them starting today? Would you relinquish those burned-down houses to His care?*

DAY 295

Living for Jesus

Finally, then, brothers, we ask and urge you in the Lord Jesus, that as you received from us how you ought to walk and to please God, just as you are doing, that you do so more and more.
1 Thessalonians 4:1

Recently Alex Honnold did the impossible. He climbed a three thousand-foot granite mountain called El Capitan without ropes. It was incredible. It was epic. It was a feat no one had ever done before.

One of Alex's friends wrote about the experience. He talked about how risky the climb was and how much mental energy was needed. He talked about how it feels to know someone who had actually done this impossible feat. I read every word and pictured the incredible climb. I was blown away, but I also couldn't help but see the comparison to what life in Christ should look like.

The longer I'm a Christian, the more I recognize just how hard the road can be, how risky it feels, yet how exhilarating to know that we are blessed when we're living for something bigger than what others are living for.

When I read about missionaries who gave everything to Jesus and died for the cross, my breath holds and my mind is blown away. While Alex Honnold climbed El Capitan alone, the promise God gives every Christian is that we are never alone. His arms will always sustain us when it feels like we're falling. He's our rock and our fortress. Living for Him is the most exhilarating life you can ever live.

Questions: *Are you living your life fully surrendered to Jesus? What's the most recent thrilling adventure God has taken you on?*

DAY 296

Be Still

Be still, and know that I am God. I will be exalted among the nations, I will be exalted in the earth!
Psalm 46:10

We all love to relax, just chill out, unwind, and do whatever it is we love to do. What do you do to relax? Some people like to exercise or go on a walk. Others love the thrill of an adrenaline pumping adventure. Still others prefer to just veg in front of the television or watch a movie. Some love to cook and some of us prefer to eat. Some love to watch reruns of our favorite shows, while others blindly shove popcorn in their faces at the movies.

But have you ever considered God's plan for your rest? It's easy and it doesn't cost you a thing except perhaps your own sense of self-importance. God's secret for our rest is that we simply rest in His presence. Because Jesus finished the work at the cross, we don't even have to work to impress Him anymore. We can rest in Christ no matter how hard we're working today.

God loves it when we run to Him to unwind. Over and over again in His Word, He invites us to come to Him when we're tired. Are you worn out and in need of rest? Don't run to the gym and refuse the temptation to veg. Won't you run to God instead?

Be still and know that He is God. That's where true rest is found.

Questions: *Are you tired today? How can you carve out some time—mentally and literally—to rest in Christ today?*

Listen Carefully

Lead me, O Lord, in Your righteousness because of my enemies; make Your way straight before me.
Psalm 5:8

There's a part in the story of David and Goliath that always gets me. Are you curious to know what it is? I'm about to tell you. When David hears that Goliath has threatened the people of God, he is horrified. He is literally beyond himself, upset that anyone could think less of God than who God is. He can't understand how anyone would defy the living God.

In an awesome act of courage, David steps out to take Goliath on where everyone else was too afraid to do it. The story goes on to say that Eliab, David's brother, got mad. Instead of supporting David, Eliab tried to shame him.

Have you ever tried to live obediently and courageously unto the Lord? Perhaps you expected those closest to you to support your choices. They won't always understand your decisions and sometimes, like in the case of Eliab, you'll find them resisting your courage to live for God. But like David, it's only when we step out in faith, even when those around us don't get it, that we'll get to see our giants defeated.

Are you facing your own Goliath today? Keep your eyes on the Lord, listen to the voice of truth, and see your giants come tumbling down no matter what every one around you is saying.

Questions: *Have you ever felt attacked by those closest to you? How does David's example motivate you to rise above the hate and do the work God has called you to do?*

God with Us

*Where shall I go from Your Spirit? Or where shall I flee from Your presence?
If I ascend to heaven, You are there! If I make my bed in Sheol, You are there!*
Psalm 139:7-8

Have you ever thought about the greatest promise God has made to you? God is a promise maker and a promise keeper. There's nothing He promises that He won't fulfill. His Word is sure.

We struggle, not because God hasn't made us any promises, but because we haven't gotten hold of His promises. Most of us don't stop long enough to think about God's promises to us. There are many awesome promises, but the best promise God has made to every Christian is the promise of His presence.

In Matthew 1 we meet Jesus, the Son of God, and He is called Emmanuel, God with us. In Isaiah 41:10 God tells us, "So do not fear, for I am with you; do not be dismayed, for I am your God. I will strengthen you and help you; I will uphold you with My righteous right hand."

God is with us. He has promised never to leave us nor forsake us. It's the promise that kept Joseph hoping while in prison and Moses going in the desert. And it's the promise that you and I can hang on to when everything feels like it's wavering.

Won't you lean on the promise of God's presence, because when it comes to this promise, God is going to keep it forever.

Question: *How can you remind yourself of God's presence today when you're too busy to notice Him or too jaded to care?*

Practical Christianity

*And when they had brought their boats to land,
they left everything and followed Him.*
Luke 5:11

It's not very practical to follow Jesus, is it? One of the most disconcerting aspects of following Jesus is that we expect it to be practical—and it's not.

When Peter and John heard Christ's call, they left their nets, dropped the family business, and followed Jesus. It wasn't practical. It wasn't easy. But no other choice was thinkable. It was the same way for Matthew, who quit his job as a tax collector when Jesus called him. And for Paul, who went to live in the desert for three years after an encounter with Jesus on the road to Damascus. His whole life was turned upside down by Jesus.

We try too hard to make following Jesus more practical. Like save enough money before stepping out in faith. Wait until your family understands the radical nature of your obedience before doing what God wants. Plan an exit strategy from your current job before jumping into missions. But perhaps it's simpler than that. Perhaps the most practical aspect of following Jesus is the impracticality of it all.

Have you *heard* God's call? Are you doing what He asked even if it sounds impractical? Now that's radical Christianity.

Questions: *What's the most radical decision you've ever made in following Jesus? What could Jesus be asking you right now that sounds ridiculous but demands you to say yes? Will you do it?*

DAY 300

Heed the Warning

Give thanks in all circumstances; for this is the will of God in Christ Jesus for you. Do not quench the Spirit.
1 Thessalonians 5:18-19

My home smoke detector beeps every once in a while. It alerts me of problems in my home, even when no one is smoking. Recently, in the middle of a storm, my electricity went off for a bit and the smoke detector took on a mind of its own. It started beeping—a lot. So I opened it up and removed the battery and eventually detached the electrical connection to shut it up. The beeping stopped, but so did my warning of an impending problem.

This illustration might sound irrelevant until you think about how we approach the Holy Spirit. Too often we try the same approach with the Spirit of God. We hear Him warning us that something is wrong. We've stepped far from God, and danger is around the bend. But instead of figuring out why the beeping won't stop, we simply detach the electrical connection in order to obtain temporary peace of mind. The problem with our strategy is that when we disconnect from God, we miss His warnings of the impending disaster.

How is your connection with the Holy Spirit? Are you heeding His beeping, or have you chosen to unplug? There may be more at stake for you than you think.

Questions: *How does the Holy Spirit warn you of the danger of your sin patterns? How have you handled His warnings?*

DAY 301

Be Healed

And the Lord restored the fortunes of Job, when he had prayed for his friends. And the Lord gave Job twice as much as he had before.
Job 42:10

What type of friends do you have? Do they build you up or tear you down? Most people can attest to the fact that we've been hurt by our friends at some point and it stings.

Job tells the same story in a book dedicated to his name. For the first 40 chapters of the book of Job, we hear the saga of a man in the midst of a horrific trial. Instead of offering him support, Job's friends heap criticism and negativity on Job. They accuse him of sinning against God. They blame him for his own misery. They offered advice upon advice that plays out to be worthless. It's exhausting to read the book. But eventually, God vindicates Job, and no one dared speak another word against the guy.

In Job 42:10 God ends the book by giving us relationship gold. God tells us that He restored the fortunes of Job when Job prayed for his friends. Until we're willing to let go of the offense pointed against us, we'll never fully experience the freedom and joy that is ours in Christ. The moment we choose to forgive, God's favor is ours to keep.

Are you holding on to legitimate hurt in your life? It might be time to let it go. Though you might have valid reasons for it, the only way to freedom is to let go of your pain and let God heal you completely.

Questions: *Are you harboring bitterness against someone in your life? Are you willing to finally let it go completely and trust God with the outcome?*

DAY 302

Undeserved Goodness

*But He gives more grace. Therefore it says,
"God opposes the proud but gives grace to the humble."*
James 4:6

I have a secret that's embarrassing to admit. There's never been a hotel I checked into that I didn't ask for a room to change in. Sometimes the room is too dark, or too close to the elevator, or it's too small, or too big. It's a habit I've developed over the years. I'm never quite satisfied.

Recently I went on a personal retreat. The hotel showed me the first room, then the second one, and finally the third. I finally gave up. I told them I was going to call it a day. But the manager seemed to understand my quirks and asked me to give her one more chance. She had just the room for me. I wasn't sure whether to believe her. I hadn't been terribly easy after all. I didn't deserve her kindness. But boy, did she surprise me! The suite she offered me was amazing. The offer was completely undeserved.

Sometimes we're tempted to settle for less than God's best. Frankly, most days we don't deserve God's best. But the crazy part about grace is that it's never deserved and always better than our best imagination.

Keep on praying and seeking God. Receive His goodness even if it feels undeserved. Then thank Him for His goodness, rejoicing in the gifts He's offered you.

Questions: *Think about God's grace in your life, and make a list of the ways He's given you far more than you've deserved.*

Sensitive to the Spirit

She replied, "Wait, my daughter, until you learn how the matter turns out, for the man will not rest but will settle the matter today."
Ruth 3:18

I tend to get stuck in a pattern. If I'm in a waiting pattern, I assume I'm supposed to wait forever. If I'm in an action pattern, I deduce it's going to be action forever. What I need to remember is that what's more important than acting or waiting is my sensitivity to the Holy Spirit.

The book of Ruth reflects this truth in a very obvious fashion. In Ruth 2:2 Naomi, Ruth's mother-in-law, offers Ruth some dating advice about her life: "Go, my daughter," she says. She instructs her to make a move toward her future husband and Ruth does. The outcome is that Ruth falls in love with Boaz and finds herself at a new crossroad. Now this time, when Ruth turns to Naomi for counsel, this is how Naomi answers: "Wait, my daughter." And Ruth did wait until God said, "Move."

There's a time to wait and a time to act, and the only way to tell the difference is to ask God about it, then listen for His answer.

Are you sensitive to the Spirit's leading, or are you still stuck in a pattern that you refuse to change?

Questions: *How can you tell you're being sensitive to the Holy Spirit in the decisions in your life? Is there something He wants you to do right now that you've been refusing to do?*

DAY 304

Press On

We are afflicted in every way, but not crushed; perplexed, but not driven to despair; persecuted, but not forsaken; struck down, but not destroyed.
2 Corinthians 4:8-9

Have you ever considered that sometimes the enemy behind us is the best thing that could happen to us in order to get us to where God wants us to go?

When the people of Israel left Egypt, God led them onward through a cloud by day and a fire by night. But most of us forget that it was also the pressure of the Egyptian army behind Israel that motivated them to keep on moving! In other words, what Satan used to defeat the people of Israel, God used to propel them into the promised land!

The same is true in your life today: What Satan uses to destroy you, God will use to transform you. Because He is with you, you don't have to be afraid of the enemy. You can remain undaunted no matter what.

God is leading you ahead, away from the enemy's reach, even while the enemy is pressing you to move forward from behind. You might feel afflicted, but not crushed; perplexed, but not forsaken; struck down, but not destroyed.

You have a treasure in jars of clay showing that the surpassing power in you belongs to God! What a promise to help you make it through today! What an awesome God we serve!

Question: *What negative pressure might God be using to move you toward where He wants you to be?*

Love Takes Time

*Love bears all things, believes all things,
hopes all things, endures all things. Love never ends....*
1 Corinthians 13:7-8

Love takes time and is not easy. Love is the distinctive that sets the follower of Jesus apart from the world. Yet we're living in a swipe right culture and it's slowly killing us.

Today when it comes to our relationships, our churches, and even our marriages, if we don't like someone, we've simply been trained to swipe left or swipe right and move on. It seems legitimate whether in dating or in the church. Most of us have developed an independence that we've convinced ourselves is enviable, and are unwilling to invest past the outside. We are quick to dismiss what doesn't appeal to us, quickly moving on to greener and better pastures.

But God's way to relationship health is far from a swipe right culture. God's way is a narrow way. His love left the comforts of heaven to be born in a manger and die on a tree. That's the way of love. Jesus instructed us to love one another. This is a love that bears all things, believes all things, endures all things, and hopes all things. If you're following the norm, you might be tempted to choose a comfortable swiping right way to relationships, but you'll end up terribly lonely.

Choose God's way of love, and you'll find the blessings of the abundant life.

Questions: *Describe your closest relationships. What makes people so hard to love? Do you ever think of yourself as hard to love?*

DAY 306

Love in Action

*Love your enemies and pray for those who persecute you,
so that you may be sons of your Father who is in heaven.*
Matthew 5:44-45

This will be hard for you to imagine, but I don't like every single person I meet. So naturally, even with my best intentions in play, I tend to treat people accordingly.

In Matthew 5:44-45 Jesus said, "Love your enemies and pray for those who persecute you, so that you may be sons of your Father who is in heaven." Jesus didn't beat around the bush when it comes to loving the people we don't like. In fact, He went so far as to say that one of the indications of our relationship with God is reflected in how we treat those we don't like.

Do you struggle with loving people in your life that you simply don't like? One of the easiest ways to show love is to find a common point of interest. Another way is to start praying for those people in your life that you find challenging. Be specific. You'll find that as you pray for their wellness and God's favor on their life, you'll start seeing them differently. You'll start seeing them with Christlike eyes and that will make all the difference in the world!

Question: *Think about someone you don't particularly like. Now make a practical plan to show them Christ's love this week.*

Signs

*This shall be the sign to you from the Lord,
that the Lord will do this thing that He has promised.*
Isaiah 38:7

I asked for a sign recently, then I missed it altogether. I had been praying for some time about a particular problem. Finally, I did the inevitable: I prayed for a sign. I asked God to show me the way by laying a fleece the way Gideon had. I prayed. Then I waited. And waited.

When nothing seemed to be happening, I cried out to God in frustration. "God, why aren't You showing me the way?" I eventually quieted down long enough to recheck my e-mails and there it was. I'd missed the sign He had clearly sent me.

Then I remembered a passing conversation I had had with a friend earlier that day that confirmed what I had prayed about. Another sign I had missed in my striving. Suddenly everywhere I looked it seemed that God had given me signs. I was just too caught up with myself to see them. I had been too distracted with the weight of my care to recognize God's hand at work and receive His answer. God had spoken and it was now up to me to act.

Would I step out in faith having been given all the signs that I needed?

Questions: *What sign are you looking for in order to step out in faith and obey God? Could He have already given you a sign and you've been missing it?*

DAY 308

See the Blessing

Blessed be the Lord, who daily bears us up; God is our salvation. Selah.
Psalm 68:19

I was scrolling through my phone recently when I saw an ad for a T-shirt with a logo that said, "Too blessed to be stressed." I laughed. I was having one of those days. It was one of those days that felt more like I was too stressed to be blessed. We can easily fall into this way of thinking.

Instead of focusing on the blessings in my life, my eyes get fixed on what I don't have. When we allow this to happen, we lose sight of all the goodness that God is pouring into our lives. We become too stressed to be blessed.

The life that is focused on God's goodness and blessing finds strength for the battle. Instead of getting angry when temptation comes, rejoice that you have been given an opportunity to fight for joy. Instead of hiding when you see that coworker walk toward you, give thanks that you are growing in love.

Indeed we are too blessed to be stressed. That's how we're meant to live. And it starts when we spend more time counting all of our blessings instead of rehashing all of our stresses.

Are you willing to live a life that's too blessed to be stressed today? Are you willing to fight for joy?

Question: *Count your blessings, name them one by one. We used to sing that song when I was growing up. Will you take time and do just that?*

DAY 309

Days of Grace

And I am sure of this, that He who began a good work in you will bring it to completion at the day of Jesus Christ.
Philippians 1:6

Once in a while when I'm lucky enough, I get to travel with my mother. As much as I enjoy it, I've started to notice a theme. Our first couple of days together are hard. She gets easily stressed and irritable. Then on the third day, like the resurrection, a new woman arises from the ashes of the travel. She transforms into a new person. She finally settles into her zone and is ready to have a blast.

I've started expecting these adjustment periods. I call them days of grace. They're days we need to give ourselves to adjust to new spaces, new people, new customs, and new time zones. Instead of getting frustrated with the people in your life during those adjustment periods, start expecting them. Instead of getting frustrated with yourself during adjustment periods, give yourself some grace too.

You can't have change and comfort simultaneously. It's usually one or the other. If you're going through an adjustment period today, slow down. Breathe and know that it's going to get better. Don't lose sight of the bigger picture. It is God who began a good work in you, and He will always complete what He started.

Questions: *Is there someone in your life right now who needs grace? How can you practically show them the grace you long for too?*

DAY 310

Stay the Course

*When the cares of my heart are many,
Your consolations cheer my soul.*
Psalm 94:19

Do you ever get frustrated and want to quit? Some days I do. Some days I just want to quit. Some days I long to shut everything down and disappear for a while, maybe to Tahiti or the Maldives.

Sooner or later, even the best of us feels like quitting. It usually happens when we're tired or stressed or pressed with time. It happens when our needs and our expectations remain unmet. We're not alone when it comes to these feelings.

Jonah tried to quit once and ended up in the belly of a whale. Elijah wanted to quit once and sat in despondency under a broom tree. Moses wanted to quit and hid in the wilderness for a few decades. Yet God met them and helped them get back up into the game. God never forgot their true calling. He never lost sight of them. Even when they felt like failures, these men learned what I'm learning: that faithfulness is not a feeling. It's a choice we make even in the middle of great frustration. It's our choosing to say yes to God even when we feel like saying no. It's trusting that God will give us exactly what we need and do exactly what's best for us because of who He is.

Stay in the game. Choose faithfulness. God's not done with you yet!

Questions: *What makes you want to quit? It's been said that faithfulness is a long obedience in the right direction. What direction are you walking in right now?*

DAY 311

Just the Right Meal

Feed me with the food that is needful for me lest I be full and deny You and say, "Who is the Lord?" or lest I be poor and steal and profane the name of my God.
Proverbs 30:8-9

In Proverbs 30:8-9 Agur wrote, "Feed me with the food that is needful for me lest I be full and deny You and say, 'Who is the Lord?' or lest I be poor and steal and profane the name of my God."

What are you having for dinner tonight? What about for lunch? Whether you favor frozen Indian meals like I do or Chinese takeout, we all have preferences when it comes to eating. And if you're a mom or dad, then you know more than anyone the importance of a balanced healthy diet. What that means is that some days you might make a meal your kids don't appreciate as much, because it's good for them. And while they might want to gorge on dessert, you love them too much to allow it.

The same applies to God. Whether it's your next meal or your future that's at stake, God is putting together the perfect story for you, and no one can steal it from you. He loves you too much to feed you anything that's not good for you, and He knows just how much of it you need to be full.

Questions: Are you satisfied with the meals God is making you in this season of your life? Talk to Him about it. Thank Him for feeding you with food that's needful for you.

DAY 312

Take a Rest

He makes me lie down in green pastures. He leads me beside still waters.
Psalm 23:2

Have you ever tried to make someone do something? It's not as easy as you might think. Making someone do something is not a walk in the park. It can be downright challenging. But if you've ever paid close attention, you'll notice the wording in Psalm 23:2. It says that *God makes us* lie down in green pastures. The emphasis is mine, and it's meant to prove a point.

God does not simply invite us to lie down in green pastures. He doesn't politely ask us to take a break. No. God makes us do it. He makes us lie down in green pastures. He forces our hand in it. And do you know why He does that? He does it because it's best for us. He does it because He knows we need it.

Have you ever gotten so caught up in your life and work that you simply can't stop? Like a treadmill that keeps getting faster and faster, you feel worn out but can't make yourself stop. It's in those times that God steps in and makes you lie down in green pastures. His action is protective. His touch is full of love. He might do it through a season of failure or disappointment. He might do it through a closed door.

He's your loving Shepherd, and He's always watching out for you. And that's a really good thing!

Questions: *Are you fighting the work that God is doing in your life? As He's making you lie down in green pastures, are you resisting Him or are you willing to trust His timing?*

Healing a Broken Heart

He heals the brokenhearted and binds up their wounds.
He determines the number of the stars; He gives to all of them their names.
Psalm 147:3-4

There's a song from the 70s that goes something like this: "How can you mend a broken heart? How can you stop the rain from falling? How can you mend this broken man? How can a loser ever win? Somebody please help me mend my broken heart and let me live again." It sounds a little bit pathetic, but truth be known, who hasn't felt that way at least once in your life?

How do you get over a broken heart? Whether it's a broken marriage that left you reeling, or a church breakup that has you wounded, most of us long to move past our own pain and brokenness. Maybe you're in the pits of a broken heart right now and need to know how to mend it. When it comes to finding healing for your broken heart, there is only one place for healing. It's at the foot of the cross. The cross is our reminder that we are loved no matter what. The cross is our confidence that we are worth His love. The best way to mend a broken heart is by turning that heart over to the Healer.

Like David often did, simply cry out to God: "Heal me, O Lord, for my bones are troubled" (Psalm 6:4). And in time, you'll see, the same God who came and healed David will come through for you. By His wounds we are healed.

Questions: *When was the last time you felt your heart break? How can meditating on the cross bring healing to your hurt?*

God Changes Us

Can the Ethiopian change his skin or the leopard his spots?
Then also you can do good who are accustomed to do evil.
Jeremiah 13:23

Have you ever been tempted to change your personality in order to be liked by someone? Someone once told me that I'd have better luck in dating if I said I was a nurse instead of a doctor. I was tempted to do it. Sooner or later we're all tempted to be someone we're not in order to be liked.

We're great pretenders. Some have pretended their way into marriage, while others are pretending their way into Christianity. It's dangerous to live as a pretender because eventually, the truth always comes out. Imagine waking up next to someone you thought was a neat freak only to find out they're a perfect mess? Or imagine getting married to a man only to learn that he's gay.

Jeremiah 13:23 says, "Can an Ethiopian change his skin or a leopard its spots? Neither can you do good who are accustomed to doing evil." The insinuation is that some things are fundamentally unchangeable without God. But God is in the business of change. He can take a heart of stone and turn it into soft flesh.

You don't have to pretend anymore. Confess your true nature to God, and watch Him transform you into the person you are meant to be.

Questions: *Have you ever pretended to be something or someone you're not? How did it play out for you? What are you hiding right now that you wish God would change about you?*

DAY 315

Change Your Habits

And those who belong to Christ Jesus have crucified the flesh with its passions and desires.
Galatians 5:24

There are days that I know I'm full. But I keep on eating. Have you ever done that too? It's one thing to overeat at Thanksgiving, but if you're like me, you're tempted to do it night after night even when you can already tell that you're full.

Sadly, most of us know how this plays out. We become too full for comfort. Why do we insist on gorging on something even when we know how harmful it can be? Why do we ignore our needs in order to grab what we want? More often than not, it's because it's our habit to indulge. We're accustomed to overeating. We're used to it.

We binge on our favorite TV shows because we've become used to it, not because we long to watch the newest show. We gorge on Facebook because we're used to it, not because we miss the people we're blindly staring at. Eventually we become so full we can't breathe.

The gift is to recognize what we need before we grab what we want. In other words, it's time to develop new habits, like opening God's Word when we're hurting and getting on our knees in the waiting.

It's time to fill ourselves with what we need instead of what we want. Before we know it, our needs will become our wants.

Questions: *What are some of the destructive habits that you've simply become accustomed to but don't need? How can you start creating new God-honoring habits?*

No More Platitudes

*From the end of the earth I call to You when my heart is faint.
Lead me to the rock that is higher than I.*
Psalm 61:2

Every day, whether we look for them or not, we're given a load of platitudes. Platitudes are those pithy remarks that we make to each other that are not always based on truth. I hate platitudes.

Here's a platitude that many singles hear: "There's someone for everyone." If I got a nickel for every time I've heard that, I'd retire. Yet we all do it. We dish out platitudes at the speed of light, giving people empty words that are meant to encourage but fall flat on hurting hearts.

What if we replaced worldly platitudes with God's promises? Instead of, "There's someone for everyone," why not give that person a true promise from God's Word like, "I know the plans I have for you, says the Lord" (Jeremiah 29:11). Or "Nothing will separate you from the love of God" (see Romans 8:39). Or "God will never leave you nor forsake you" (see Hebrews 13:5).

While we can't hang our hats on platitudes, we can hang our whole hearts on God's promises. As you learn to put your weight on God's promises, you'll find them strong enough to handle your fears, your failures, and your disappointments.

Platitudes won't get you through hard times, but God's promises will help you get stronger.

Question: *Which promise of God are you going to hang your soul on today? Write it down and say it aloud to yourself.*

Provider

And my God will supply every need of yours according to His riches in glory in Christ Jesus.
Philippians 4:19

I was driving around with my three-year-old nephew one day. It was raining and I needed to find a parking spot close to the store. I was worried about transferring him out of his car seat into the elements and must have spoken my worry out loud.

After a beat I heard Sam's sweet little voice chime up from the back: "Hey, Lina, want me to ask God to help us find a parking spot?" I smiled and nodded yes, partly full of faith and partly nervous he'd pray in vain. He prayed a short prayer. His words were sweet and so simple. Our eyes were open and suddenly you guessed it; the perfect parking spot opened up right in front of the door.

Did you know that God is as much in the mundane as He's in the miraculous? He loves hearing His children pray. He loves giving us answers when we come to Him as little children. Perhaps it's because little children believe what our jaded hearts have forgotten—that God listens and hears us when we pray. He cares about even our parking spaces.

No matter your need today, ask God to provide. Who knows? You might just get your answer.

Question: *What's on your prayer list today? Write down a couple mundane needs, and watch God provide everything you need today!*

DAY 318

Guard Your Mind

Finally, brothers, whatever is true, whatever is honorable, whatever is just, whatever is pure, whatever is lovely, whatever is commendable, if there is any excellence, if there is anything worthy of praise, think about these things.
Philippians 4:8

I love quotes. I heard a great one the other day and want to share it with you: "Whatever we irrigate in our imagination will grow." Our imaginations have a greater impact on our behaviors and moods than we think.

In Philippians 4:8 Paul says, "Finally, brothers and sisters, whatever is true, whatever is noble, whatever is right, whatever is pure, whatever is lovely, whatever is admirable—if anything is excellent or praiseworthy—think about such things." God gave us this command because He knows it's what we need to thrive.

What thoughts are you watering these days? Most of us spend our days irrigating negativity and discontent. Instead of watering our imaginations with the truth, we water them with seeds of jealousy and bitterness. Instead of thinking the best about people, we think of their worst habits. Then we wonder why our hearts are hurting all the time. Let's root out the weeds of sin in our lives, and choose to fix our thoughts on all that is excellent and praiseworthy. It's not only possible; it's the key to our survival.

Will you choose what is good and lovely?

Questions: *Take an inventory of your thoughts from the last few days. What are some of the weeds you need to root out, and what are some of the thoughts you need to plant afresh?*

Say Yes

"And the master said to the servant, 'Go out to the highways and hedges and compel people to come in, that my house may be filled.'"
Luke 14:23

We all have excuses and we use them liberally. When we're invited to go places we don't feel like going, we say we're too busy. When we're asked to volunteer for service, we don't have the time. When we're included in a new venture, we excuse ourselves because of our limited resources. We're too chicken to say yes. It's easier to hide.

In Luke 14 Jesus told a parable of a man who gave a banquet and invited a bunch of people. One by one they made excuses: "I just bought a business." "I've got too much to do." "I just got married." Do you know what the man in the story did? He went on to find others who would come to the celebration.

The parable is a picture of God inviting His people on a journey with Him. Alas, they were too busy. They didn't have the time. They had more important things to do. The party did happen. Others were invited instead. The ones with excuses just missed out on all the fun.

You've been invited into a deeper walk with the Lord. Stop making excuses. You don't have to run from Him. Come home. No more excuses. It's time you get serious about God's invitation. Say yes.

Questions: *What adventure has God been inviting you on? Will you stop making excuses and jump in? Say yes to God right now. Tell Him you're in.*

Get Stronger

For while bodily training is of some value, godliness is of value in every way, as it holds promise for the present life and also for the life to come.
1 Timothy 4:8

How committed to working out are you? I have a friend who's at the gym all the time. He's committed to working out. I know it because every time I check Facebook, he's got a picture of himself pumping iron. When I run into him at the grocery store, he's in gym clothes. No matter where I turn, this guy is working out. Even at church on Sundays he's got his bag with him, and he's ready to go. My friend is committed to staying in shape. It's inspiring and a little bit annoying.

And while exercising is good for the body, there is something even better. In 1 Timothy 4:8 Paul says that "while bodily training is of some value, godliness is of value in every way." It's not that working out is bad, but too many of us are far more concerned with bodily exercise than with soul training. Too many of us are more committed to looking good than to becoming more godly. The only way to become more godly is to invest in our souls. It happens when we're not on a treadmill, but on our knees.

Only time with God through His Word will give us the strength we need when we're up against a trial.

Questions: *How much time and energy are you committed to building up your soul muscles? What spiritual exercise regimen might you start to get stronger?*

DAY 321

Make Friends

Two are better than one, because they have a good reward for their toil. For if they fall, one will lift up his fellow. But woe to him who is alone when he falls and has not another to lift him up!
Ecclesiastes 4:9-10

Friendships take work. The older I get, the more I recognize it. It takes work to develop real friendships. It takes a willingness to be open and authentic. It can sometimes even be risky. Most of us yearn for deep friendships and that yearning increases with time.

God created us after all for relationship. That relationship need is first met with God. He offered us friendship with Himself through Jesus. He's also offered us fellowship in the Spirit. And even more practically, He's given us a family—a community of people meant to encourage us and journey heavenward with us. That community is called the Church.

But it takes work to build lasting friendships. It takes stepping out of our comfort zones, and reaching out to others with our needs. It takes being sometimes vulnerable and sometimes available for others when they're in need.

Are you willing to risk your comfort for real relationships? Ask God to lead you as you look for godly friends. Ask Him to give you wisdom in choosing right friends; and get involved in your local church, the best place to find the kind of community you were created for.

Questions: *What is your relationship with the local church like? What risks are you willing to take in order to deepen your friendship with other Christians?*

DAY 322

Redeeming Failure

To give them a beautiful headdress instead of ashes, the oil of gladness instead of mourning, the garment of praise instead of a faint spirit.
Isaiah 61:3

Think about the last time you failed at something. Maybe you feel like a failure right now.

I was going through a difficult season when I read about this guy and was deeply encouraged. He had a difficult childhood, and less than one year of formal education. He failed in business at age 31. He was defeated for legislature at 32, and failed again in business at 33. He was elected to the legislature at 34. His fiancée died when he was 35. He was defeated for speaker again at 38.

At 42 he married a woman who became a burden, then defeated for Congress at 43, defeated for Senate at 55, defeated for VP at 56, and defeated for Senate at 58. Then after all of these failures, he was finally elected for President. That's Abraham Lincoln, of course. Can you believe his story?

You might feel like you're going through a tough season, but remember that God redeems every failure for good. The Scriptures are full of men and women who looked like failures until God stepped in and redeemed their story.

There is no setback too wide for Him to restore. Keep Him at the center of your life, and in time every purpose of the Lord still stands.

Questions: Why do you think God uses so many people who looked like failures as part of His big story? In what ways has God already redeemed parts of your story?

Fear of Man

Stop regarding man in whose nostrils is breath, for of what account is he?
Isaiah 2:22

Most of us love to be affirmed. When someone compliments me, it doesn't matter what it is I've done, it fills my heart with joy. It motivates me to work even harder. I suppose you can say that words of affirmation are my love language. In the very same breath, if we're being honest, most of us have the opposite effect when we're criticized. When someone tears what we did apart, our hearts plummet and anxiety takes over.

What if we blew our chances for a better future? What if they don't ask us back again? What if we don't get the job? We let people control us and forget that God is sovereign over our lives.

In Isaiah 2:22 God says, "Stop regarding man in whose nostrils is breath, for of what account is he?" It's true. People come and people go, their words build us up or they tear us down; but at the end of the day, only God's purposes for us will stand.

Are you controlled by the fear of man? You don't have to be. It is God who rules every moment of your day. You're safer than you feel. As long as you're walking in His will, it's going to be okay.

Questions: *Are you living in the fear of God or the fear of man? How can you tell?*

DAY 324

Ripple Effect

And He said to all, "If anyone would come after Me, let him deny himself and take up his cross daily and follow Me."
Luke 9:35

When was the last time you played dominos? I was given the game for Christmas and reminded of how much I love it. Have you ever lined up the domino pieces in order, then bumped just one of them, sat back, and watched the whole thing tumble down? It's amazing the impact that one domino can create simply by falling.

Too often in my life I lose sight of the big picture. I see my life day in, day out, hardly making a dent in this world. I try to be faithful, but if I'm being honest, my impact feels limited. Then I think about Jesus.

Jesus gathered twelve guys around Him, and only three were His closest friends, and one was His enemy. He poured into them and loved them. His circle of friends didn't look like much. No one thought they would change the world. But just like in the game of dominos, one by one the disciples watched Jesus take that first fall and eventually everything changed. A ripple effect was started that keeps on going today.

You may not feel like a world changer right now, but all God asks you to do is to impact the one life He's placed in front of you.

Be willing to die to yourself, and who knows what might happen when we're willing to follow the example of Jesus?

Questions: *Who has God placed in your life right now that you might be able to impact? In what ways can you reach out to that person in love?*

Set Free

So if the Son sets you free, you will be free indeed.
John 8:36

If I ever get thrown in jail, there would probably be a pretty good reason for it. The one thing I can promise you is that I would want to be bailed out.

While few of us realistically will spend any time in jail, the truth is that we probably deserve to. We deserve a lifetime in prison. God's Word tells us that we were born sinners with a death sentence on us, separated from God forever.

Yet despite the odds, and regardless of whether we deserve it, God lovingly bailed us out of jail through Jesus Christ. He paid the price for our sin so that we could be free. He did it by sending Jesus to die on the cross for our sins.

The sad reality is that despite being freed, many of us are still hanging around the prison cell, refusing to be bailed out.

Have you received Christ's payment for your sin? Have you been set free? And having been set free, are you walking in the freedom that has been purchased for you? Are you living unto God? For freedom Christ has set us free.

Let every day be a new opportunity to show our gratitude to a God who loved us enough to send His Son to die for us and set us free.

Questions: *In what ways do many Christians still live like they're in prison? In what ways do you still live like you're in prison?*

DAY 326

Don't Nitpick

Do all things without grumbling or disputing.
Philippians 2:14

I've never met a nitpicker I didn't recognize. I can be a nitpicker if I'm not careful. Nitpickers. We all know them. Some of us *are* them. We can't let things go. We claim we want excellence, but like hyper perfectionist woodpeckers on a tree, we nitpick until we get what we want the most.

To nitpick is to be excessively concerned with or critical of inconsequential details. We've all been there. Some of us are there right now. We nitpick our churches, we nitpick our bosses, we nitpick our spouses, we nitpick our friends.

In the Old Testament, the people of Israel nitpicked every single thing they didn't like about the life God had given them. They couldn't see the goodness of God, and nitpicked their way through the wilderness. The result was often tragic for them.

The result is equally tragic for us if we don't break the habit of nitpicking. The Bible calls nitpicking murmuring and complaining. Let's transform our nitpicking into praise. The result could be lifesaving, not just for us, but for those around us too.

Questions: What are some of the things you nitpick the most about? Can you look for ways to praise God in those areas instead?

Stop Sinning

*Now the law came in to increase the trespass,
but where sin increased, grace abounded all the more.*
Romans 5:20

It amazes me how often I act like I should be the exception to the rule. I assume that someone somewhere should understand my dilemma and make an exception for me just this once. It's arrogant and rude. Typically, the Lord will find ways to correct me, and I am grateful for it.

When it comes to sin, many of us approach God as if we should be the exception to the rule. We claim we were tired. We complain that we were bored or didn't know any better. We plead ignorance. In our arrogance we assume that God will overlook our sin. We conclude that we're not as bad as everyone else. We want to get off easy. But it doesn't work that way.

Jesus paid the penalty for our sin. He died so that we would stop sinning. While God gives grace abundantly, the only way to overcome sin is to humbly admit to God that we're wrong, to ask for His forgiveness, and to beg for His help.

As we receive His grace, we begin to understand that there are no exceptions to the rule. Sin must stop, and grace is ours if we're willing enough to receive it.

Questions: *Do you struggle with habitual sin? What excuses have you made to God when you choose to sin? Will you receive God's grace and ask Him to help you find liberty from sin?*

Choose Life

*Choose this day whom you will serve...
But as for me and my house, we will serve the Lord.*
Joshua 24:15

There was a crazy show on TV for a while called *Man versus Food*. The concept was nuts. The host would show up to well-known eating places and order the biggest thing on the menu, and eat until he nearly exploded. It was man versus food. Who would win? The people standing around him would cheer him on.

While it's sort of funny, the truth is that many of us treat our thought lives like man versus food. We glutton on negativity, seeing how much jealousy and anger and criticism we can shove down our throats and wonder why we feel so sick all the time. Typically we have no problem finding people around us to cheer us on, pushing us even further into the pit of self-pity and misery.

The only way to move past a man versus food lifestyle is to change the channel. It's not as difficult as it sounds. Turn your back away from the pile of sin in your life and find life. Surround yourself with people who will cheer on your godly choices.

While sin might seem entertaining for a season, in the end it brings nothing but misery.

Questions: *Who are your balcony people? Are they cheering you on in the faith? Have you openly asked them to pray for you in your struggle with sin?*

DAY 329

Good Friends. Great Choices.

Do not be deceived: "Bad company ruins good morals."
1 Corinthians 15:33

I have to confess something. There's something that I sometimes do that I'm not very proud of. On occasion, especially when I'm lazy or when it's cold, I put my recyclables in the green non-recyclable trash bin.

I have a friend in my small group who once found this out and almost unfriended me. I told her I wanted to change. I sort of meant it. I wish I could say that I did change, but even with my good intentions, I still catch myself bending the rules on that one. I also hide from Andrea every time I see her. I know that given enough time, she's going to ask me about my trash struggle.

When it comes to certain sins in our lives, many of us adopt the same mentality. We want to change, but not really. We like the idea of change better than the idea of hating our sin. Eventually we keep on sinning and just hide our sins from others. We sort of adjust to a new stealth way of living. At first we don't notice the difference, but in time, putting recyclables in the nonrecyclable bin will kill you. It doesn't honor God and it's lazy.

Are you wishy-washy about the choices that you're making? Are you settling for a lifestyle that's going to kill your soul in the end? It's not too late to change.

Question: *We all need an Andrea in our lives. Who is your Andrea— that friend who will hold you accountable even when you'd rather simply avoid her?*

Watch Yourself

So you also must consider yourselves dead to sin and alive to God in Christ Jesus.
Romans 6:11

I told my mom I didn't have a choice as I flew past the car to my left to avoid falling into the ditch. It didn't stop her from hollering out in fear from her seat. The truth is that I did have a choice. I could have slowed down and yielded to the car next to me, but that would have cost me too much. It would have meant giving up my pride. It would have meant admitting I was wrong. It would have meant ceding my rights.

When we convince ourselves that we have no choice in our actions, we become powerless. We leave God out of the equation and we lose—every single time.

There's always a choice to make when it comes to doing what's right. And there's always a price to the choices we make. The question we must ask ourselves is this: Are we willing to make the right choices no matter the cost? There are people around us whose very lives will depend on how we answer that question.

My old pastor used to say, "Choose to sin, choose to suffer." He was right. God has given us the freedom to choose. While it might cost you your pride, the price to live righteously has already been paid. It's up to you to realize it.

Questions: *In what specific ways have you ever suffered because of your persistence to continue in sin? How would you choose if you lived in a greater awareness of the gospel in your life?*

Language of Praise

Let the word of Christ dwell in you richly, teaching and admonishing one another in all wisdom, singing psalms and hymns and spiritual songs, with thankfulness in your hearts to God.
Colossians 3:16

Because I was born in Lebanon, I speak several languages. Four to be precise. There was a season in my life where I noticed I'd picked up a new language, and one that I am not very proud of. It was the language of ungratefulness. Its main tone is complaining. You might be familiar with it. Maybe you're fluent in it too. It's an easy language to learn, and it's hard to shake once you get used to it.

Complaining is the language of the ungrateful. It becomes more pronounced when we set our eyes on the things we want but don't have. It forgets all the good things that God has generously given us. It's a universal language that too many of us are fluent in. It's time to learn a new language.

I have started learning the language of praise. But here's a secret: It takes lots and lots of practice to learn a new language. So if you're like me and want to learn the language of the grateful, start praising God as much as you can. Pretty soon you'll be fluent in the language of praise.

Questions: *Stop right now and give God praise. Ask a friend you see a lot to point out how often you revert to the old language of complaining. Ask God to help you change.*

DAY 332

Never Alone

He was despised and rejected by men, a Man of sorrows and acquainted with grief; and as One from whom men hide their faces He was despised, and we esteemed Him not.
Isaiah 53:3

Loneliness. Even the word is depressing. We're living in an era of epic proportions when it comes to loneliness.

I got an e-mail from someone once who admitted, "I hate loneliness." And who doesn't? No matter who you are and where you live, odds are that you've felt the sting of loneliness that led you down the path into self-pity. Before long you convince yourself that no one really cares about you, certainly not enough to call you. You start to question the value of your life.

Why does God allow us to be lonely? And why does loneliness feel so… lonely? While I don't have all of the answers, there is one thing I know: God understands our loneliness. He feels our pain. He is near to us when we turn to Him for comfort. Jesus was described as a Man of sorrows and acquainted with grief. He is able to sympathize with our need.

Instead of trying to numb your loneliness with what feels good in the moment, turn to Jesus. Find in Him the friend you need when no one else seems to care. He loves you and He cares.

Questions: *When do you feel most lonely? What are some of the sin patterns you turn to when you're lonely? Ask God to help you sense His presence when you come up against loneliness.*

DAY 333

Good Days and Bad

And he said, "Naked I came from my mother's womb, and naked shall I return. The Lord gave, and the Lord has taken away; blessed be the name of the Lord."
Job 1:21

I have good days and I have bad ones. I bet you do too. When my days are good, I feel happy with God and recognize His favor on my life. But on the bad days, I get aggravated with others, with myself, and even with God.

If you've ever read about Job, then you know how resilient that man was. On the worst day of his life, after losing everything and everyone he cared about, he bowed his face to the ground and said these famous words that we all love to sing: "The Lord gave, and the Lord has taken away; blessed be the name of the Lord."

I want to be able to say the same words that Job used on my bad days. When my pain is steep and my hurt is agonizing, I want to praise God with all my heart. God's goodness does not rely on our circumstances. His favor is not temporal. When we choose to trust God on our bad days, we declare to a watching world that our God is great and worthy of our praise. You can tell the condition of your heart by how you respond to God when life doesn't go as planned.

How are you doing when it comes to worshipping God? Do you recognize His goodness no matter what you're going through?

Questions: *What makes praising God so hard on the bad days? What made Job able to praise God even when his whole world was falling apart?*

DAY 334

Fitting In

But our citizenship is in heaven, and from it we await a Savior, the Lord Jesus Christ.
Philippians 3:20

Do you struggle to fit in? I've always had a hard time fitting in. I know this comes as a shock to you given my natural charm but it's true.

In high school, lunch was my least favorite hour because I never knew where to sit. Thirty years later, I still feel like I'm dancing around the outside of a circle, struggling where I fit in. I want to belong, but I am not quite sure where. I'm too single for the marrieds, too Christian for the world, too smart for my own good. And on and on it goes.

It's easy to get discouraged if you constantly feel like an outsider. But think about it from God's point of view: We are called to be in the world, but not of it. We are reminded over and over again that this world isn't our home. We are citizens of heaven.

It occurs to me that we're not supposed to fit in here on this earth. The only harbor to anchor our hearts on right now is in the safe arms of Jesus. He's the One to whom we belong, and heaven is the only place that will feel like home.

Turn to Him when you feel on the outskirts, and find rest for your soul.

Questions: *Where do you find it hardest to fit in and why? How can you find rest in Christ the next time you feel like an outsider?*

DAY 335

Stop Worrying

Finally, brothers, whatever is true, whatever is honorable, whatever is just, whatever is pure, whatever is lovely, whatever is commendable, if there is any excellence, if there is anything worthy of praise, think about these things.
Philippians 4:8

As an ER doctor I run into hypochondriacs all the time. They are your quintessential worry warts. They think they're dying all of the time. They want to talk about their symptoms all of the time. How do you get a hypochondriac to stop worrying? I have learned that it is only patience and reassurance that will calm a hypochondriac's heart.

The truth is that I've never met a hypochondriac I didn't love. The truth is that I, too, am a worry wart. I worry about everything. And the older I get, the more I am learning that only God's persistent reassurance will move me past my worry and into a place of peace. I can't muster enough energy to overcome worry on my own. But God faithfully loves me, and gently reminds me that no matter what happens, He's my Father and will never leave me alone! It's in the shadow of God's love that my worry finally disappears.

If you're a worry wart, take heart. God is with you to the end. He's got you and will never let you go.

Questions: *If God were to reassure you in your worry today, what would He tell you? What would He remind you about Himself?*

Satan's Lie

Be sober-minded; be watchful. Your adversary the devil prowls around like a roaring lion, seeking someone to devour.
1 Peter 5:8

Did you know that Satan is a liar and wants to steal your peace? Go all the way back to Genesis, and you'll find Satan with one purpose in mind: to destroy Jesus and anyone who belongs to Him.

He started with Adam and Eve. Satan filled their minds with doubt about the goodness of God. They fell for the lie that God didn't care about them. They were deceived and took matters into their own hands, thinking that God had kept something special from them. They found out they were wrong. They'd fallen for Satan's lie.

We Christians battle the same temptation today. Satan wants us to believe that God doesn't care about us and is keeping back from us that which is good for us. It's a lie. God's Word is truth. It tells us that God loves us and knows exactly what we need. He who began His work in us won't stop until He's done.

Everything will work out for good for the follower of Christ. That's the truth, and don't let anyone take it away from you.

Questions: *What circumstances in your life make it easy for you to doubt God's love? How can you fight those doubts with the truth of who God is?*

Submit to One Another

Submitting to one another out of reverence for Christ.
Ephesians 5:21

Submission is a word that carries so much baggage, doesn't it? As a single Christian I've noticed that many singles act like they have been set off the hook when it comes to submission. Yet submission isn't a word just for the marrieds. In Ephesians 5:21 Paul writes, "submitting to one another out of reverence to Christ."

The truth about submission is that it's Christlike. It's for both men and women, single or married. No one demographic has a monopoly on submission. We all get to practice it. God intends for all of us to practice a humble attitude of mutual submission to one another.

At the end of the day, submission is all about yielding. It's about giving up our rights for the sake of the other. It's about trusting God with the outcome. It's about dying to self over and over and over again. Submission is at work in every marriage, every work relationship, and every church interaction. See, submission is about godliness.

Let's look for ways to practice mutual submission to one another as we are willing to die to ourselves for the sake of Christ.

Question: *In what specific ways can you die to yourself today? Think about practical ways to do just that in marriage, at work, and in your church.*

DAY 338

Keep Waiting

But they who wait for the Lord shall renew their strength; they shall mount up with wings like eagles; they shall run and not be weary; they shall walk and not faint.
Isaiah 40:31

There's a house on my street that went on sale forever. It was pretty and functional and I liked it. Finally, after what felt like ages, a sign went up that said the sale was pending. I breathed a sigh of relief for the owners. But as luck would have it, the sale fell through and the house was back on the market.

A few months later, the house did eventually sell, and this time for real. I saw the owners move out and all seemed well. As I think about that house, I am convinced that the house took longer to sell than its owner anticipated or wanted. I'm sure the process created more anxiety in their hearts than expected. But the bottom line is that the house did eventually sell.

It's the same with most of our waiting. We go through a period of time where we give up. We expect the worst. We don't see the light at the end of the tunnel. But eventually the house sells, and all our fears become lost in the rearview mirror. It might not happen exactly when we thought it would or how. It might involve some near misses and disappointments along the way.

But as we wait on the Lord, He always provides exactly what we need and when we need it. Keep waiting. The best is yet to come.

Question: *In what area in your life are you currently waiting on the Lord? Think about the things God might be teaching you in this season of your life and give thanks.*

Forgiven and Free

For you were called to freedom, brothers. Only do not use your freedom as an opportunity for the flesh, but through love serve one another.
Galatians 5:13

My nephews babysat a dog named Nellie for the longest time. Nellie was an "interesting" dog. She seemed afraid of her shadow. She'd approach you cautiously and feel her way around you not very sure of herself. Nellie wasn't the cutest dog ever, but she grew on you!

When I asked my nephews about Nellie, they told me the rest of her sad story. Poor Nellie had been hurt earlier in her life, and had developed a natural guardedness around people. Poor, poor Nellie, and yet so like us. We get wounded by someone, perhaps an ex, a church, or a pastor. And just like Nellie we learn to build walls around our hearts. We learn to hide. There is a better way.

Jesus can heal our hurt. He died on a cross to overcome our insecurities. He loves us so deeply and unconditionally. When He takes over our life, we become free to love others. We are safe because of Him. We become able to open our hearts to others no matter what they've done to us before. It's called forgiveness, and it's only possible because we've been forgiven too.

Questions: Who are some people that you feel unsafe around? How do Jesus and the gospel change your pain into freedom to love and forgive?

Heroes of the Faith

Therefore, since we are surrounded by such a huge crowd of witnesses to the life of faith, let us strip off every weight that slows us down, especially the sin that so easily trips us up. And let us run with endurance the race God has set before us.
Hebrews 12:1

We all have heroes. People we look up to and admire. People we try to copy. Who's your hero? An athlete, a movie star, a rock legend? What makes a person your hero?

I want to tell you who my heroes are. They're names hardly anyone hears anymore. They're names like David Livingstone, the great missionary doctor, and David Brainerd, the missionary who died of TB at age 29 while serving the Lord. Then there's Amy Carmichael, the single missionary who spent her life in India and one of the first women to fight child prostitution and win. She adopted over one hundred children who were going to be sacrificed to the gods.

My heroes are people like Jim Elliott and Hudson Taylor and Adoniram Judson and William Carey and Gladys Aylward. None had it easy, but each had a tale of persevering faith. Each gave their lives to Jesus and refused to give up. Each has their names written in heaven's Book of Life.

Lots of people are posing to be a hero today, but only a few are heroes in heaven as well. So...who's your hero?

Questions: *Who is your modern-day hero? How about your biblical hero? What makes your hero your hero? Are you living a life that inspires someone to keep on keeping on?*

DAY 341

Try Something New

He who calls you is faithful; He will surely do it.
1 Thessalonians 5:24

I once stared at a food I didn't understand. "Go ahead, try it," my friend advised me. I wasn't sure about it. It didn't look like something I'd love. But after a few nudges, I figured I had nothing to lose. I did try it and, boy, did I ever love it! It has become my go-to snack on days when I'm looking for something healthy. I bet you're dying to know what it is, but the truth is that it doesn't matter what "it" is; it's the principle that matters.

We're all afraid of trying something new. We troll around the edges of a new adventure, a new ministry, a new opportunity, a new church. We're afraid to take a risk; we're afraid we might hate it. But what if...what if the very opposite happened? What if instead of hating it we loved it? What if it became the very heartbeat of our soul? When I think back, that's how I became a Bible teacher. One day, I was asked to try it. I did, and I fell in love with the Bible.

I wonder what it is you'd love if you were just willing to try it.

Questions: *What new opportunity might be waiting for you to take if only you mustered up the courage to try it? What keeps you from taking that step of faith?*

DAY 342

Drop the Labels

Judge not, that you be not judged. For with the judgment you pronounce you will be judged, and with the measure you use it will be measured to you.
Matthew 7:1-2

Do you know what a frequent flyer is? Or a bounce back? No, I'm not talking about the airlines. I'm talking about the ER. When someone comes to the ER over and over again, we call him a "frequent flyer." And when someone comes back too soon, we call him a "bounce back."

Does it bother you to hear these labels? Do you bristle at the stereotypes? We all hate labels, and we should. Yet we use them all the time. We spend two seconds gathering data, then without a second thought we give it a label: single for a reason, plus size, over the hill, Republican, Democrat, illegal, gay. If you can think of it, we've got a name for it.

But what if we dropped the labels? What if instead of squarely categorizing people, we got to know them instead? What if we looked for the face of God in them, and looked past the surface? I wonder what we'd find if we looked past the label. I have a feeling we might find people who are hurting, in need of a Savior. I have a feeling we'd find people exactly like us.

Questions: *Do you tend to be quick to judge people and put them in a box? Why do you think we do that? What are some ways to overcome stereotyping others?*

Healer

He Himself bore our sins in His body on the tree, that we might die to sin and live to righteousness. By His wounds you have been healed.
1 Peter 2:24

Jesus' response to pain is always the same. Whenever He encountered someone who was hurting, He was always moved with compassion. He never turned them away. He never spoke a harsh word to someone because He was worn out or done for the day.

Sometimes when I'm tired, I get calloused about other people's pain. Sometimes when I'm busy, I get dismissive of other people's pain. Sometimes when I've been hurt, I get cynical about other people's pain. Granted, when the circumstances are right and I have a stethoscope around my neck or my hand on my Bible, I tend to be much more compassionate about other people's pain.

Yet our Savior didn't need a reminder of who He was. Even now, Jesus is never dismissive or cynical or too busy for our pain. No matter the reason for our pain, Jesus is always deeply moved because of it. Even more, Jesus can heal us when we're hurting.

If you're in pain today, turn to Jesus. He always has time for you. You can trust Him to heal you and deliver you from pain.

Questions: *How can you become better at remembering your true identity as the child of God? How can you develop patience for other people's pain?*

DAY 344

Send Me

And I heard the voice of the Lord saying, "Whom shall I send, and who will go for us?" Then I said, "Here I am! Send me."
Isaiah 6:8

There's an awesome passage of Scripture in the book of Isaiah where the prophet hears God ask this Question: "Whom shall I send, and who will go for us?" Isaiah immediately responds, "Here I am. Send me!"

You've probably heard these words before, and maybe even said them once or twice when you were at a Christian camp. You felt God calling you to go somewhere or do something, and you told Him you'd go anywhere.

Most of us who have answered God's call assume that He will surely send us somewhere exciting, glamorous, and big. Yet His call might surprise us. His call might simply take us to the house next door.

What if God has called you, and you did say yes? But what if instead of sending you to Honolulu, God is sending you to the homeless shelter down the street? Would you still do it? And what if, like Isaiah the prophet, all you ever did see during your lifetime was nothing more than closed hearts and eventual destruction? Would you still trust that God is in it?

Only the follower of Jesus who is willing to die to self can truly keep on saying, "Here I am, Lord. Send me."

Questions: *Have you ever felt disappointed by God's call for your life? Have you ever been surprised by it? What can you learn from Isaiah the prophet to encourage you to go on?*

DAY 345

You Are Loved

The LORD appeared to him from far away. I have loved you with an everlasting love; therefore I have continued My faithfulness to you.
Jeremiah 31:3

My mother once tried to teach my nephew Samuel how to say "I love you." He was two at the time and very precocious. Every single conversation she had with him, she encouraged him to say it: "Samuel, say 'I love you.'" His answer was always the same. He would just giggle out loud. After several months he still couldn't quite say the words, but one thing became evident: He knew how deeply loved he was. The words eventually did come, but the process was a joy to watch unfold.

So it is with our relationship with God. He's told us over and over again how much He loves us. Sometimes He does it through a sunrise or a sunset. Sometimes He does it through others. Ultimately, He did it through His Son Jesus who gave His life for us on the cross.

Day after day God uses little moments in our lives to pursue us and remind us how much He loves us. Slowly we begin to understand how deep the Father's love is for us. And little by little our smiles tell Him we get it, until eventually our words catch up and we're able to say it out loud: Father, we love You. Have you told Him how much you love Him today?

Question: *What are some of the ways that God has shown you lately how much He loves you?*

Not a Failure

"You are My witnesses," declares the Lord, "and My servant whom I have chosen, that you may know and believe Me and understand that I am He. Before Me no god was formed, nor shall there be any after Me."
Isaiah 43:10

Do you ever feel like a failure? Have you ever noticed that there is very little correlation between *feeling* like a failure and actually failing? I know many people who have failed and are still happily plugging away while others have achieved more than I can imagine and still feel inadequate.

Our feelings, especially when it comes to failure, cannot always be trusted. One of the biggest lies we tell ourselves is that the best way to stop feeling like a failure is to succeed. You can apply this to any area of your life. You might be tempted to feel like a failure because you haven't seen your dreams come to pass yet. You might believe that getting married or bearing a child or getting a promotion is your antidote to feeling like a failure. But what if you're simply believing the lie that your feelings are telling you?

Our feelings are based on the stories we tell ourselves and the stories the world tells us. Maybe it's time we start listening to the story God tells us about us. His is a story of good news when we put our faith in Jesus!

You are a success when you're living faithfully for Jesus no matter the outcomes here on this earth.

Questions: *How do you measure your success? When do you feel like a failure? How do you think God measures success based on the example of Jesus?*

DAY 347

Talk about Jesus

*Let the words of my mouth and the meditation of my heart
be acceptable in Your sight, O Lord, my rock and my redeemer.*
Psalm 19:14

I once had a very interesting two-hour flight. I had just settled into my window seat when I caught bits and pieces of the conversation next to me. I tried to ignore the conversation but couldn't. For the entire 120 minutes, I listened to the two women next to me talk about mold. Yes, they spent the entire trip talking about mold.

It turned out that these women were experts on mold and were headed to a conference about mold. They were quite passionate about mold. They had given their lives to study mold. They did research on mold, and wrote papers about mold. By the end of the flight I felt like I was one big piece of mold.

Since that flight I haven't been able to quit thinking about the intensity with which my seatmates pursued their passion. It reminded me of Paul who said that he decided to know nothing except Jesus Christ and Him crucified.

What would our lives look like if we invested all of our energy, not to study mold, but to focus on Jesus Christ, our Savior? How would it change our world if we gave Jesus and His Word our all?

Questions: *What do those around you hear when they eavesdrop on your conversations? How much time each day do you spend thinking and talking about Jesus?*

DAY 348

Why, God, Why?

This God—His way is perfect; the word of the Lord proves true;
He is a shield for all those who take refuge in Him.
Psalm 18:30

When difficult circumstances come my way, it's easy for me to ask why. Why, God, why is this happening to me? Have you ever asked yourself the question?

It's easy to wonder how good God is, or whether He is able to keep bad things from happening to us. Why haven't You provided a partner for me, Lord? Why am I not getting a raise despite being so faithful in my giving? Why are my kids still running away from You? Why haven't You answered my prayers, Lord? And the hardest of them all: Why am I still waiting, Lord?

The surest way to fall into self-pity and misery is to keep on asking God why. Trusting God means trusting that while God could change my circumstances, if He hasn't yet, then He must have a really good reason for it. Start asking Him about that reason. Instead of asking why, ask Him what He's trying to teach you in this present trial. In Psalm 18:30 David reminds us that "this God—His way is perfect; the word of the Lord proves true."

If you're stuck asking God why, resolve to surrender to what God is trying to accomplish in your life today, trusting Him with both process and outcome.

Questions: *What could God be trying to accomplish in your life through your present trials? What character traits and fruit of the Spirit is He trying to grow?*

DAY 349

Guard Against Self

For by the grace given to me I say to everyone among you not to think of himself more highly than he ought to think, but to think with sober judgment, each according to the measure of faith that God has assigned.
Romans 12:3

We live in the most narcissistic culture ever. In Greek mythology, Narcissus was a very handsome guy who, because of his disdain toward others, was punished by the gods by falling in love with his own image. He became so enraptured by his beauty that he was unable to pull himself away from his own reflection and wasted away and died.

Most of us are at risk of dying of narcissism. We are living in an age where each of us has a page dedicated to me, myself, and I. We are self-absorbed, egocentric, and way overestimate our own importance. We are the exact opposite of what God tells us to be in Romans 12:3. Paul wrote that we ought to not think of ourselves more highly than we ought to think but to think soberly. In other words, God wants us to forget about ourselves and live for Him first and for others. We must pay even more attention to guard against narcissism as we seek to follow the example of Jesus.

While it sounds easy, dying to self requires that you intentionally put others ahead of yourself today. Are you willing to do it?

Questions: How much of your life is spent thinking about "me"? How might the culture have influenced the way you think about yourself?

DAY 350

Back to the Basics

You keep him in perfect peace whose mind is stayed on You, because he trusts in You.
Isaiah 26:3

The bane of my existence is that moment when I'm supposed to remember a password for one of my many online accounts and can't. Even with the updated phones and apps to help the memory process, I still find myself facing a password crisis at least once a month. And when I'm up against a wall, I do what you likely do too. I reset the password one more time and start all over again. No matter how hard I try to remember, every so often, I simply have to go back to square one and reset my password in order to go on.

When it comes to the things that matter in my walk with the Lord, I've found it to be the same. No matter how hard I try, I tend to forget the basics. Every so often, just like with my password, I have to reset my account and start afresh. I simply have to go back to the basics. I have to reset my brain and remember that God loves me so much and has a plan for my life. I have to reset my thoughts and remind myself that He hasn't forgotten me and that no weapon formed against me will succeed.

Once I remember the basics, everything else quickly falls into place too.

Question: *What are some of the basics you need to reset in your mind in order to go on?*

DAY 351

Live in Confidence

Behold, I have engraved you on the palms of My hands; your walls are continually before Me.
Isaiah 49:16

What are you afraid of? Some people are afraid of snakes. Some are afraid of heights. Some are afraid of closed spaces or pandemic illnesses or traveling to unsafe regions. Me? I'm afraid of the future. What if God doesn't show up for me the way I want Him to? What if He lets me down?

Do you ever fear the unknown? The Bible teaches us that perfect love casts out fear. The surest way to fight off the kind of fear that mislabels God is by setting your mind on God's love. The surest way to settle your mind on God's love is to remember the cross. Jesus gave His life on the cross simply because of love. He didn't have to die for our sin, but He did. He gave His life for me. He loves you so much that He died for you too. Don't ever forget that.

The same God who gave us Jesus can do far more than our minds can imagine. He loves us eternally. Our names are printed on the palms of His hands! Do you know this God? Do you love Him? Then you have no reason to fear anymore!

Question: *Why is it so hard to remember how much God loves you? Rest in His love for a moment before rushing into the day.*

DAY 352

Hear God Speak

Call to Me and I will answer you, and will tell you great and hidden things that you have not known.
Jeremiah 33:3

"Go ahead," my nephew said, "open to any page and put your finger somewhere. Now read the verse out loud, and you'll know what God wants." I laughed. There was a time in my life when I would have tried that technique.

I used to think that reading God's Word was about finding ammunition for whatever plan I had in mind. I used to think that reading God's Word was a strategy to get what I want from God. As I've gotten older, I know better. I understand that reading God's Word is about relationship. It's about finding out who God really is and what He loves and about knowing His heart. It's about growing closer to my Father, the God of the universe. It's about seeing where I fit into His story, the story of redemption.

It's natural to want to put my finger on a verse and get a "fortune cookie" verse for the day, but that's not what walking with God is all about. It's human to want tangible answers to our questions.

Faith grows when we grow confident in who God is and rest our all in His promises, even when we can't see the answer.

Question: *If God were to speak to you today, what area in your life do you need Him to give you a word for? Go ahead and tell Him about it, and expect Him to provide you an answer in His Word!*

Step into Community

And they devoted themselves to the apostles' teaching and the fellowship, to the breaking of bread and the prayers.
Acts 2:42

Most single people complain about being alone, yet if truth be told, there are times in our lives that we want to be alone. And when we can't carve out alone time, it's easy to isolate ourselves from others even while we are with them. We simply build an invisible shield protecting our hearts from everyone else.

Even married people can fall into that trap. We tell people what we want them to hear depending on our moods. We sometimes resort to a silent treatment. But the more I study the life of Jesus, the more I see the example of Someone who refused to settle for superficiality in His relationship with others. Jesus lovingly broke down barriers and intentionally got to know others beyond the superficial. The result was life-changing for anyone who encountered the Messiah.

On those days when I'd rather be alone, I think about God's plan for me to be in community, and I resolve to step out of my circle of comfort and into the unknown. Who knows what might happen when I am willing to live in community when I'd rather be alone?

Questions: *How can you make your time with others relationally rich? What can you learn from Jesus about tearing down the barriers that protect you from others and love others instead?*

DAY 354

Love Everyone Always

Greater love has no one than this, that someone lay down his life for his friends.
John 15:13

I had a dog once for a day. Her name was Madam Bailey the Third. I thought I was going to love that dog, and I sort of did—for a day. Then she woke me up in the middle of the night and made a mess on my white carpets. By the end of that day Madam Bailey got upgraded to my friend's ranch house.

Before you point your finger at me and accuse me of animal intolerance, think about this for a minute. We all love to talk about love. Love is easy when it's convenient. Love is easy when everything is clean and convenient and fits into our little boxes. But what happens when we start to notice the mess? What happens when the person God has plopped into our life steps on our toes? Yeah, love is easy when it maintains space. Love is swell when it stays in its parameters. But God has called us to something much bigger than a fickle kind of love.

God has called us to love when it's inconvenient and hard. It's the kind of love that demands sacrifice. It's the kind of love that Jesus showed us on the cross and that's ours in Christ.

Do you know His love? Are you sharing His love with the people in your life, especially when it's hard?

Questions: *Who in your life is hard to love? In what ways can you extend Christlike love to them today?*

DAY 355

Christmas Details

Before they call I will answer; while they are yet speaking I will hear.
Isaiah 65:24

When was the last time you stopped to think about the birth of Jesus? Most days in my life I'm too busy and distracted to stop and consider the obvious.

When it comes to the birth of Jesus, so many little things had to happen for His birth to take place. There had to be a barren Elizabeth and her husband Zachariah, and there had to be a Mary and a Joseph. There had to be a star shining brightly, and three wise men and a wicked king. There had to be a census, and no room at the inn, and there had to be fourteen generations from Abraham to David and another fourteen from David to Jesus. Every little detail mattered before the coming of the King.

You and I forget that God is always doing ten thousand things while we wait on Him to deliver the one. Who knows what all He might be planning while we wait on Him for that one?

Take hope today as you consider the story of the birth of Jesus. God is at work in every detail of your life whether you recognize it or not.

Questions: *Think about the big answers to prayers in your life. Can you see how God was weaving a greater story in the waiting? How does that encourage you to keep waiting on the Lord right now?*

Great News

Fear not, for behold I bring you good news of great joy that will be for all the people. For unto you is born this day in the city of David a Savior who is Christ the Lord.
Luke 2:10

What's the best news you might get today? For some of you, the best news you could ever receive is news of a first date, or perhaps news to your own wedding invitation. Perhaps for you, it's the dream of a winning lottery ticket that would send you to the moon, or news of a free all-inclusive vacation on the beach somewhere that would make your day. Our lists are endless. We long for good news.

But consider this: The best news we've ever been given is found in Luke 2:10. We're told: "Fear not, for behold I bring you good news of great joy that will be for all the people. For unto you is born this day in the city of David a Savior who is Christ the Lord." The best news we could ever receive is the news that we've been given a Savior. That God became man and died for our sins.

No wedding cake or bucket list vacation will ever compare to the joy of knowing Jesus the Messiah. God with us. Emmanuel. There is no greater news.

Questions: *What do you long for with all your heart? Would you ask God to satisfy your heart and your deepest longings with Jesus?*

DAY 357

Christmas Truth

For to us a Child is born, to us a Son is given; and the government shall be upon His shoulder, and His name shall be called Wonderful Counselor, Mighty God, Everlasting Father, Prince of Peace.

Isaiah 9:6

What do you want for Christmas this year? When it comes to Christmas, most of us can get pretty cynical very quickly. Mistletoe is overrated. Hallmark movies are for single ladies with cats. The entire season is one big financial drain.

Instead of joy, most of us feel stressed in the days between Thanksgiving and Christmas. Maybe you're one of the few remaining romantics who can't wait to snuggle up to your Hallmark movie marathons while the rest of us roll our eyes and smirk.

It's easy to get distracted with negative emotions around the holiday season, but it's critical to stop and remember that Christmas isn't about us at all. It's not about the mistletoe and the eggnog. It's not about all my dreams becoming true. No—Christmas is about Jesus. Christmas celebrates the birth of a King whose life would eventually lead Him to the cross for the sake of our sin.

Maybe it's fitting to feel bittersweet around this time of the year. And maybe Jesus understands it.

Questions: How does the holiday season make you feel? How can you keep from getting self-centered around the holiday season?

Hope

And the Word became flesh and dwelt among us, and we have seen His glory, glory as of the only Son from the Father, full of grace and truth.
John 1:14

Hope. It's the word that comes to mind when I think about Christmas morning. Hope that God has not forgotten His people even after 400 years of silence. Hope that joy can be found in a barn when welcome can't be found elsewhere. Hope that there is light in the darkest of nights. Hope that our questions have answers and that evil will never win. Hope that fear has no place in the presence of a Savior.

Hope that the waiting will always be worth it, especially if you're an 84-year-old woman named Anna. But mostly hope that because of Christmas we have a Savior named Emmanuel who has come to be with us forever. Hope that someday soon we will get to see Him face-to-face and that until that day joy is ours and peace has come and the glory of the Lord continues to shine.

Wherever you are and whatever you're doing, I wish you the happiest of Christmases. Hope is yours in Christ today!

Questions: Do you know the hope of Jesus this Christmas morning? Take a minute and meditate on all that is possible today because Jesus was born in a manger.

Never Disappointed

"Come, everyone who thirsts, come to the waters; and he who has no money, come, buy and eat! Come, buy wine and milk without money and without price."
Isaiah 55:1

Do you ever feel disappointed on the morning after Christmas? More people face disappointment the day after Christmas than you might think.

Once I got a red blanket for Christmas. That was my big gift. Maybe this year you were hoping to get a breadmaker but got a crockpot instead, or maybe you were hoping to get a proposal and got a breakup instead. Whatever it is you were hoping to get and didn't, today is a day for hope and rejoicing!

There is a gift that will never disappoint you. It's the gift of putting all your hope and expectation in Jesus. He's the only One who will fill your soul completely and bring you unceasing joy. David said it this way in Psalm 62:5: "For God alone, O my soul, waits in silence, for my hope is from Him." Jesus is the only answer to the heart that's still waiting. Jesus is the fountain that never runs dry.

Won't you drink from the well that will satisfy you forever, and find freedom to overcome the disappointment you're holding on to?

Questions: *What is at the root of your feelings of disappointment? In what practical ways can you drink at the fountain that will always satisfy you?*

DAY 360

God's Favor

"The Lord bless you and keep you; the Lord make His face to shine upon you and be gracious to you; the Lord lift up His countenance upon you and give you peace."
Numbers 6:24-26

We like to talk about God's favor a lot in the Church. When things go well for us we point to His favor. For singles, marriage seems like God's favor. For professionals, promotion feels like God's favor. For the financially struggling, a raise feels like God's favor. For the parent of a toddler, a day without bedwetting feels like God's favor. But I wonder if we're confused about God's favor. I wonder if it's time to redefine His favor.

God's favor on Jesus led Him to the cross. God's favor on Paul led him to the prison. God's favor on Peter resulted in his crucifixion upside down. And God's favor on the beloved disciple allowed him to spend years in exile alone.

God's favor is not defined by our version of the American dream. God's favor is far better than a big house and a fat retirement account and a hot husband. God's favor is our peace no matter what we're going through today. God's favor is His promises no matter what we're facing. God's favor is Jesus—Emmanuel—God with us.

The people of Israel prayed this prayer of God's favor on one another: "The Lord bless you and keep you; the Lord make His face to shine upon you and be gracious to you; the Lord lift up His countenance upon you and give you peace." I pray it over you today.

Questions: *How would you define God's favor in your life? Where in your life have you felt like God has not given you His favor? Can you see it from a different perspective today?*

DAY 361

Christ Is Yours

If any of you lacks wisdom, let him ask God, who gives generously to all without reproach, and it will be given him.
James 1:5

At my hospital we have a lounge for doctors. Every day it's stocked full of sandwiches for lunch. The lounge is open to any doctor with a badge who tries to access it. If we use the badge to get into the lounge, we are free to eat as many sandwiches as we want.

What amazes me is how little I take advantage of the lounge. I show up to work with a lunch I've just paid for or with plans to spend a few bucks on a sandwich from a take-out place. Why would I spend money on something when it's already mine for free? It doesn't make sense how quickly I'm willing to waste money for what's already mine for free.

When it comes to our walk with the Lord, it's exactly the same thing. We're offered loads of free benefits simply because of our relationship with God through Jesus Christ. But instead of enjoying the joy and peace that is ours in Him, we work harder and harder trying to create a sense of peace on our own.

If only we'd learn to access His throne of grace freely and boldly to get all that we need! Won't you try it today?

Questions: *What is yours in Christ for free that you haven't accessed yet? Will you ask Him to give you eyes to see and a heart to receive all that is yours in Christ?*

DAY 362

Invisible Touch

Give, and it will be given to you. Good measure, pressed down, shaken together, running over, will be put into your lap. For with the measure you use it will be measured back to you.
Luke 6:38

It hurts to feel invisible. None of us like that feeling. But have you ever considered that there are blessings in being invisible too?

Once in a blue moon I get an anonymous donation or a card that's signed, "A loved one." No name is given—simply a word of encouragement. My heart explodes with joy. I love those moments of anonymous generosity by invisible givers. It magnifies the act when the focus is on the gift.

Jesus often told those He healed not to tell anyone about it. He instructed us to give quietly, not letting our right hand know what the left one gives. There's a beauty to anonymous acts of generosity, in a lack of insistence on being noticed. There's a Christlikeness to this kind of sacrificial servanthood.

If you feel invisible, I challenge you to start giving out generous acts of invisible touch. Bake pies and send cards and write notes and do what needs to be done invisibly, but completely seen by our heavenly Father in whose name we do these acts of kindness.

Let's be a movement of invisible generosity to a world hungry for grace.

Question: *What are some invisible acts of generosity you can extend to someone today? Make a list of two or three ways and do it!*

Into the Deep

*And beginning to sink he cried out, "Lord, save me."
Jesus immediately reached out His hand and took hold of him.*
Matthew 14:30-31

Starting a new year always feels like we're stepping into the deep. We don't know what's to come, but our expectations are high and our hope is alive.

There may be storms all around us, but in the beginning of the new year, everything feels possible. We feel unstoppable—sort of like Peter did right before he stepped out of the boat and onto the water. What a moment that was! But it didn't take long before Peter started sinking. Only a handful of steps and his eyes saw the storm and he became afraid. The good news is that Jesus was right there to catch him. Peter was safe even in midst of the storm.

As you are about to step into the deep with new resolutions for the upcoming year, you might be afraid. You don't have to be. Jesus is with you every step of the way. Step out into the deep and know that if you fall, His arm will reach out to save you. He's never going to leave you alone.

Questions: *What makes you most afraid as you begin this new year? How does knowing Jesus is with you always encourage you to take the next step anyway?*

New Beginnings

*Remember not the former things, nor consider the things of old.
Behold, I am doing a new thing; now it springs forth, do you not perceive it?*
Isaiah 43:18-19

This is my favorite time of the year: time to make some changes, time to resolve again to live what we say we believe.

We're about to start a new year. One of the more popular practices I've enjoyed in the last few years has been the practice of looking for a one-word theme for the new year. I like starting the year by asking God to give me a verse, a promise for the new year. As I set up a brand-new Bible reading plan, I typically buy a new journal and commit to starting a new page with God.

In Isaiah 43:18-19 we're told, "Remember not the former things, nor consider the things of old. Behold, I am doing a new thing; now it springs forth, do you not perceive it?" Anything can happen this new year! God is waiting for you to seek Him more intentionally this year, to know Him more intimately.

Will you do whatever it takes to make time for God? Will you commit this new year to Him?

Questions: *What steps are you going to take this year to deepen your walk with the Lord? Will you ask the Lord to help you find a word and a verse for this new year?*

About Lina AbuJamra

Lina AbuJamra is a pediatric ER doctor, now practicing telemedicine, and founder of Living With Power Ministries. Her vision is to bring hope to the world by connecting biblical answers to everyday life. A popular Bible teacher, podcaster, and conference speaker, she is the author of several books including *Thrive, Stripped, Resolved* and her most recent book, *Fractured Faith: Finding Your Way Back to God in an Age of Deconstruction.*

Lina ministers to singles through her Moody Radio show, *Today's Single Christian,* and is engaged in providing medical care and humanitarian help to Syrian refugees and others in disaster areas in the Middle East.

Her ministry also provides spiritual retreats for women at The Hope Ranch.

Born in Beirut, Lebanon, Lina now calls Chicago home. She is single and a huge Packers fan and would not survive without her iPhone. Learn more about her at livingwithpower.org.

For additional information on Lina and her ministry, go to:
www.livingwithpower.org.